KeyWords
FOR LIVING

Devotional Thoughts to Unlock Life's Purpose

D1367521

1

Sincere Appreciation Expressed

As a child and teenager, I was privileged to attend a Judeo-Christian school for ten of my formative years. The school's motto was *"Omnia Ad Dei Gloriam"*—**all to the glory of GOD.** This statement captures my highest driving purpose for writing this work.

I hesitate to limit the influence of so many who have impacted and shaped my writings, however there are several who deserve special recognition because of their tireless support and prayers throughout this project. Foremost is my wife, **CLARE BRYAN** without whose personal example and her previous book publications, I might never have persevered.

MICHAEL GUIDO was a mentor and a genius in writing one-minute devotionals to a worldwide audience. I was blessed to be one of his students and protégés. He encouraged me continually.

Without the ongoing assistance of **MINDI ASHBURN**, this work may have never been started. For many years she has relayed the weekly KeyWord recorded versions to radio stations throughout Georgia and has kept meticulous records while transcribing the original written drafts.

Early on, I was offered a perfect setting in which to write multiple segments through the generosity of **JIM & MARLENE GREENE.** My visits to their Saint Simons Island retreat was positively inspirational and productive.

In more recent years, **PAM SCHILDECKER** used her editing, writing and creative skills to clean up and improve my documents while organizing the drafts into printable form. Pam was assisted by **JULI HOLTZCLAW** who used her abilities in matching all scripture references into a single version.

When it came down to formatting and final editing, **EDDY OLIVER** was my choice. For months we molded the work into its present form. His experience and giftedness pressed me to completion.

I am grateful to share these devotionals with you believing that your life will be challenged and enriched through reading and applying the spiritual principles which are discovered through these key single-word expressions.

Carpe Diem!

Introduction

Keys are important. With a key, I can unlock my home, my car, my office, my safe deposit box, my gym locker, my gate, my truck, or just about anything that's locked up. A key is a tool of entry allowing us to go places and do things that otherwise would be impossible.

Words are also keys. They unlock the opportunity to transmit our thoughts, our attitudes, and our desires. God's words are life-changing and the keys which open purpose and meaning for our lives.

Clear and concise communication has been a life goal for me as expressed through years of conversations, teaching, writing, and media broadcasts. My first experiences with regular public speaking began over four decades ago while helping lead a church in downtown Atlanta, Georgia. We were televised weekly and I was challenged to share short audio and video presentations.

Later I became Senior Pastor of a large congregation in Augusta, Georgia. The live services were broadcast regularly, but I felt we could reach a broader audience through writing and producing short, one-minute inspirational spots. Since that time, I have continued to create hundreds of these now heard on multiple stations.

The names or titles for my broadcasts have changed over the years, but the concept has not. This book is a compilation of those writings along with additional personal challenging questions and quotes from various sources and walks of life.

The purpose of my *KeyWord Ministry* remains steady—to clearly communicate the Good News of the Gospel to inspire, challenge and offer spiritual transformation for those who seek a deeper purpose in life.

Devotional Contents At-A-Glance

A - Acceptance, Acronyms, After, Air, Always, Angst, Animals, Answer, Anxious, Arrive, Attitude

B - Balk, Bark, Bedlam, Belief, Believe, Belt, Birds, Bite, Blackball, Bless, Blinds, Blow, Body, Bowling, Boycott, Brain, Brand, Bread, Breakers, Breastplate, Breeze, Bridegroom, Brother, Budget, Bug, Burn, Bush

C - Calculate, Calm,, Cave, Census, Chains, Change, Child, Children, Christ, Clean, Cleaning, Clicks, Clouds, Clutter, Collision, Colors, Comfort, Conceit, Control, Count, Coverage, Crash, Crashed, Creation, Creator, Cross, Crown, Cry, Cup, Cure, Curfew

D - Dance, Date, Day, Death, Decisions, Delay, Desire, Dessert, Difference, Dip, Diploma, Discharge, Discount, Dog, Dreams, Dress, Drift, Drive, Driver, Drugs

E – Early, Earshot, Eccentric, Economy, Emotions, Empty, Escape, Escapes, Exchange, Expectancy, Expectant, Expectation, Extra, Extremes

F – Faith, Falsehood, Family, Fare, Feet, Fiasco, Fight, Fighting, Figs, Final, Fire, First, Fish, Flight, Flying, Floor, Flowers, Fog, Food, Formula, Fortress, Freedom, Fresh, Fruit, Fruitful, Fulfill, Full

G – Gamble, Garbage, Garden, Gifts, Giving, Glass, Go, Goal, Goblin, Good, Gossip, Grass, Grave, Great, Growth, Gum, Gutters

H – Hair, Hear, Heart, Heckle, Helmet, Heyday, Hog, Hole, Holly, Hot, Hour, House, Hurt

I - Identity, Idol, In, Influence, Integrity, Inventions

J – Jewels, Josh, Journey, Jumbo

K – Key, Kick, Kindness, King, Kingdom, Kiss, Kite, Know

L- Labor, Lake, Lame, Last, Law, Lemons, Lewd, Life, Lightning, Listen Lists, Losers, Lounge, Lumber, Lunch

M – Make, Mark, Meek, Meetings, Mercy, Milk, Mind, Moon, Mountains

N- Nag, Name, Nature, Newness, Nice, Nose, Not, Nothing, Nutrients

O- Obey, Off, Organism, Out, Overwhelm

P- Pain, Panic, Paparazzi, Patience, Pension, Perfect, Perseverance, Pester, Phrases, Pierce, Plant, Power, Praise, Prayer, Preparation, Presents, Pride, Prison, Produce, Profit, Purchase, Purification, Pursuit, Puzzle

Q – Quick, Quiet, Quietness

R- Radio, Rain, Rainfall, Reed, Rest, Results, Retire, Return, Revision, Ring, Roar, Rock, Rule, Rules, Rummage

S –Sabotage, Sail, Salt, Scapegoat, Scent, Seas, Secret, Seeds, Serving, Shield, Shine, Ship, Shop, Shore, Shrimp, Silence, Silent, Sincere, Skin, Sky, Sleep, Smell, Smile, Snob, Something, Speech, Spirit, Staff, Stare, Stark, Stars, Still, Stillness, Stocking, Straight, Street, Strength, Stroke, Strong, Substitution, Sunset, Surf, Swell, Switch, Sword

T- Tax, Tears, Tension, Test, Thanksgiving, There, Thimble, Thirst, Thoughts, Threshold, Tired, Tomorrow, Touch, Treasure, Tree, Trees, Tribulation, Trip, Trophies, True, Turn

U – Umbrella, Unity, Utopia

V- Vandal, Victory, Vine, Visa, Vision, Vista

W- Warm, Wash, Watch, Weak, Wealth, Weather, Weeds, Why, Wind, Word, Work, Worship, Writing

X – eXercise, X-Ray, Xmas

Y – Yearn, Yes, Yesterday, Yield, Yoke, Yolk, Yore, Yule

Z – Zany, Zealot, Zenith, Zigzag

A

ACCEPTANCE

To be accepted means to fit in, to be loved, and even to be appreciated. However, the harsh fact is that many of us work hard at gaining acceptance, but feel unaccepted.

We all want to be accepted and we work hard for approval. In the home, we comply with the assigned chores. At school, we accomplish the expected academic exercises. At work, we fulfill the tasks given between employer and employee. Even in the realm of recreation, we compete to make ourselves appear more complete through the acceptance of others.

God's plan is to "accept one another, then, just as Christ accepted you, in order to bring praise to God" (Romans 15:7). It's a reciprocal routine. Jesus accepts you through forgiveness, and we, in turn, are to forgive and accept others. As hard as this seems, it is harder to ignore this spiritual solution in our continual quest for acceptance.

In spite of your sinful soul, God extends His love and will accept you as you are because of who He is.

KeyPoints to ponder:
- Have you accepted the forgiveness of God, our heavenly Father?
- Do you feel accepted today?
- Are you showing others acceptance through your forgiveness?

"Jesus accepts you the way you are, but loves you too much to leave you that way."– Lee Venden

ACRONYMS

Acronyms can be ridiculous and even redundant. For instance, ATM means Automatic Teller Machine, so why do we say, "ATM machine"? Then there's "LCD display" for Liquid Crystal Display or "OPEC countries," an acronym for Organization of Oil-producing Countries. It's ridiculously repetitious.

Think of these letters for a moment – EGO. From a spiritual perspective, it can be either good or bad. E-G-O could mean Edging God Out, which is what many of us do. However, we should choose the positive power of E-G-O as Exalting God Only.

The point is not for you to define ego or to initiate a Sigmund Freud psychoanalysis, but rather to help you think through who you are before God.

Which way is it for you? The Bible says, "Be exalted, O God, above the heavens ..." (Psalm 108:5). The Apostle Paul proclaimed, "...Always Christ will be exalted in my body" (Philippians 1:20).

Leave your selfish ego behind and begin to exalt the One True God above.

KeyPoints to ponder:
- Am I exalting God only?
- In what areas of life am I edging God out?
- Is my ego pride-filled or one which pursues the heart of God?

"A proud man is always looking down on things and people; and, of course, as long as you are looking down, you cannot see something that is above you."– C. S. Lewis

AFTER

With great anticipation we always await the beginning of a new year, but what comes after? The truth is that "after days" have even greater potential than the "day of" because there are more of them to right the wrongs of yesterday.

"After" is not only a definition of time, but a determinant of direction. Here's what I mean. The Bible described King David as "a man after God's own heart; he will do everything I want him to do" (Acts 13:22). His direction of life was aimed toward the Almighty. This defined his days afterwards because his heart matched the heart of the Holy One.

Jesus rebuked His disciples following His resurrection "for their lack of faith and their stubborn refusal to believe those who had seen him after he had risen" (Mark 16:14). The Bible tells us this happened after Christ had appeared before Mary Magdalene.

What you do with your after days is not just important – it's essential.

KeyPoints to ponder:
- Is your direction after the heart of God?
- Will you go after others whose hearts are hard?
- What will you do after pondering this message?

"Where God guides, He provides." – Author unknown

AIR

We simply cannot live without it – air. The air we breathe is a perfect combination of chemical compositions that, if disturbed, would bring sudden death. God's control of the elements is a sign of His love for life.

Take a moment to breathe in for three seconds. Now exhale to empty your lungs completely. This simple exercise is a reminder of the rhythm of life and the routine which renews another moment of survival on this globe.

Yet, the air we enjoy today is temporary because we are subject to the "ruler of the kingdom of the air, the spirit who is now at work in those who are disobedient" (Ephesians 2:2). The devil is a deceiver who would have us think that this life is all there is.

The polluted air we breathe here is a preparation for the better breathing to be had with a heavenly Father in a future of forever. In the beginning of time, God breathed into the nostrils of mankind the breath of life (Genesis 2:7). With His air we have the opportunity to accept an eternal life which offers total forgiveness. Following His resurrection, Jesus breathed on His disciples and said, "If you forgive anyone's sins, their sins are forgiven ..." (John 20:23).

KeyPoints to ponder:
- Have you breathed the air of forgiveness from our Lord?
- Will you take a moment to exhale polluted thoughts and actions?
- Are you praising God with the breath He has given you?

"If we really want to learn how to love, we must learn how to forgive." – Mother Teresa

ALARM

The hypothalamus is the part of the brain that regulates our "body clock," which, if we're fortunate, helps us wake up on time even if our bedside alarm fails to go off. I have a double back-up system. My bedside clock is reinforced by my alarm watch, strategically set across the room to force me out of bed. However, most of the time, I'm already up and going before either alarm begins to sound.

What gets you up and going each day? More than a system of alert, it should be the Spirit of the Almighty. Just because you're on your feet does not mean that you have power and a purpose for the day. God intends for each of us to awaken with a readiness to serve Him through a refreshed body that He has loaned to us.

The Bible tells us to "Sow your seed in the morning, and at evening let your hands not be idle, for you do not know which will succeed, whether this or that, or whether both will do equally well" (Ecclesiastes 11:6). Wake up!

KeyPoints to ponder:
- What time is it in your life right now?
- Are you awake and alert to the possibilities associated with your remaining time?
- Would you be alarmed if Jesus returned today?

"Courage is almost a contradiction in terms. It means a strong desire to live taking the form of readiness to die."
– G. K. Chesterton

ALWAYS

Always is a long time. It's an eternity. Yet, we all know that when friends or family promise "always" it's not necessarily so. We want relationships and rewards to last forever, but many don't. However, our disappointment shouldn't bring discouragement or even doubt, because not all promises pass away.

God said He would love you – always.
God said He would be with you – always.
God said He would forgive you – always.
God said He would have a home for you – always.

Our problem is that we don't trust the truth – always. We've been hurt by someone, somewhere and it's taken a toll on our belief, which has affected our behavior.

Jesus offered assurance when he declared to His disciples, "And surely I am with you always, to the very end of the age" (Matthew 28:20b). He said this as He challenged His followers to freely share their faith. He wanted them to understand their efforts were only effective with His presence and power which is promised – always.

KeyPoints to ponder:
- Do you believe God's promises are always true?
- Do you believe God's promises are always for you?
- Won't you trust God to provide His power for your day in all ways?

"God never made a promise that was too good to be true."
– Dwight L. Moody

13

ANGST

Angst is a strange word. It just sounds like it hurts. If you were looking for noise to scream when pained, you might exclaim, "Angst!" but then most people would look at you funny. Maybe some synonyms might be better understood, such as agony, anxiety, or awful. However you say it, there's no doubt when you feel it.

God gave us feelings for a purpose. Our emotions are not to be ignored but initiated. When bad feelings occur or angst arrives, instead of cussing, fussing, and fuming, we could be learning from the circumstance by leaning on God.

Every hurt happens for a reason. Every bad can be turned to good and everybody can choose to make right choices.

How are you handling your angst? Jesus knows your weaknesses and wants you to turn to Him for your strength. The Apostle Paul wrote, "I can do all things through Christ who gives me strength" (Philippians 4:13). He should know, as he was beaten, jailed, shipwrecked, slandered, and stoned – all because he believed.

KeyPoints to ponder:
- Are you in angst?
- What's your greatest hurt that you are harboring?
- Will you give it to God—now?

"The more you pray, the less you'll panic. The more you worship, the less you worry. You'll feel more patient and less pressured."
– Rick Warren

ANIMALS

Certain times of the year I see squirrels jumping from limb-to-limb in my back yard. Some people consider them to be pests; others think of them as quite cute. Though they don't usually attack people, except in cases of trying to get food, a little known fact is that they are immune to rabies and cannot transmit it to human beings.

Ever wonder why squirrels seem to follow the same paths as they pounce and play? It's because they excrete a scent from glands between the pads of their feet, and they literally "mark" trees as their own.

The Bible reminds us that God made all animals, and each is unique in His creation (Genesis 1:24-25). He even gave man the privilege of naming them (Genesis 2:19-20). That would have been both fun and challenging. Whoever thought up the name of platypus must have been up too late the night before!

All of God's creation is intended for one powerful purpose, and that is to name the name of Jesus as Savior and Lord.

KeyPoints to ponder:
- Do you believe God created you for a purpose?
- Have you discovered His purpose for you?
- Will you call on the name of Jesus to show you His way—today?

"The mystery of human existence lies not in just staying alive, but in finding something to live for." – Fyodor Dostoyevsky

ANSWER

When someone gives an answer, it is either in response to a question or a command to respond. Grammar gurus would term the responses as either nouns or verbs, depending on the usage. In mathematics, an answer is the solution to a problem, and problems are plentiful.

To whom do you turn for answers? "The Lord is near to all who call on Him" (Psalm 145:18). Your answers come when you call. God even invites you in His request to "Call to me and I will answer you and tell you great and unsearchable things you do not know" (Jeremiah 33:3).

Our problem is that we search for answers in all the wrong places. Answers don't come through anxiety, nor are they found in fretfulness. We would do well to remember that God cares, and he hears our hurts. To prove it, He said, "Before they call I will answer; while they are still speaking I will hear" (Isaiah 65:24).

Our desire is to get quick answers to quick questions, but sometimes this is not what we need at all. It's the process of discovery that is, at times, more valuable than the product.

God not only has the answers; remember that He is the answer!

KeyPoints to ponder:
- What is the greatest problem you face?
- What answer do you seek?
- To whom are you turning for solutions?

"Within the covers of the Bible are the answers for all the problems men face."– Ronald Reagan

ANXIOUS

Anxiety is one of the leading causes of medical concern today. Prescription drugs are readily available to ease our anxious thoughts in an effort to regulate our behavior. However, the cure doesn't always come.

The problem is not just physical because anxiety evidences itself in our spiritual lives as well. What's the solution? Who's got the lasting answer?

The Apostle Peter said, "Cast your anxiety on him (Christ) because he cares for you" (1 Peter 5:7). That's easier said than done.

The wise writer of Proverbs said, "An anxious heart weighs a man down, but a kind word cheers him up" (Proverbs 12:25). One answer to anxiety is in giving and receiving kind words.

The Apostle Paul wrote: "Do not be anxious about anything, but in every situation, by prayer and petition, with thanksgiving, present your requests to God" (Philippians 4:6). Another answer to anxiety is to pray.

Okay, so what's the payoff? What can you exchange for anxiety? God's promise for us is peace which He says will guard our hearts and minds (Philippians 4:7). I like that deal – my prayer for God's peace. Instead of anxious thoughts I can have God's guidance. Try it.

KeyPoints to ponder:
- What makes you anxious today?
- Where will you go for peace?
- Whose worry can you help to heal?

"It is our work to cast care, and it is God's work to take care."
– Thomas Watson

ARRIVE

When you arrive you've come from where you've been to where you wanted to go. We are usually glad to be there, especially if it happens to be home.

You cannot get there without first leaving. Some of us need to let go of the comfortable and leave the convenient so that we can join the journey. Jesus invites you to leave your Christian comfort zone and He's even provided a map (the Bible) to guide you as you go.

Our world tells us we have arrived when we get the applause and acceptance of our family, friends, and even our foes. We're told that success should drive our lives, when living for significance is a much better choice. A significant life is discovered through giving more than grabbing, being more than doing, and loving more than living.

Christ said, "I am going there to prepare a place for you...and take you to be with me..." (John 14:2-3). He has initiated our escape and now invites us to arrive. More than a simple solution, this arrival offers spiritual satisfaction unparalleled to any attempt established on earth.

KeyPoints to ponder:
- Have you arrived?
- Are you willing to leave the comfortable and convenience of the now?
- Will you join Jesus on His journey?

"Letting go doesn't mean that you don't care about someone anymore. It's just realizing that the only person you really have control over is yourself." – Deborah Reber

ATTITUDE

Everybody has an attitude. How's yours today? Recently, I overheard a woman comment to a friend with disgust about another woman, "She's got such an attitude." The truth is that we all do, whether it's right or wrong.

"Your attitude should be the same as that of Christ Jesus ... the very nature of a servant, being made in human likeness" (Philippians 2:5,7). What we think about determines our direction in life, and our attitude is like a rudder that guides the journey.

God's Word tells us, "Whatever is true, whatever is noble, whatever is right, whatever is pure, whatever is lovely, whatever is admirable – if anything is excellent or praiseworthy – think about such things" (Philippians 4:8). What are you thinking about right now? Your attitude is determined by your thought life.

It is also like clothing. You made a choice about what to wear today, and you can choose to change at any time. When we become God-followers, we are told "to be made new in the attitude of your mind; and to put on the new self" (Ephesians 4:23-24).

Your attitude will determine your altitude. If it's low, you're bound to crash; if it's high and holy, you can fly above the storms of life with joy.

KeyPoints to ponder:
- How's your attitude today?
- Are you climbing higher or about to crash?
- Will you stop right now and ask God for guidance?

"We can complain because rose bushes have thorns, or rejoice because thorn bushes have roses." – Abraham Lincoln

B

BALK

Balk is a word to stop for – literally. Many sports fans consider a balk as something that a pitcher performs if he stops his windup short of throwing the baseball. But the origin of the word goes far back, beyond a ball and a bat. It literally means to stop short before proceeding, coming from the Old English "balca," or beam.

In days before locks, beams were placed across the door to block intruders. Because the beam stopped or stalled those seeking entry, the meaning of the word carries over today.

Have you balked with God? There are times when we stop short of what He wants for our lives. We'd rather do it our own way; we prefer not to be prodded or pushed.

Jesus told His followers to "Go and make disciples of all nations..." (Matthew 28:19). If we stop or stall at this command of Christ, we create a balk against God.

Evaluate your actions today toward the Almighty and get going for God.

KeyPoints to ponder:
- What plan of God have you stopped short of?
- Have you stalled on fulfilling a promise to another?
- Will you stop stopping and start starting today?

"You may delay, but time will not." – Benjamin Franklin

BARK

When I hear the word "bark," two thoughts come to mind. One is the sound of a dog; the other is the side of a tree. We hear dogs bark, and hold onto tree bark.

It's funny how the same word with such different meanings can have the same purpose. The purpose is for protection. We want our dogs to bark when strangers approach, and we want our trees to keep their coat of bark as a layer for life.

We also need protection. The Bible warns us that there is a thief who comes to "steal and kill and destroy" our lives (John 10:10a). God tells us that there is one who "prowls around like a roaring lion looking for someone to devour" (1 Peter 5:8). That's the devil.

God's power and promise of protection will keep us safe from Satan and secure us in our Savior's care, if we ask for it. Someone or something is barking at you right now. Be sure you don't get bitten because of unbelief.

KeyPoints to ponder:
- What area of your life needs protection?
- Who are you depending on to provide it?
- Do you believe the bark of God is better than the bite of Satan?

"May the perfect grace and eternal love of Christ our Lord be our never-failing protection and help." – Saint Ignatius

BEDLAM

In referring to a madhouse, the word bedlam can be taken quite literally. There was a place in London in the mid-thirteenth century with that very name. Originally, the site was a priory called St. Mary's of Bethlehem and then later, Bedlam. Some three hundred years later, the site became a house of detention for the mentally insane.

Does your life seem like a madhouse right now? What once started as your Bethlehem, has now become your Bedlam. The Christ child was born in Bethlehem to bring peace, but exited this world by man's panic. Jesus made men mad over His claims to be God, which is still happening today.

The prophet Isaiah said, "For to us a child is born, ... and he will be called Wonderful Counselor, Mighty God, Everlasting Father, Prince of Peace" (Isaiah 9:6). Is He your Prince of Peace or are you bothered by a world of bedlam?

Trust God with your bedlam and allow Him to turn your burdens into blessings.

KeyPoints to ponder:
- What is maddening about your world right now?
- Are you seeking the Prince of Peace or a quick fix from the pain?
- Will you trust God to heal you? When will you ask Him?

"When you close your eyes and think of peace, what do you see? Confusion and chaos, or calmness and contentment?" –Anonymous

BELIEF

A belief is something in which you put your faith and feelings. When a person says he has a belief, it is usually substantiated by an experience. We believe what we have received in some form or fashion from our five senses.

A person who is thoroughly indoctrinated with a belief, one who believes in a cause through and through, and who leaves no gaps, holes, or openings for any change is said to be "dyed in the wool." This funny expression comes from those who work with wool because they know that if you attempt to dye an item after it has already been spun into cloth, the odds are slim-to-none of having an even, colorfast result.

Is there any matter over which you are "dyed in the wool?" Surely we all have areas of obstinacy which affect our objectivity.

"The simple believe anything" (Proverbs 14:15). Jesus said, "The one who believes in me will live, even though they die; and whoever lives by believing in me will never die" (John 11:25-26).

KeyPoints to ponder:
- Are you living by faith or feelings?
- Is there a gap in your belief about God which needs bridging?
- Will you put down your pride and believe that Jesus is your best answer?

"A man's real belief is that which he lives by. What a man believes is the thing he does." – George McDonald

BELIEVE

Do you believe? Sure you do – we all do. Everybody believes in something or someone. If we didn't, we would have no basis upon which to share an opinion, because our opinions are based on our beliefs.

What you believe is more important than the fact that you do believe. "You believe that there is one God. Good! Even the demons believe that – and shudder" (James 2:19). It's not enough to believe that there is a God; it is vital that you believe in who He is and why He came.

We are warned NOT to believe every spirit, but to test to see whether it is from God (1 John 4:1). How do we know what's real and what is not, or what is true and what is false?

Jesus said, "I am the resurrection and the life. The one who believes in me will live, even though they die..." Then he followed His divine declaration with this question, "Do you believe this?" (John 11:25-26).

Well . . . do you? For years, I studied about God at a Christian-based school, but it was not until I was a college student that I put my faith and life into His hands. I believed, and because I did, I now have the promise to receive a life worth living here and in the hereafter.

KeyPoints to ponder:
- In what or whom do you believe?
- Do you believe only because you have seen, felt, heard or experienced it?
- Are you willing to trust God by believing what you may not yet understand?

"Sometimes I look up and say, 'I know that was you, God. Thanks.'"
– Anonymous

BELT

A belt is both functional and fashionable. It holds our clothing, and it makes a statement at the same time.

In earlier times when tunics were worn, it was impossible to run without a sash or belt. Your efforts to race would end in disaster as you tripped on your tunic.

Today, belts are big business. The belt industry thrives on specialty brands that meet every desire and whim. If you wear a Harley Davidson belt, you attract some looks of disgust and some looks of love. If you wear a belt with a Christian cross or a Star of David, the same holds true.

One belt that shouldn't bother anybody is the belt of truth and faithfulness. The Bible refers to it as "girding your loins" (Isaiah 5:11 and Ephesians 6:14, KJV). In other words, our spiritual clothing is held together by our fidelity in telling the truth. Otherwise, what we do and what we say will only trip us up along life's way.

You might be interested in who's watching the statement that your belt is making today.

KeyPoints to ponder:
- Do you feel like you've been tripped up lately?
- Is your spiritual belt of truth holding you together?
- Will others be attracted to how well you run the Christian race today?

"Your faithfulness makes you trustworthy." – *Edwin Louis Cole*

BIRDS

Most birds are beautiful. They beckon us with song, and they soar with the wind, defying the law of gravity. What I love about birds is that they seem so free. Nobody tells them how high to fly or when to rest – they are creatures of choice.

There are over 800 species of birds in North America. We feed them, call them, watch them, listen to them, and can learn from them. As in all of creation, they provide a God-link for us.

Jesus complimented birds while warning His disciples who would want to follow Him. "Foxes have dens and birds have nests, but the Son of Man has no place to lay his head" (Luke 9:58). His point was simple and succinct. God-followers have no lasting security on earth. Though birds have homes here, our intended home is in heaven.

"In my Father's house are many rooms" (homes), said Christ (John 14:2). Jesus said this because He knew He was returning there and providing us a way to join Him through His sacrificial death and His miraculous resurrection.

KeyPoints to ponder:
- Do you have a solid sense of His security?
- Are you flying high here on earth with no place to land?
- Are you certain that you have a heavenly home waiting for you?

"There is no security here on this earth. There is only opportunity."
– Gen. Douglas MacArthur

BITE

Here's a question for you: What do a mouthful, a munch, and lunch have in common? Answer: Each of these activities demands that you take a bite to enjoy it. A bite can bring delight or destruction depending on who's the biter and who gets bitten.

The word "bite" comes from the Dutch bijten and the German word beissen. Both led to our modern transliteration from the Old English word bitan. No matter how you say it, you can always feel it.

Most all of us have been bitten by the words of others and have experienced hurts which need healing. You might be ready to bite someone's head off even now!

God's got a better plan. His name is Jesus. He took the bite out of death to save us from the sting of sin. Now He's waiting for you to receive His relief.

The Bible states it best as the Apostle Paul wrote, "Where, O death, is your victory? Where, O death, is your sting?" (1 Corinthians 15:55). If you don't want to be bitten, then you must believe.

KeyPoints to ponder:
- Are you still bleeding from someone's bite?
- Do you have a scar that reminds you how much it hurt?
- Will you turn to the Healer to get His comfort and cure?

"Show me your hands. Do they have scars from giving? Show me your feet. Are they wounded in service? Show me your heart. Have you left a place for divine love?"– Fulton J. Sheen

BLACKBALL

During my college days I had to face the possibility of being blackballed from a fraternity. I made it, but unfortunately many didn't. This vetting practice dates back to early English social clubs that voted for their initiates by dropping white balls or marbles into a ballot box. Those voting against a candidate dropped black balls – hence the term. One black ball and you were voted out. It was not too fair and certainly not too fun for the rejected.

Not so with God. His system is both fair and forgiving. He offers life to all who will believe and receive His Son as a substitute for sin. The Bible gives the condition and provides a cure when it states, "Everyone who believes that Jesus is the Christ is born of God..." (1 John 5:1).

Aren't you glad that God isn't prejudiced or prone to pick His favorites? He wants everyone to experience His love and to claim lives worth living. His fraternity lasts forever and His favor is not based on someone's opinion or optional vote. Are you ready to join? God's been waiting for you with a willing heart and with patient persistence.

KeyPoints to ponder:
- Who has blackballed you in life?
- Who have you blackballed?
- Who will you pursue to persuade them of God's favor?

"That is just the way with some people. They get down on a thing when they don't know nothing about it."
    – Mark Twain, "The Adventures of Huckleberry Finn"

BLESS

Have you ever wondered why we hear people say, "God bless you" after a sneeze? The explanation comes from understanding that, in the same way that some people believe we can separate our body and our spirit, the ancients believed a good sneeze could literally blast your soul right out of your body! To ensure that no bad spirits moved into the vacancy, "God bless you" was said to clear the way so soul and body could reunite.

But the truth is that the blessing of God is not entirely based on our behavior. The favor of our heavenly Father is given to those who live their lives in obedience to God's Word and not by superstition fashioned after man's way. God blesses us not because we deserve it, but because He enjoys it and because we need it.

Blessings, however, are a two-way street. The Psalmist proclaimed, "Bless the Lord, O my soul: and all that is within me, bless his holy name" (Psalm 103:1, KJV). So the truth is that God has blessed you, but the question remains, are you blessing God with how you live, how you love, and with what you learn?

KeyPoints to ponder:
- How am I blessing others?
- Am I blessing God?
- Next time I sneeze, will I thank God for His blessings?

"Make me a blessing, O Savior I pray, make me a blessing to someone today." – Ira B. Wilson

BLINDS

When I open my blinds at home I can see more clearly that which was hidden. If I were blind in sight I could not see at all. However, if I'm in a duck blind, I'm hidden from the hunted so I can try to shoot them from the sky.

Being blind has its advantages and its awfulness. Jesus healed the blind. He used many ways to show His sovereignty. Once He collected a clump of clay, then molded it into mud and anointed the eyelids of a lad (John 9:6). Why? To prove the sight-giving power of God. The four gospels share six stories of Christ curing the blind. It's obvious that He is interested in each of us seeing more clearly.

I think it's a matter of spiritual sight that makes God glad. Even if our eyes see fuzzy, God wants our conscience to see clearly. He's committed to clarity. Are you? He wants us to see life as He does.

If you are blind and need some sight, it's time to turn to Christ for a cure.

KeyPoints to ponder:
- What are your blind spots?
- Have you asked Christ to cure you?
- Would you be surprised if He did?

"There is a condition that is worse than blindness, and that is seeing something that is not there." – Thomas Hardy

BLOW

Winds blow, smoke blows, and when I get mad – my mind blows. And if I anger another person enough we might even come to blows. Whatever you have experienced, blows bring about some form of change from what was once constant.

Something is blowing around in your life right now. Change is inevitable, unpreventable, but very prevalent these days. Joblessness, homelessness, along with financial and physical fires all seem to be blowing across our lives in America and around the world.

These can be days of discovery, not gloom and doom. We must seek God's favor through faithfulness instead of reacting in fear. As the winds of change blow, we would do well to remember that Jesus Christ is constant: He is "the same yesterday and today and forever" (Hebrews 13:8).

This doesn't mean that our changing world does not matter to God. Rather, it serves to remind us that He serves as our source of stability for our unstable lives. It's time to evaluate who we are, what we are doing and where we're going. Be sure the thing you're living for is worth dying for.

Don't be blown away – stay strong in the Savior – He's not going anywhere!

KeyPoints to ponder:
- Have you come to blows with anyone recently?
- Do you feel blown away? By what or whom?
- Will you trust Christ as the only constant in your world of change?

"You can change your life by changing your heart." – Max Lucado

BODY

Did you know that the average body has between 14 and 18 square feet of skin? Our skeletons account for less than 20 percent of our average body weight, while the muscles in a man's body compose around 40 percent of his make-up. It's 30 percent for most women.

Your body is a beautiful creation of God – intricate and fascinating in its construction and function. The Bible reminds us that our, "body is the temple of the Holy Spirit" (1 Corinthians 6:19). Therefore, we are to honor God with how we treat our bodies. They are divine gifts from the Giver.

Jesus delivered his body for death so that our bodies would receive the reward of eternal life – if we have faith in His forgiveness (Luke 22:19). Even the church is called a "body of believers" as they become linked to our Lord (Colossians 1:24).

How you treat your body shows God and others what you believe. If you ignore it, you fail to follow God's desire and design for His gift of life on loan to you.

Though our earthly bodies will not last forever, we must heed the inspired intent of God and use them for His glory, not abuse them for our gain.

KeyPoints to ponder:
- In what shape is your body in God's eyes?
- What needs to change to make your body beautiful for Christ's sake?
- Will you begin today to spiritually exercise the gift of your body?

"Do not grudge the Hand that is molding the still too shapeless image within you. It is growing more beautiful, though you see it not, and every touch of temptation may add to its perfection."
– Henry Drummond

BOWLING

More than two-thirds of the 100 million persons who go bowling at least once a year live in the United States. Who said that baseball was the only great American pastime?

One interesting fact is that bowling is fairly equally enjoyed by both genders. In fact, only 3% more men bowl than women.

All of these fun facts are reminders that a sport that focuses on knocking things down is widespread in our country. While this is true physically, it is also true spiritually.

We have become a people who enjoy taking down each other through gossip, competition, and deceit. It seems we've made a game of it at the expense of others.

But the Bible tells us to "Be kind and compassionate to one another, forgiving each other, just as in Christ God forgave you" (Ephesians 4:32).

So, the next time you feel like knocking down something or someone – take your frustrations to the bowling lanes, not to the bodies and lives around you.

KeyPoints to ponder:
- Do you feel knocked down right now?
- Have you been knocking down anyone else?
- Will you cry out to God to help you stand up with His strength?

"If you're going through hell, keep going." – Winston Churchill

BOYCOTT

The term boycott derives its name and meaning from the first victim of its practice. In 1880, an absentee Irish landlord by the name of Lord Erne employed Captain Charles Boycott to manage his estates. When Boycott pressed his tenants for unreasonably high rates, they refused to pay. In protest, the Irish Land League adopted the phrase to commemorate the action, and boycotting today gets its meaning from this event.

I am so glad that God doesn't boycott us when we refuse to pay the high cost of redemption to gain forgiveness. God never ignores a person whose life needs rescue – even if we push Him away in our pride and self-sufficiency.

In fact, God's sacrifice should be sign enough that He wants us to get more from life and not less. The Bible offers proof: "Therefore, there is now no condemnation for those who are in Christ Jesus, because through Christ Jesus the law of the Spirit who gives life has set you free from the law of sin and death" (Romans 8:1-2). Since God won't boycott you, your response of belief will be certain to bring you relief.

KeyPoints to ponder:
- Do you feel like a victim?
- Are you seeking victory over an oppressor?
- Won't you turn to the One who will offer you His gift of grace without payment?

"The biggest disease today is not leprosy or tuberculosis, but rather the feeling of being unwanted." – Mother Teresa

BRAIN

Do you remember the scarecrow character in the story of "The Wizard of Oz"? Sure you do! He was belittled because he wanted a brain. We're all born with brains. It's how we use them or abuse them that makes a difference.

The expression of "racking one's brain" is derived from the German word "recken," which means to stretch or draw out. This is exactly what was happening in the mid-1400s in a cruel torture first introduced in the Tower of London. From then until now, this common figure of speech has remained.

The Bible tells us to, "Set your mind on things above, not on earthly things" (Colossians 3:2). It's hard not to ponder the present, but many times, as we do, this often creates a fretful feeling, which can rob us of God's fantastic future.

God gave us brains to think, to respond, to remember, and to reflect. He fully expects us to use them and not abuse them when we become consumed with our concerns and fail to give them to Him. Use your brain to think about that today.

KeyPoints to ponder:
- What or who are you thinking about right now?
- Are your thoughts of bringing help or harm?
- Won't you pause to pray for God to give you wisdom to serve others and Him?

"Man's mind is like a store of idolatry and superstition; so much so that if a man believes his own mind it is certain that he will forsake God and forge some idol in his own brain." – John Calvin

BRAND

Not until recent times did anyone try using a hot iron to leave a permanent mark or brand. The custom arose during the days of medieval cattle trade. "Brand" comes from an old Saxon term for "flaming stick," which of course left an identifying mark. Later in time, an entrepreneur started branding wine barrels by burning his mark on them, and by 1750 most wooden containers were branded similarly.

Do you know that you are branded as well? If you believe in Jesus Christ as God's Son, you're branded as a Christian. The origin of this identity dates back to the first century as the Bible states, "...the disciples were called Christians first at Antioch" (Acts 11:26). It was initially a derogatory term meaning "little Christs."

Then, as now, everyone carries a label or wants to put one onto others. We categorize, generalize and polarize our world too often. A Christian should be a reflection of the personality and character of Christ. If you claim the name, then spread His fame. Do not be ashamed of being branded a believer. You belong to a big God who offers a bright future and who brands us for His blessings. A label for the Lord speaks loudly!

KeyPoints to ponder:
- Is there a mark on your life which others can see?
- Is it a brand of belief in Jesus or a character flaw marked by foolishness?
- Will you ask God to help you to reflect Him as a "little Christ"?

"The best index to a person's character is how he treats people who can't do him any good, and how he treats people who can't fight back." – Abigail Van Buren

BREAD

The Bible says, "man does not live on bread alone" (Deut. 8:3), but, if we're honest, bread alone can make life more lovely. My wife used to have a bread machine, and our home would be filled with the delicious aroma as she baked it. But when we all gained weight, we sold it at a garage sale.

Bread is so good that when it's really good, we'll pay a premium to get it. I remember a time when my father-in-law wanted fresh-baked bread so badly that he paid $11 for the delivery of a $3 loaf!

Bread is a staple of life. Jesus broke bread with His disciples as a symbol of His body to be broken for us (Luke 22:19). In fact, Jesus said, "I am the bread of life"
(John 6:35).

God knows that we need bread, but just the right amount. The Model Prayer reads: "Give us today our daily bread" (Matthew 6:11). Our problem is we often want more!

So if we do not live on bread alone, then what does bring longevity for life? The answer is, "every word that comes from the mouth of the Lord" (Deuteronomy 8:3b; Luke 4:4).

KeyPoints to ponder:
- Where are you getting your greatest spiritual nourishment?
- Would it be worth sharing with another?
- Is it stale or savory?

"Eaten bread is forgotten." – Thomas Fuller

BREAKERS

There are deal breakers, back breakers, jaw breakers, and even ocean wave breakers. A breaker is something or someone who crashes into a setting and interrupts the serene. Is there something that is breaking into your life right now?

To be truthful, we need to be broken at times. Brokenness forces us to get fixed. The Bible reminds us that all have sinned and we all need fixing (Romans 3:23). We've been broken. God our Father has a fix – His name is Jesus (Romans 10:9).

Recently I dropped a porcelain figurine of great value. It shattered and I shouted! When I applied Gorilla Glue on the broken bits of china, it dried clearer and stronger than the original. Yes, the evidence of the accident was still visible, but the result of the repair is beautiful.

What will you allow God to glue in your broken life? His solution is simple: He has given us a sin-breaking Savior to make our lives solid again.

KeyPoints to ponder:
- What is broken in your life?
- Have you asked God to be the glue to repair it?
- Are you willing to be broken again so God can prove His Power?

"God uses broken things. It takes broken soil to produce a crop, broken clouds to give rain, broken grain to give bread, broken bread to give strength." – Vance Havner

BREASTPLATE

A breastplate is a warrior's way of protecting his heart. Behind the breastplate is the life-giving organ that pumps blood throughout the body. If our hearts are hurt, we are wounded forever.

Each year, Valentine's Day places hearts at the forefront of our thoughts. They're everywhere! Cards, commercials, radio, television, and billboards beckon us to buy more to prove our love. But this kind of love doesn't really last.

Considering that the average heart beats around once every second, by the time a person reaches seventy years of age, his heart would have pounded out 2.8 billion beats. Wow! That's a part of our body worth protecting.

God knows there is a part of our heart that is more vulnerable. It's the spiritual self that needs the greatest protection. That's why the Bible tells us to "put on the breastplate of righteousness" (Isaiah 59:17; Ephesians 6:14).

When we're right with God, our hearts don't get hard. We are safe and secure behind the belief that He has our hearts in His hands.

KeyPoints to ponder:
- In whose hands is your heart today?
- Is it fully protected or pierced?
- Won't you thank God for sharing His Son's heart to make your heart whole?

"There is a wisdom of the head, and a wisdom of the heart."
– Charles Dickens

BREEZE

If a light or gentle wind is gusting, I call it a breeze. If something is easy or quick to accomplish, I can say, "It's a breeze."

Whichever way life takes you, there is a way through the trial or test, even when you feel blown away. You don't have to give up or give in to the forces which bring you fear. God's got a better plan. He knows how tough you have it. He knows that life is not always a gentle breeze. He knows your every hurt and what it takes to heal you.

The Bible tells us to count it all joy when you experience trials and troubles (James 1:2). Is this practical, realistic or even really possible? Yes! However, you cannot make it alone. You're going to need God's help. His promise is actually a provision, as God said He would never leave you nor forsake you (Deut. 31:6; Joshua 1:5).

The joy you can discover in times of turmoil is found when you call on Christ to come alongside you. He wants to walk with you through your trauma and trouble to help you experience better breezes as you believe and trust in Him.

KeyPoints to ponder:
- What's blowing you down right now?
- Has it blown you away?
- Will you ask Jesus to send His breeze of peace into your life?

"The Lord's mercy often rides to the door of our heart upon the black horse of affliction."– Charles Spurgeon

BRIDEGROOM

In days gone by, a groom was a person who performed any menial task. Technically a groom is a male servant or stable boy responsible for the care of horses. Early marriage ceremonies were often followed by feasts which lasted many days. The newly married man was expected to act as a table waiter for his bride and thereby began to carry the name of a bride's groom, contracted in popular speech to a bridegroom.

Jesus is a bridegroom in His marriage to the church called the bride of Christ (Revelation 19:7). His desire to serve His bride was proven through His willing persecution and ultimate death on our behalf.

He did not demand divinity; He sacrificially serves us because of His love for us. "Greater love has no one than this: to lay down one's life for one's friends" (John 15:13). That's how much Christ cared for you!

Someday the Bible tells us that there will be an ultimate marriage feast where God will gather the faithful in the Holy City "prepared as a bride beautifully dressed for her husband" (Revelation 21:2). This celestial celebration will reunite God's true church with the Savior for a marriage literally made in heaven.

KeyPoints to ponder:
- Do you hear wedding bells?
- Are you seeking new ways to serve, rather than to be served?
- Have you joined the bride of God's church to await the coming of Christ, the ultimate Bridegroom?

"As a bridegroom rejoices over his bride, so will your God rejoice over you."– The Prophet Isaiah (62:5b)

BROTHER

I have one brother. He's 13 years my senior and for years we lived in separate cities. When I was born, I was probably more of a bother to him than a beloved brother. After all, babies do cry and teenagers do complain.

The Bible says that a true friend is one who sticks closer than a brother (Proverbs 18:24). Just because brothers are biologically born doesn't always guarantee that the relationship will be close. In fact, some brothers are fonder of fighting than forgiving and being friends.

Jesus introduced the world to His Heaven Father and told us if we love and follow Him, we are family. And since this is true, then I actually have millions of brothers and sisters across the globe.

If your family is falling apart, you can come join mine where God is a Father who will never leave you and will always love you (Joshua 1:5). He's inviting you to believe and to become a brother or a sister to the mighty God who wants you to belong.

KeyPoints to ponder:
- Do you have someone who you call brother?
- Are you close or is it clumsy?
- Do you have the same Heavenly Father?

"A friend loveth at all times, and a brother is born for adversity."
– King Solomon

BUDGET

Much is being said these days about "the budget," whether it is national or personal. These tight times demand a more frugal response from all of us. Legislators and corporate leaders are not the only ones who have been loose in their spending. The average American is tens of thousands of dollars in debt and getting deeper every day.

Where should you turn with your troubles? There's not a bailout plan big enough or a surge in the stock market which is strong enough to meet our every need. We actually have only one Source who has enough substance to sustain us. He is God – the Maker and Creator of everything for everybody.

Why do we avoid the obvious while looking for a loophole? How long will it take before we take a longer look at the One who watches us as we worry?

The Bible offers a balanced budget as it states, "The Lord will keep you from all harm– he will watch over your life; the Lord will watch over your coming and going both now and forevermore" (Psalm 121:7-8).

The battle of the budget is really more of a battle over your belief in the One to whom you really belong.

KeyPoints to ponder:
- Do you believe God can balance your budget?
- Have you given Him the key to your heart and your safe deposit box?
- Will you cry out to the Lord to help you to give Him your stuff and yourself?

"How much pain have cost us the evils that have never happened."
– Thomas Jefferson

BUG

Bug is a fun word because it's equally effective as a noun or a verb. A bug can crawl and fly or someone can be a bug. Bugs can even bug you.

Maybe another way to say bug is to say bother. I used to bug my sisters when I would listen in on their telephone talks with boyfriends. And then, we all know how bugs can bother you, especially when they bite.

It's a great thing that we are not a bother to God. He loves us no matter how much we bug each other and even Him. The Bible reminds us that "God is love" (1 John 4:16).
It also tells us that He loves us with an "everlasting love" (Jeremiah 31:3).

Much of the time we love whatever is lovely, but God's kind of love reaches beyond the prejudice and pride that we so easily project. His love is patient, kind, forgiving, persevering, and even perfect (I Corinthians 13). How comforting it is to know no matter how we bug God, He is never bothered to the point of letting us loose. For those who believe, you are held in His holy hand (John 10:28).

KeyPoints to ponder:
- What's bugging you?
- Who are you bugging?
- Will you love God and others enough to show appreciation for the One who loves you most?

"I like long walks, especially when they are taken by people who annoy me." – Fred Allen

BURN

Burns are bad, whether they are on a piece of toast or from staying in the sun too long. Burns are hurts that come from heat when something gets too hot and you get too close. I don't believe anyone tries to get burned – it just happens; and when it happens, you want relief, not a repeat.

What do you do when you get burned emotionally? Someone slanders your name; another person gossips with a lie that ruins your reputation. How about the boss who promised a raise and seems to forget what was said? Then there are those who say you mean everything to them until you discover that actually you mean nothing at all. Ouch! Burned again.

God's goal is to build us up, not to burn us. His plan has a purpose and offers a provision. His purpose is for us to live lives of abundance and eternity (John 10:10b). His provision was to send a Savior who offered His life to forgive us of our sin which separates us from Him (John 3:16).

The ultimate burn of hell will come to those who refuse to repent and believe (Matthew 13:50). It's an unholy hurt that has no cure for those who wait too late.

KeyPoints to ponder:
- Have you been burned by someone or something recently?
- Do you need a salve from our Savior?
- Are you certain of your security through believing and behaving for Christ's sake?

"So live that you wouldn't be ashamed to sell the family parrot to the town gossip."– Will Rogers

BUSH

A bush is more than the last name of past Presidents. A bush or shrub is a growth that is larger than a seedling and smaller than a tree. It is best described as a leaf-filled object that can add ornamental beauty to any landscape. But what about people who we say are "beating around the bush"? The phrase comes from a customary hunting procedure long ago. A hunter would beat the bush to scare out game to shoot.

Once God lit a bush on fire, but it never burned. He did this to get the attention of Moses by means of the miraculous (Exodus 3:3). It was God's divine call to Moses in preparation to lead His people.

Isn't it wonderful how the ordinary things in life can be used for the extraordinary work of God? You might think of yourself as simple, but God knows you as someone of strength. He wants you to be looking and listening for His call. He wants you to grow in Him as well as to know Him.

KeyPoints to ponder:
- What evidence is there of spiritual growth in your life?
- Are you adding beauty to the landscape which surrounds your life?
- Will you ask God to plant you deep and water you heavily for rapid spiritual growth?

"Do not think that love, in order to be genuine, has to be extraordinary. What we need is to love without getting tired."
– Mother Teresa

C

CALCULATE

If I calculate correctly it means my system of accounting is sound. Today's advantage of calculators and computer software make the task easier and more accurate than ever. But this has not always been the case.

The vast and intricate enterprises of the Roman merchants demanded some form of reliable bookkeeping; however, the cumbersome system of Roman numerals made addition and multiplication all but impossible.

The Roman solution used for centuries was to arrange little rows of limestone pebbles or "calculi" to keep up with shipments and receipts for merchandise. That's where and how we get our word – calculate.

Jesus never had a calculator, but He keeps perfect accounting of our every activity in life. Not only does He know people by name, He also knows their nature. He knows your pluses and your minuses as well. He sees you stumble, and He sees you stand. No amount of human reasoning can add up to redemption. It's a gift from God based on His calculation of our need for forgiveness. God invites you to join Him as He says, "Come now, let us reason together ..." (Isaiah 1:18).

KeyPoints to ponder:
- Is your life in the plus or minus column right now?
- Are you living by reason or by faith?
- What do you need to do to truly count for Christ?

"It will cost a man the favor of the world. He must be content to be thought ill of by man if he pleases God." – J. C. Ryle

CALM

When the winds whip and the trees bend, it brings chaos to our calm.

Most of us wish for smooth sailing, quiet waters and fair skies. Well, dream on. You can control the weather about as easily as you can control all of your circumstances in life. We pay big bucks for meteorologists to give us their predictions and then we get outraged when they forecast rain. Our desire for control and calm at times becomes comical, but nobody's laughing.

The miracle of calm was illustrated by Christ one time on board a boat. He was sleeping in the midst of the storm when the disciple tried to shake him awake.
He brought perfect peace with one word as they screamed to Him, "Lord, save us! We're going to drown!" (Matthew 8:25).

I don't know what kind of storm you are in right now, but I do know this. God is your calm for chaos. Jesus will save your soul, but you have to ask him.

KeyPoints to ponder:
- What kind of storms are you experiencing today?
- How long has it been since your life could be described as calm?
- Won't you cry out to Jesus to prevent you from perishing?

"Do everything quietly and in a calm spirit. Do not lose your inner peace for anything, even if your whole world seems upset."
— St. Francis deSales

CAVE

I discovered a cave recently in the northwest mountains of Georgia. The land developer and owner of the expansive property told me it was the seventh longest cave in the nation. I was impressed.

It took me awhile to find it as I crisscrossed a plunging stream, hiking uphill on a leaf-covered trail not well marked. When I found it, I ran to the entrance and crawled into the dark mouth, which eventually opened into multiple rooms as if going into the belly of the earth. I stopped short of my desired spelunking exploration, however, because it was too dark. Though a bright, cloudless day was outside, the inner crust covered with rocks and paths was as dark as midnight on a moonless night. I stumbled to get back out because I could see nothing. At best, I had to feel my way back to the light.

Life is sometimes like my brief adventure that day. We manage well when we see where we're going; we fall down, even crawl in the dark. The Bible reminds us that, "The Lord is my light and my salvation, whom shall I fear" (Psalm 27:1). Often, I stumble in sin as I crawl in my own cave of activities. My only source and salvation is to go to the Light for "God is light" and He patiently waits on me to turn to Him (1 John 1:5).

KeyPoints to ponder:
- Have you fallen into a dark cave of life?
- Are you ready to explore the expanse of God's world?
- Do you think you have been deceived in the darkness of this day?

"Darkness cannot drive out darkness: only light can do that."
– Martin Luther King, Jr.

CENSUS

America's ten most populous states account for more than half of our nation's total population. A lot of people live in a little amount of space. While the city of Atlanta boasts over five million residents, it was not until 2003 that the state of Wyoming's entire population broke the half million mark.

Counting people is fine as long as we don't forget that people count. God created every single person as unique and wonderful and He put us in diverse places for a purpose. It's not by random chance that we were chosen to reflect His character. We were made in God's image to bring him pleasure, not pain.

How are you handling your God-given life? Do you consider yourself insignificant as a part of the whole in comparison to the billions of bodies that walk this world?

You are important. You have a purpose. You are a part of a larger plan. And, if you'll get with God and seek him, you will discover the divine difference that you can make in our world that is waiting for your action.

KeyPoints to ponder:
- Have you discovered God's purpose for your life?
- Do you see yourself as one of millions or one in a million?
- What will you do to make a mark by how you live and love?

"I believe significance comes when you add value to others – and you can't have true success without significance." – John Maxwell

CHAINS

Chains are usually described as linked pieces of metal that form a line or circle. They can be either ornamental or operational. We wear chains for fashion and use chains to pull or secure something.

In an earlier time of American history, southern states began using chain gangs prior to the Civil War, a continued practice of nearly one hundred years. Georgia became the last state to outlaw this method of prisoner punishment in the late 1940s. The decline was due as much to automation as to public protest. New machinery used to build and repair roads did not require as many workers.

The Apostle Paul proclaimed that he was in chains for Christ, speaking of his literal arrest for faith and also his chosen bondage to God for his beliefs. The spiritual irony is that his outward imprisonment gave him greater inward freedom.

Paul's power is expressed as he said, "Remember Jesus Christ, raised from the dead, descended from David. This is my gospel... of being chained ... but God's word is not chained" (2 Timothy 2:9). That's good news!

KeyPoints to ponder:
- Are you a prisoner to unholy habits?
- Do you want to be set free?
- Will you ask Jesus to break the chains which bind you?

"The secret of living a life of excellence is merely a matter of thinking thoughts of excellence. Really, it's a matter of programming our minds with the kind of information that will set us free." – Charles R. Swindoll

CHANGE

The word "change" has multiple meanings. To some it's the coins in one's pocket or purse. To others it refers to a turn-around in life. Some of us like change; most of us hate it. We get comfortable in life; we enjoy a sense of being settled in. "Why change?" we scream. "I like life where I am." Mark Twain quipped that the only one who really enjoys changing is a baby with a soiled diaper!

Our world is constantly changing and so are our lives, whether we like it or not. In the Old Testament book of Malachi (verse 3:6), God said, "For I the Lord do not change." In the New Testament, we read that "Jesus Christ is the same yesterday, today and forever" (Hebrews 13:8).

Today, when you change clothes or change locations, or even get the oil changed in your car, think about the stability that God offers. Remember His unchanging love for you. Be reminded that no matter how much we despise change, someday we will all be changed in the twinkling of an eye and at the sound of God's trumpet (1 Corinthians 15:51).

KeyPoints to ponder:
- Are you ready for a change?
- Have you settled into satisfaction and maybe even success?
- Will you allow Christ to change you today?

"Once you bring life into the world, you must protect it. We must protect it by changing the world." – Elie Weisel

CHILD

Children are beautiful. They are innocent, unspoiled, and mostly pure. Children have a way of showing their emotions unlike most of us as adults. They will cry openly. They will laugh spontaneously. They will give without reservation and take without invitation. Children are a cool creation of God.

Do you think that "age" defines a child? Think again – it's attitude and position. Here's what I mean. We can be child-like in mind, heart, and emotion even when fully grown. And in another way, we can be children forever when we choose to be adopted by a heavenly Father.

The Bible says, "The Spirit himself testifies with our spirit that we are God's children" (Romans 8:16). Our opportunity to create a lasting legacy as a child comes from above as we remember that God said, "I will be a Father to you, and you will be my sons and daughters" (2 Corinthians 6:18).

Be a child again. Keep on loving, learning, playing, and praying. Your Father in heaven enjoys it.

KeyPoints to ponder:
- How old do you feel?
- Is it time to play again?
- Will you ask your Heavenly Father to help you laugh and love through Him?

"Happy is he who still loves something he loved in the nursery: He has not been broken in two by time; he is not two men, but one, and he has saved not only his soul but his life." – G. K. Chesterton

CHILDREN

I have three children who have grown to become men and begun to have children themselves. The cycle of life leads us to encourage the endurance of mankind from generation to generation.

As much as I might want to claim credit for my sons' lives, I cannot. Every child is a God-gift. The Psalmist spoke rightly in proclaiming to God, "For you created my inmost being; you knit me together in my mother's womb" (Psalm 139:13).

Your life didn't begin in a hospital years ago, somewhere at some point in time. You are a product of the power of God from the moment of conception until your present perception of His mighty miracle.

Children are "a heritage from the Lord . . . a reward from Him" (Psalm 127:3). How we treat our children is how we treat the Giver of life. God calls us His children if we will become born spiritually through faith in His Son. This second birth is even better than the first because you can claim its everlasting effect without worry.

KeyPoints to ponder:
- How were you treated as a child?
- How are you treating the children in your life?
- Have you become a child of God?

"Three things never to give up when you grow up: licking the bowl, dancing in the rain, and feeling safe when someone you love is nearby." – Anonymous

CHRIST

Christmas Day is meaningless without Christ. It is diminished to a holiday instead of its intended amplification of a holy day. Years ago, Greeks used the letter X (chi) as a symbol of faith. The X-mark or chi marked the places of worship and became well known among believers.

Over the last sixty years in America, there's been a buzz about substituting an X for the name of Christ in Christmas. Many have screamed that it is yet one more signal of the commercialization of this holy day.

There is a sense of irreverence associated with this move. Yet, in the mid-1800s, retailers readily used Xmas because a sizeable number of Americans could not read.

All this is to say that you can shorten Christ's name, use Greek letters, embolden it, shout it, or even whisper it. However, you cannot have a Christmas celebration without the Christ Child. He's not a good thing – He's a God-thing! Let Christ be the center of your head, heart, and home.

KeyPoints to ponder:
- What mark have you made for the name of Christ?
- Is Christmas a holy day or have you made it a holiday only?
- How will you put Jesus in the center of your celebration?

"How many observe Christ's birthday! How few, His precepts!"
– Benjamin Franklin

CLEAN

What I like most about taking a bath or shower is coming out clean. I look better, I feel better, and I smell better. Being clean is a good thing and can even be a God-thing.

Because God forgives us when we ask Him, we can be clean of guilt and guile. This is a powerful promise from Christ, who alone can cleanse us from our sin.

Nehemiah said, "You are a forgiving God, gracious and compassionate, slow to anger and abounding in love" (Nehemiah 9:17). Who of us does not need to be clean in a world of dirt, deceit, and depression? We all need the fact and feeling that God will forgive and forget what we have done to harm Him, others, and even ourselves.

It may cost you four quarters to self-clean your car at a car wash, but it cost Christ His life to get God's power to clean us up spiritually – here and in the hereafter.

KeyPoints to ponder:
- Is it time for you to bathe and clean up?
- Do you feel too dirty to try?
- Won't you trust God to be your spiritual soap today?

"Better keep yourself clean and bright; you are the window through which you must see the world." – George Bernard Shaw

CLEANING

Cleaning is a chore. Some of us are forced into the necessity, and some of us enjoy it. We love the results, but the process can be a struggle. I love it when it's over, but I loathe it while I work.

Think about your house. Whenever you have company coming, you hurry to dust and vacuum and wipe and polish. You seek to secure help in your hurry because you want everything to be just right when your guests arrive. Somehow, my adrenaline changes my attitude to clean more of my clutter when this is happening.

The same is true of our spiritual lives. Whenever we get dirty from selective sin, we scurry to clean up before others see our filth. But sometimes we cover up more than we clean up.

God has a better plan. He invites us to come clean completely, and He offers to do the dirty work. His Word says, "If we confess our sins, He is faithful and just and will forgive us our sins and purify us from all unrighteousness" (1 John 1:9). Now that's a divine deal. God promises to clean up our messes and to forgive as well.

KeyPoints to ponder:
- Do you need His cleansing today?
- What specific dirt of life has collected around you?
- Will you ask the Lord to give you a spiritual bath?

"God doesn't seek for golden vessels, and does not ask for silver ones, but He must have clean ones." – Dwight L. Moody

CLICKS

I can click on a lamp and I can click my tongue against my teeth. A click is an action which causes a reaction, depending on whether you are the one to do it or the one to hear it. However, to click with someone has more to do with a relationship, like with a neighbor, rather than a response, as with a noise. Clicks are used every day to gain attention and ignored by many who want to remain anonymous.

What's clicking in your life? For many of us, not much; for others, it's too much. Christ didn't click with the religious righteous of His day, but He came to help us get in sync with God. His whole purpose was to turn us on to God's love and to turn off our sense of selfishness.

The Christ-click is an action which demands our reaction. He is making necessary noises to move our world from sin to salvation, from selfishness to selflessness, and from prideful to powerful. As with any sound, we can choose to ignore it or to acknowledge it. The choice rests in your response.

KeyPoints to ponder:
- Are you listening for His appeal?
- Does the sound bother you or bless you when God calls you?
- Will you respond immediately as soon as you hear the Savior today?

"To every action there is always opposed an equal reaction."
– Isaac Newton

CLOUDS

I remember learning cloud descriptives in my early science classes: Cirrus, cumulus, cumulonimbus, stratus, nimbostratus, altostratus, and the like – each developing at different altitudinal levels. Clouds form when water vapor rises from the earth, cools, and condenses.

God used clouds to guide Moses and His chosen nation out of Egyptian bondage toward freedom in the Promised Land (Exodus 13:21). During a devastating drought, God gave Elijah a spiritual sign of a hand-sized cloud to signal a coming storm (1 Kings 18:44). The Scriptures teach us that empty lives are like "clouds without rain" (Jude 12).

But what about the clouds of life? When do they form? What rain pours from them, and how can they be dispelled? None of us are immune to these, and there's no Weather Channel to warn us of their arrival and intensity.

The truth is that we need clouds. We won't always have sunny days, and that's good.
The next time you see clouds, think of how God can use them to remind you of Himself and His never-changing love in our ever-changing world.

KeyPoints to ponder:
- Is it cloudy in your life right now?
- Do you understand that this may be a good thing?
- Is the Son of God shining for you?

"Men give advice; God gives guidance." – Leonard Ravenhill

CLUTTER

One of my New Year's resolutions was to clean out the clutter from our closets and storage rooms. What I thought would be a few hours turned into a few days. Now here's the truth: clutter clings to itself and it multiplies – especially when you are attempting to clean it up.

My wife has her items organized in our house; I have my "organized piles" where I choose to put my stuff. Now, I'm not messy, I'm just not meticulous. The problem with my procrastination in picking up is that the piles pile up until I choose to clear the clutter.

What happens in the home can happen in the heart. Little by little we ignore the clutter of unclean living until it becomes an unholy habit. One Bible saint named David cried out to God, "Create in me a pure heart, O God..." (Psalm 51:10). Maybe your cluttered life needs to make the same appeal to the Almighty.

What's cluttered between you and your family? Your friends? Your work associates? God? Why don't you clean it out before it takes you out?

KeyPoints to ponder:
- Will you ask God to show you your clutter?
- Do you have the opportunity to help someone else to clean up?
- Will you do it today and quit putting it off until tomorrow?

"Three Rules of Work: Out of clutter find simplicity; From discord find harmony; In the middle of difficulty lies opportunity."
– Albert Einstein

COLLISION

I remember my first car wreck as a 16-year-old boy. I thought I was an expert driver with my vast experience of five months driving skills, and then it happened. I was cutting through a parking lot, thinking about my girlfriend whose house I had just left, and suddenly someone put a concrete light post in front of my car – in the parking lot – on purpose, just so I would hit it!

My collision was more than a crash of my car; my pride was also punished. How could I explain how I totaled my 1962 Impala going 20 mph in a parking lot? Of course, that lesson was minor in comparison to the greater collisions of life: the unexpected crashes in school, among friends, family, at work and elsewhere. Collisions are contagious and maybe you are having one right now.

God can do more than fix it – He'll even forgive it. Our foolish mistakes become opportunities for Him to reach in with a remedy. When life comes crashing down, it's time to look up!

The Psalmist says it best, "I will lift up my eyes to the hills – where does my help come from? My help comes from the Lord, the Maker of heaven and earth" (Psalm 121:1-2).

KeyPoints to ponder:
- What is colliding in your world today?
- Are you learning from it or loathing it?
- Will you take your crumpled pride and crushed life to the Lord?

"Experience: that most brutal of teachers. But you learn, my God do you learn." – C.S. Lewis

COLOR

Color is a life-giving word. Without color our world would be dull and dead. From getting my first box of Crayola crayons until today, I have loved adding color to life.

A funny fact about crayons reveals that the names of the colors, as they appear on the labels, are always lowercase because tests reveal this is easier for elementary students to read. But some colors smell – sure they do! Stick your nose in a box of Crayola's and take a deep breath. If you're like me the smell evokes childhood memories.

What color is your world today? God made the rainbow with all the primary colors as a reminder of His protective love and covenant to care for you (Genesis 9:13). Jesus came to earth to give you a life filled with color and joy (John 10:10b). The Bible says that Christ was, "the light of men ... the true light that gives light (color) to every person ..." (John 1:3, 9).

Pick your colors carefully before you draw today's picture for your life.

KeyPoints to ponder:
- Is it time to brighten up your choices?
- What will you draw with what has been given to you?
- Will you turn to Jesus if you have lost your joy?

"When your life seems black and white, make sure you dream in color." – Anonymous

COLORS (Christmas)

Green, red and gold are three colors that announce the return of the Christmas season each year. Yet, they are more than rich colors; they represent the rich history of the most celebrated holiday on earth.

Green represents a life that remains vital and beautiful, even during the darkest of trials. Red symbolizes Christ's blood shed so that human souls could be reconciled to God. Gold promises the gift of eternal life. These colors ring true at Christmastime and throughout the year.

This holiday rainbow of colors reminds us that the season is more than glitz and glitter, shopping and spending, giving, and getting. It's a time to reflect and to remember. We reflect on God's love and remember that Jesus was born to die. His death brings our life, and his resurrection brought our reason for redemption.

What color will your Christmas be this year? Will it be dark and dreary or bright and beautiful? It's not a matter of how you decorate, but more a matter of how you demonstrate your love for Jesus.

KeyPoints to ponder:
- Have your colors faded at Christmas?
- Will it be brighter this year than last?
- Will you allow the Savior to color your world again?

"A world without Christ is a world that is always winter, and never Christmas." – Unknown

COMFORT

We all have "comfort zones." They are those areas of life that when disturbed, we cry out in protest. "It's not fair," we scream. "I don't like this." Instead of seeking our own comfort, imagine what this world would be like if we were looking more to comfort others? That's what God does for us.

The 23rd Psalm says of God, "Your rod and Your staff, they comfort me" (Psalm 23:4b). God has every right to demand that we bring Him comfort, but instead, He reaches out in our times of hurt to bring us His healing.

When Jesus Christ returns to this world again at the sound of God's trumpet, every believer will be united with the Lord. This passage of promise concludes with a sentence of security: "Therefore, comfort one another with these words" (1 Thessalonians 4:18).

Comfort conjures up thoughts of ease and inactivity. Yet, the most comfortable we can be is in the center of God's will and purpose for our lives. Many times this makes us extremely uncomfortable. Instead of looking for a way out of your current circumstances, why not look up to the Christ of Comfort who will help you, heal you and make you whole?

KeyPoints to ponder:
- Are you comfortable right now?
- Is anyone else uncomfortable because of you?
- Do you need to pray for God's comfort today?

"Now, God be praised, that to believing souls gives light in darkness, comfort in despair." – William Shakespeare

CONCEIT

Too many of us think more highly of ourselves than anybody else. It's called conceit. We brag and boast when we'd do better to pray and ponder. What is it that makes us have to prove that we're better than we are?

The powerful prophet Isaiah warns us with these words: "Woe to those who are wise in their own eyes and clever in their own sight" (Isaiah 5:21). Pride is the probable root of our problem. Yet, it only takes one trouble to turn our sense of significance into sorrow.

Don't get me wrong; we should have self-confidence and a sense of realistic value. The trouble begins when we believe that we do not need others or God to help us.

We're born as dependent people, progress to become independent, then learn our greater potential as interdependent. We can become our best, however, when we return to become dependent once again.

On whom do you depend? We need God – we need each other!

KeyPoints to ponder:
- Do you think more highly of yourself than you should?
- Have you progressed from independence to dependence on God?
- Will you be willing to confess your conceit?

"If a man thinks he is not conceited, he is very conceited indeed."
– C.S. Lewis

CONTROL

Who's your boss? To whom do you yield your allegiance? For some, it's a parent; for others, it's a supervisor at work. For all of us, it needs to be God.

When life seems out of control, it is usually when we're trying to control it. Why don't we let the Lord do for us what we cannot do for ourselves?

Most of us think that our reasoning and rationale is at a higher level than our religion. We certainly don't like the sound of someone "lording" over us. We're independent and prideful, but the truth is that this type of arrogance leads to disaster.

We need to be led by the Lord. He promises to "provide for our every need" (Philippians 4:19), to protect us (Psalm 21:1), and to point us in the right direction for life (Proverbs 3:5-6).

The key to receiving this gain from God is to trust him. It's time to let go of your control today and ask the God of the universe to guide you.

KeyPoints to ponder:
- Who controls you?
- Whom are you trying to control?
- Are you out of control and willing to call out to Christ?

"You cannot tailor-make the situations in life, but you can tailor-make the attitudes to fit those situations." – Zig Ziglar

COUNT

How high can you count? My 3½-year-old granddaughter and I had a recent contest of counting. I think she must have won because she kept saying numbers that I had never heard before.

More than a matter of pronunciation, many times it is a matter of punctuation. It matters where you put the commas when you count. Numbers are known by how many zeroes there are behind the leading digit.

Let me test you. How much is the number "google"? It was first used by a 9-year-old named Milton Sirotta in 1940. It's the number one (1) followed by 100 zeroes. Little Milton's uncle brought it to the public in his book entitled, "Mathematics and the Imagination."

More important than how high you can count is to understand that you count to Christ. You are important, not your age or your abilities – just you! You are unique and special to God.

"Know that the Lord is God. It is He who has made us, and we are His; we are His people, the sheep of his pasture" (Psalm 100:3). You count!

KeyPoints to ponder:
- Do you feel like a zero?
- Are you numbered among God's children?
- Do you really understand how much you count to Christ?

"One touch of Christ is worth a lifetime of struggling."
– A.B. Simpson

COVERAGE

There's cloud coverage in meteorological terms, man-to-man coverage in football and basketball, news coverage on a hundred different cable and satellite stations, and then there's God's coverage.

If someone asks, "Are you covered?" you usually think of insurance. My house is covered, my cars are covered. And in the case of my unexpected death, I guess one might say that my family is covered. The benefits of these kinds of coverage or protection come as blessings in the case of crises.

God's got a coverage plan far greater and far grander than what we can buy. His protection is based on His promises and is backed up by His power. "He will cover you with his feathers, and under His wings you will find refuge..." (Psalm 91:4).

Are you covered? The premium for this kind of coverage has already been paid through the crucifixion and resurrection of Jesus Christ. If you believe and receive His plan, then protection will be provided for you throughout eternity. What a deal!

Don't allow God's perfect policy to lapse. Decide today.

KeyPoints to ponder:
- Who is protecting you?
- Are you assured that you are insured by God's protection plan?
- Won't you ask Him for His coverage – right now?

"Our 'safe place' is not where we live; it is in whom we live."
– Tom White

CRASH

You can crash a car, crash a party, or even crash on a couch. What you don't want to do is crash your life.

As a young driver, I didn't know how to go slow until I crashed. I learned my lesson, however, because the expense of the error lingered. It took a long time before the repairs were made to return my car and it cost me months of work to pay the price.

Have you crashed recently? Are you still learning a lesson which has lasted throughout your life?

We all crash from time to time. Even Christ crashed when He met with the religious guard of His day. They tried to wreck His work for the glory of God. The difference which brought repair occurred when He turned to ask for His Father's favor. Will you?

Jesus said, "Come to me, all you who are weary and burdened, and I will give you rest" (Matthew 11:28). The promise of His protection is big enough to repair your crash and to restore your soul. Trust Him today.

KeyPoints to ponder:
- What repairs need to be made in your life?
- Who are you asking to fix them?
- Are you willing to work to pay the price for restoration from a recent crash?

"By a Carpenter mankind was made, and only by that Carpenter can he be remade." – Desiderius Erasmus

CRASHED

My first crash was catastrophic. I accidentally crashed into a light post with my car while I was cutting through a parking lot. Some people crash on a couch after a wearisome day. That crash is less catastrophic and more therapeutic than mine was.

However you crash, there's one strong commonality--change. A wreck will change your life; so will getting needed rest. Changes and crashes – they seem synonymous, but they are not.

A life with God calls for change. Sometimes our lives have to be crashed before we're willing to be changed--a broken relationship, financial downturn, divorce, family division, health issue; you name it. Life's crashes can bring about Christ's cure. He wants to use the worst that we experience to bring about the best. The Bible says, "All things work together for good, to those who love God and who are called according to His purpose."

Won't you let God change you even though you cannot control your circumstances?

KeyPoints to ponder:
- Have you crashed in life lately?
- Do you feel like a wreck right now?
- On whom will you call to get straightened out?

"What lies behind us and what lies before us are small matters compared to what lies within us." – Ralph Waldo Emerson

CREATION

I find it amazing that God can put something together, and it works, but when I try, it sometimes falls apart. He can make it happen, even when it never did. The Bible opens with the statement, "In the beginning God created the heavens and the earth" (Genesis 1:1). It continues by exclaiming that all this was done from a "formless and empty" world. Now that's awesome!

Recently, I was putting together a bed that I bought at a local wholesale warehouse. What a deal – I saved some big bucks. But what I didn't calculate was the nearly two hours I struggled to put it together, only then to discover it was missing a side rail. What good was that?

Not so with God. No missing parts when He puts life together. "For everything God created is good . . ." (1 Timothy 4:4).

In fact, you and I were created in His image (Genesis 1:27). Even if we don't think we are of value, we are.

God put Himself into us in giving life, and now it's our turn to give our lives back to Him. Think about that.

KeyPoints to ponder:
- What have you put together lately?
- Did everything come together as it should?
- Won't you call on Jesus to re-create your life with His love?

"The purpose of life is a life of purpose." – Robert Bryne

CREATOR

One Christmas morning, to my delight, I awoke to the answer to my many months of desire and requests – an erector set! Of course, as a young boy, I had no idea that this elaborate box of metal bars, including a million screws and an electric motor, was invented by A. C. Gilbert who had a resplendent resume. He was a graduate of Yale Medical School as well as an Olympic Gold Medalist in the pole vault.

What I wanted most was the opportunity to create. I quickly spilled out the contents and began to build a tall tower accompanied by a battery-powered hoist, which was my imaginary elevator.

All of us were created to create. We blossom when we build. Accomplishments are far better than accumulations. What we do is more important than what we have and who we are supersedes all else. "In the beginning God created the heavens and the earth" (Genesis 1:1) and He created you in His own image (Genesis 1:27). He made us to live to the max and expects us to make the most of every minute.

How are you building your life and what are you contributing in the construction of others? Our Savior longs to create in you a life of purpose, because you were born to believe.

KeyPoints to ponder:
- What have you built lately which gives you joy?
- Are you a creator of joy in other people's lives?
- What will you ask the Creator to create in you today?

"If life is not a celebration, why remember it ? If life – mine or that of my fellow man – is not an offering to the other, what are we doing on this earth?" – Elie Wiesel

CROSS

The word "cross" has several meanings. It can be the intersection of two lines or roads, it can define an angry attitude expressed through "cross words," or it can become a reminder of our Redeemer who sacrificed His life for our sin.

Let's look at the cross of Christ today. As an ugly, hideous instrument of death, it became a sacred symbol of love. "For God so loved the world, He gave His one and only Son so that whoever believed in Him may have eternal life." (John 3:16)

Man's attempt to crush Jesus Christ became God's opportunity to crush sin. The Roman's rule of the day was no match for God's sovereign rule over all of our days. What mankind intended for harm to one Man, became God's healing for all men.

Wherever your roads lead you in life and no matter how angry your attitude, do not forget the greater cross that proved the power of God over life and death.

Jesus died for you but lives today for your life to have His protection, His power, His purpose, and His potential.

KeyPoints to ponder:
- Are you cross with anyone today?
- Have you learned to carry your cross for Christ's sake—daily?
- Won't you pause to praise our Lord for going to the cross to crucify your sin?

"To endure the cross is not tragedy; it is the suffering which is the fruit of an exclusive allegiance to Jesus Christ."
– Deitrich Bonhoeffer

CROWN

"Crown" is a royal word. It makes you think of a king or queen or, at worst, a dental appliance that covers your entire tooth. Crowns identify royalty and cover the heads of those in authority. They are a signal of significance.

The Bible says that someday the faith-filled believers will receive crowns "that will last forever" (1 Corinthians 9:25). Compare this promise to the temporary adornment offered to those in political, athletic, social, and even religious positions.

Athletes practice and train to get the prize, whether it's a medal, a ribbon, or simply recognition. However, a spiritual sprinter is more concerned with the ultimate reward over the immediate trophy.

What's it like for you today? Are you a slave to your schedule, running on a never-ending track of time? Do you feel less royal and more like a puppet in the hands of circumstances?

God has a design for your life, and it's to become a child of the everlasting King. Jesus is King of Kings and Lord of Lords (Revelation 19:16). He invites you to become a part of His royal family, and it comes by your choosing.

Christ wore a crown of thorns (Matthew 27:29) so that we could have crowns of eternal life (Revelation 2:10). Remember that God has given you the privilege to be crowned with honor and glory (Psalm 8:5).

KeyPoints to ponder:
- What will you do with your royalty?
- Will you use it to rule over others or share the power without pride?
- What ways can you share your King with others?

"Character is power."– Booker T. Washington

CRY

No one likes a crying baby. Crying and whining grates on our nerves and forces us to seek silence. But not all cries are caustic. A baby's first noise is not a nuisance, it' a welcomed gasp for growth, which comes from the gift of air.

If someone cries out for help in times of trouble, we reward them with a rescue. To cry is a plea for help or a pronouncement of a warning.

Jesus cried several times while on the earth during his first visit. He looked over the city of Jerusalem, a promised people, and he wept over it. His heart was burdened for God's people who had strayed very far from his favor.

When his friend Lazarus died, Christ cried again. His heart hurt for Mary and Martha, the sisters of the deceased. Though he proved His power by raising the dead, his head was still suffering for those sisters.

This God-given emission of emotion is not always a sign of weakness. It can be a signal for strength. Because you care for something or someone, you can cry. Jesus did.

KeyPoints to ponder:
- How long has it been since you've cried?
- Is someone crying out for your help?
- Are you ready and willing to respond?

"Crying is all right in its own way while it lasts. But you have to stop sooner or later, and then you still have to decide what to do."
– C. S. Lewis

CUP

A cup is a common dispenser of liquid that is either poured or stored until needed. However, a cup is also representative of our lives. For example, in Psalm 23, King David proclaimed, "My cup overflows." Surely, he wasn't talking about his liquid, but his life.

How's your cup today? Is it overflowing or is it empty? Do you find yourself thirsty for more life and love or satisfied in all that you're experiencing?

Jesus had a wonderful way of sharing how life becomes beneficial to ourselves and to others. He reminded His disciples, "If anyone gives even a cup of cold water . . . because he is my disciple, he will certainly not lose his reward" (Matthew 10:42).

See how it works? We give by helping; we get by giving. That's a great promise with a rich reward.

Your cup of life may be shallow, but it will certainly fill up and even overflow as you choose to share and care for others, rather than complain and cry over your own concerns.

KeyPoints to ponder:
- Is your spiritual cup full or empty today?
- Has your cup spilled out on others?
- How will you purpose to fill the cups of others?

"Wherever a man turns he can find someone who needs him."
– Albert Schweitzer

CURE

Don't you wish you had the cure for cancer or AIDS or any disease that destroys life and longevity? Everyone dreams of a day when our immune systems aren't attacked in such a way as to bring sickness.

I have a cure – His name is Christ. No, He does not choose, nor does He offer to take away every malady with His spiritual medicine. Instead, He can provide a cure for us from the inside out, instead of our usual cry to be cured from the outside in.

We live in a world of disease and personal disaster because it is an imperfect world which is guided by guile and soaked in sin.

Our Savior does not promise a cure from our problems; however, He does offer hope for our hurts. "The Lord upholds all those who fall and lifts all who are bowed down," says the Scripture (Psalm 145:14).

Our hearts may hurt, and our bodies may be broken, but God gives the cure of peace and serenity in the midst of our suffering. Ask Him!

KeyPoints to ponder:
- Are you sick?
- Is it serious?
- Do you understand that every illness is serious to our Savior, especially sin?

"The sovereign cure for worry is prayer." – William James

CURFEW

The word curfew comes from the French *couvre feu*, which means "cover the fire." Its origin is linked to the time when you had to extinguish fires, snuff out candles, or turn down the wicks of lanterns.

The Bible teaches us about the importance of time. "For everything there is a time" – a season for every reason (Ecclesiastes 3:1).

What time is it in your life? If you're young, you think it's early; if you're old, you might think it's too late. However, God's curfew call comes at His choosing and not our own. It is not how long we live, but rather how well we live.

When the flame of your life is covered, what legacy will you leave? Many people think that having more is better, but it's not really what you get that makes a difference; it's what you give away.

KeyPoints to ponder:

- Isn't it time for you to live for the Lord before your fire goes out?
- Do you know it's never too late to turn your life back to the Lord?
- What will you do with the time you have left to leave a lasting legacy?

"The measure of a Christian is not the height of his grasp, but the depth of his love."– Clarence Jordon

D

DANCE

To dance is to move rhythmically, usually in sync with some type of music. Some dances are named for their pattern of movement; some after real or fictional persons. The Fox Trot got its name from Harry Fox, The Urkel from Steve Urkel, The Freddie from Freddie and the Dreamers, and The Soupy Shuffle from Soupy Sales.

God guided us to a dance of life when David dedicated the temple saying, "You turned my wailing into dancing ..." (Psalm 30:11). We are also reminded by the writer of Ecclesiastes that there is "a time to mourn and a time to dance" (Ecclesiastes 3:4). So what time of life are you in today?

If you are discouraged or depressed, it's time to change your dance. You've probably spent too much time with the wrong people or involved in the wrong programs.

You need to rearrange your steps to discover God's guidance. His rhythm is always in sync with our needs and never goes out of style.

KeyPoints to ponder:

- Who is your best dance partner?
- Will you ask Jesus to join you as the Master Instructor?
- What steps will it take for you to stay in sync with the Savior?

"Today is your day. Your mountain is waiting, so get on your way!"
– Dr. Suess

DATE

A date is more than a mark on the calendar or the name of a sweet fruit often mixed with nuts. A date also refers to the relationship fostered by friends with the intent to grow more together.

I dated my wife over six years before we married. We met in high school and grew to love each other even more with time. My dating days were easy, but *not so in the last century*. Farm boys worked from dawn to dusk and were lucky to have any time other than Sunday afternoons to court their sweethearts. If a boy wanted to take a girl out, he had to plan it long in advance; he had to set a certain "date" which led to our use of the word today.

Do you believe that God has a desired date for you? He planned your birth and He knows the time of your death. He also desires that you use your days wisely which He has given in between.

Someday, the Bible says, Jesus Christ will return to earth. We don't know the exact date, but "in a flash, in the twinkling of an eye, at the last trumpet ... the dead will be raised imperishable, and we will be changed" (1 Corinthians 15:52).

KeyPoints to ponder:
- Are you ready for that day?
- Do you have a relationship with the Redeemer?
- What responses are you giving to the Creator who is courting you?

"Live so that when the final summons comes you will leave something more behind you than an epitaph on a tombstone or an obituary in a newspaper."– Billy Sunday

DAY

A day is divided into 24 hours, while seven days make a week. It takes 365 days to create a year and 3,650 days to determine a decade. Every day is important, though some seem more important than others.

Not long after the calendar was created, it became the custom of monks and religious leaders to mark saints' days, holidays, and festivals in red ink. These days were usually festive and to be remembered. We carried the term "red-letter day" to its present meaning.

How we handle our days can be divine or demonic, depending on our attitude and our actions. If today is not a red-letter day, then it probably has more to do with our character rather than our calendar.

The Bible reminds us that, "This is the day that the Lord has made, let us rejoice and be glad in it" (Psalm 118:24). Are you rejoicing today or regretting this day? Christ gives you a choice, so choose wisely.

KeyPoints to ponder:
- What's your day look like so far?
- Will you determine to make it better or be satisfied to take whatever comes?
- What specific steps will you take to guide your day to glorify God?

"It is not length of life, but depth of life." – Ralph Waldo Emerson

DEATH

Death and taxes are two unavoidable consequences of life. Let's deal with death, though most of us spend a lifetime avoiding it.

Death is inevitable, but it doesn't have to be dreaded; it can actually bring delight. "Oh, really?" you ask. Listen to the promise that death brings from the lips of our Lord. Jesus said, "In my Father's house are many mansions (or dwelling places) ... I go to prepare a place for you" (John 14:2). If my only passage to paradise is through death, then I'll choose to see it as an opportunity to claim, rather than a challenge to avoid.

Don't get me wrong, I'm not anxious to speed up the death process for you or myself; it's just that when I die I want full assurance that there's more there than here. Maybe that's why we call it the hereafter.

Dealing with death may not be easy for any of us; however, avoiding the topic makes it even tougher. The heavenly home we have coming is a place where "there will be no more death" – ever (Revelation 21:4).

KeyPoints to ponder:
- Do you fear death?
- Are you prepared to meet the Master?
- If you knew you had 24 hours to live, what would you do differently?

"Though I walk through the valley of the shadow of death, I will fear no evil."– (Psalm 23:4)

DECISIONS

For some, decisions come easily. Others have to be *hurried*. Indecisiveness has lost many opportunities and produced problems since the beginning of time. What we want, we worry over, and what we dread, we are willing to let linger to make a choice. It's a cycle of uncertainty that screams for instant interruption.

What do you do when you don't know what to do? Seeking the counsel of friends is comforting but does not always bring us the best. Gaining more knowledge may nudge us closer to conclusion, but still this can be shallow. Is there a source of wisdom that can give us the answers for life? Yes!

"If any of you lacks wisdom, you should ask God, who gives generously to all without finding fault, and it will be given to you" (James 1:5). God says, "Call to me and I will answer you and tell you great and unsearchable things you do not know" (Jeremiah 33:3).

Our Source is also a Savior who wants to rescue you in times of trouble and turmoil. He not only has the answers to your decisions, He is the answer!

KeyPoints to ponder:
- What decision are you struggling with today?
- Who have you asked for help?
- Have you prayed about it and are you obeying what you've heard?

"Let principles make decisions." – Jack Hyles

DELAY

When you see the sun from earth, you're not seeing its current location, but where it was eight minutes ago. It takes that long for the light from the sun to reach our eyes.

There are many delays in sight and sound which surround all of us. But perhaps a worse delay is when people procrastinate. We've all heard the cliché, "Do not put off until tomorrow what you can do today."

Procrastination is nothing new. We are a people with preferences, but many times our delays will cause disaster. Not getting a doctor's diagnosis or rejecting a certain cure sounds foolish. But there's a human condition which causes worse consequence. It's called sin.

God promises to cleanse us of our sin if we confess it and ask for His forgiveness. The problem comes when we deny it, and even disguise it, which only delays His offer of help. It is time for you to turn to Christ for His cure. Do it ... without delay!

KeyPoints to ponder:
- Are you a procrastinator?
- What have you put off doing which you should do today?
- Are you willing to confess this before God and ask for His help?

"Aren't you glad Jesus never said, 'Just a minute! I'll get around to it in a bit!'" – Anonymous

DESIRE

Desires are God-given, but when misdirected, they become distractions rather than delights. The Psalmist said, "Delight yourself in the Lord, and he will give you the desires of your heart" (Psalm 37:4).

Instead of pursuing our fantasies, perhaps we should examine our fears. "The Lord is near to all who fear him ... He fulfills the desires of those who fear him ..." (Psalm 145:18-19). To fear God means to respect and revere Him – not to be afraid of Him. He loves you and wants the very best for your life.

Until I understood His plan for me, I did not understand that God had a desire for my life. The prophet Jeremiah spoke for God when he wrote, "I know the plans I have for you ... plans to prosper you and not harm you, plans to give you hope and a future" (Jeremiah 29:11).

Our hope for the future is built on God's grace, not our own goodness. You will never be good enough to deserve God's forgiveness. His desire is that you would come to Him in faith. When you do, He responds with love that lasts.

KeyPoints to ponder:
- Is it truly your desire to do the will of God today?
- What are your greatest fears which keep you from faith?
- Have you discovered God's plan for your life and do you desire to follow it?

"All things are lawful for me," but not all things are helpful. "All things are lawful for me," but I will not be enslaved by anything."
(1 Corinthians 6:12)

DESSERT

It was the French who gave us both the word and custom of dessert. By definition, their word *"desservir"* means "to clear the table," which originally consisted of clearing both dishes and tablecloth to make way for the final presentation.

Most often that final food course was a pastry or ice cream, but by all means, it was something sweet. The easy excuse was given that sugar provides a rush of energy to facilitate quick and successful digestion of the meal.

What's sweet to you? Is it just what you eat or is it also what you experience? To me the sweetest times of life are enjoyed knowing I have peace with God. That lingers longer than any dessert.

The power of peace is demonstrated through a life lived with purpose. Jesus said, "I have come that they may have life, and have it to the full" (John 10:10). If your life isn't sweet enough, then you need something more. God is ready to serve you this meal course when you ask for it.

KeyPoints to ponder:
- Are you what you eat and is it sweet?
- Have you eaten and enjoyed a sweet treat from God's Word today?
- What will you do to prepare for God's final presentation of Himself to His world?

"Life is what we make it, always has been, always will be."
– Grandma Moses

DIFFERENCE

I remember a marriage seminar speaker who said, "The difference makes the difference!" What he meant was that because men and women differ in thought, body type, and personality – this is good. Too much of the same would be boring and lead to complicated competition.

Some differences are less obvious than others. For instance, the average male brain weighs about five ounces more than a female. No wonder I'm so thick-headed! Red-green color-blindness is seven times more common in men than it is in women. Outward differences of physical proportion are more obvious.

God's design of differences should not be disturbing. Rather, it should be affirming. It affirms that we are all unique and yet similar as we were made in His image and likeness (Genesis 1:26).

Whatever differences you have with God can be made right by turning to Him and trusting in Him. Even though we are not perfect, we are still expected to use our God-given bodies and brains to serve our Creator and celebrate our differences among His creation.

KeyPoints to ponder:
- What's different in your life from this time last year?
- Are you celebrating your differentness with others or using it to bring chaos?
- Are you making a difference in sharing Christ with different people?

"Find out who you are and do it on purpose." – Dolly Parton

DIP

One of my first summertime jobs was to dip ice cream for customers who couldn't make up their minds, as I was serving 31 flavors. To relieve my frustration from this early vocation, I would ride my bicycle to a pool and take a dip. However, my favorite teenage temptation was to eat a French onion dip with chips.

You can dip your head, your hands, your hat or even your heart. But whatever you choose, a dip is one direction – and that is down.

What is your direction today? Are you up or down? Maybe you've gotten sideways with someone. If you are honest, you'll admit that these are desperate times of life when you dip down.

But there is a way up, which you can know and experience. The Bible teaches "...whatever is true, whatever is noble, whatever is right, whatever is pure, whatever is lovely, whatever is admirable...think about such things" (Philippians 4:8). God's purpose is to take you from life's dips to His divine destination. So, make your choice today – follow Jesus who wants to take you up, both now and later.

KeyPoints to ponder:
- What will you do to think through what you need to do?
- What is your direction today?
- How far down has your life dipped?

"Keep your mind going in the right direction, and your life will catch up with it. It will get better." – Anonymous

DIPLOMA

The word diploma originates from the Greek meaning "a doubling." Its reference is to a paper folded in half, which came to be known as an official document, conferring a privilege. Diplomats had diplomas giving them societal status. All of this historical background leads us to what we now know of a diploma as a document which acknowledges a degree.

Do you have a diploma? Is it from high school, college, or graduate school? Is your diploma prominently displayed or hidden away from public view? A diploma signals a graduation and acknowledges an accomplishment.

Someday each of us will graduate from this life to another. The Bible says we will either go to be with God or be separated from Him due to our sin (John 6:47). The choice is ours while we work on earth.

If we ask forgiveness and confess our needs, we will get clean and gain a graduation gift from God (1 John 1:9). The alternative comes when we ignore the warning and live a life that is lacking.

KeyPoints to ponder:
- Have you been repeating the same grade level for years?
- Are you working to graduate from the school of life with honors?
- Heaven is God's graduation gift to those who believe – do you?

"The greatest accomplishment is not in never falling, but in rising again after you fall." – Vince Lombardi

DISCHARGE

To discharge means to let go or to release. You can discharge a gun by firing a bullet or the Army can discharge a general by taking away his brass. Either way, what once was in place is no longer.

There is both an honorable discharge and a dishonorable one; this depends on your actions and your attitude while serving as a soldier. The same is true in a spiritual sense. We can either honor our Savior by living life with love or dishonor Him through hatred and hurt. Which is true for you?

The good news is that God will never discharge you needlessly. The Psalmist extended God's great promise when he wrote, "Though he may stumble, he will not fall, for the Lord upholds him with his hand" (Psalm 37:24).

God's grip on you will not slip. He is firm and faithful as well as forgiving. However, He expects us to believe and to behave. Before you discharge Jesus Christ from your life, remember that He gave His life to offer you peace and purpose. Don't discharge His divine love from above.

KeyPoints to ponder:
- In what ways are you honoring Christ in your everyday life?
- Do you know of times you have stumbled and have felt the grip of God?
- Whom have you discharged lately that needs a reload into your life?

"We must learn to let go, to give up, to make room for the things we have prayed for and desired." – Charles Fillmore

DISCOUNT

We all want to get a good deal, but as the saying goes – you can't get something for nothing. The next best thing is to get something for less – a discount. Actually, the saying comes from *d'escompte,* a French word meaning "taken from the count." Apparently, the early practice consisted of selling merchandise by count and setting aside a portion when computing its cost.

God gives us a divine discount when it comes to forgiveness. He sets aside our sin when we confess it and computes the cost based on Christ's compassion displayed at Calvary's cross. Because Jesus gave His life for our sins, our belief brings banishment from our guilt. Now that's a bargain.

There is nothing cheap about faith because it cost Christ His life. There is, however, something sacred about forgiveness when applied to a life which seems less than the best. The Bible tells us that, "If we confess our sins, He (God) is faithful and just and will forgive ... and purify (us) ..." (1 John 1:9). That's the best deal ever – a discount from discouragement, doubt, drudgery, and depression. It's our Savior's offer for you to take.

KeyPoints to ponder:
- What price are you willing to pay for peace?
- Do you think you'd get a discount if you earned it?
- Would you be willing to list the ways in which Jesus paid the price for your peace already?

"When all is said and done, the life of faith is nothing if not an unending struggle of the spirit with every available weapon against the flesh." – Dietrich Bonhoeffer

DOG

A dog is said to be man's best friend, but "dog days" are man's worst enemy. The reference is to those hot, sticky summer days. Actually, the words were first coined by Romans as "*carniculores dies*," which is Latin for days of the Dog Star. It's a reference to Canis Major, in which Sirius is the brightest star. Sirius, known as the Dog Star, is so brilliant that the Roman people believed its rising contributed to the sweltering heat of summer.

Some days are like dog days all year long. You muddle your way through them in search of relief. You seek ways to get cool and wonder when you will ever get a break.

God knows all about tough times. He sent His one and only Son to suffer humiliation and death to identify with our times of trouble.

Our human souls are saved because of Christ's dog days of death and the bright and morning star of hope which shown through His resurrection. He said, "Come to me ... and I will give you rest" (Matthew 11:28).

KeyPoints to ponder:
- Will you come to Him?
- What will you say to Him once you come?
- Are you ready for His rest?

"The life of inner peace, being harmonious and without stress, is the easiest type of existence." – Norman Vincent Peale

DREAMS

Dreams are strange. They either bring delight or dismay and sometimes a combination of both. Psychologists tell us that dreams are a mixture of reality and latent fears. Some people put too much emphasis on their supposed meanings; others ignore them altogether.

Joseph had it right about dreams when he said, "Do not interpretations belong to God?" (Genesis 40:8). True, but God reveals His answers through some of us. Before Joseph interpreted the dreams of a Pharaoh's court, he was accused by his brother of being "a dreamer" (Genesis 37:19).

But he's not alone in this labeling. There was Daniel (Daniel 1:17) and another Joseph, the earthly father of Jesus. Even Joel, the prophet, foresaw a day when "old men will dream dreams" and "young men will see visions" (Joel 2:28).

Sometimes God chooses to speak to us through dreams as a warning or as a way to wake us up from going wayward. Sometimes it's the late-night pizza or chili that sets the mind to racing. Next time you have a vivid dream, ask God to tell you the meaning. If there is none, let it go. If there is a message, invite Christ to help you to fulfill it.

KeyPoints to ponder:
- Have you been dreaming lately?
- Do you think God might be trying to tell you something?
- How will you act on what you know you need to do?

"All our dreams can come true, if we have the courage to pursue them." – Walt Disney

DRESS

A dress is both something one wears and the process of putting it on. How we dress differs from culture to personality to economic affordability.

To "dress up" usually means to put on your best clothes. To be "dressed to the nines" is actually a mispronunciation, though it has risen to become a popular expression for years. Contrary to some opinion, it does not mean that on a scale of 1 to 10 that you are dressed almost perfectly. The expression is English in origin and when spoken correctly it was actually, "dressed to thine eyes." This is an obvious reference to being spiffed up from head to toe.

One day there will be a wedding of Christ in his church. The Bible says, "Let us rejoice and be glad and give Him glory! For the wedding of God's lamb has come, and His bride has made herself ready. Fine linen, bright and clean, was given to her to wear" (Revelation 19:7-8).

How we dress or act is of the utmost importance to God, both now and later.

KeyPoints to ponder:
- Are you dressed for the wedding where Jesus will be the ultimate Bridegroom?
- Is there an area of your life where your spiritual clothes are shabby?
- What items in your spiritual life do you need to take off in order to dress up for Christ's coming?

"I've always been a girl who loves to dress up."—Gwen Stefani

DRIFT

To drift means to wander. A piece of driftwood by a seashore has wandered from the water to the beach. A drifter is someone who never stays but wanders place to place.

Do you drift in life? Do you ever wonder why you wander? There's a reason for your restlessness and it's recorded in the Bible. You drift because you doubt.

When you ask God for wisdom in your ways, He will answer, but when you ask, Scripture says you "must believe and not doubt, because he who doubts is like a wave of the sea, blown and tossed by the wind" (James 1:6).

Our world is ever-changing, yet our great God is changeless. He's a constant in the midst of change. He remains when we are prone to wander. He is stability when you have a problem standing.

Which way will your life be blown today? If you believe the Bible and don't doubt, the promise of divine direction can be yours. It's time to stop your drifting and start believing.

KeyPoints to ponder:
- Have you drifted from the Lord?
- Do you feel washed up on the shore?
- How will you begin today to stabilize?

"We sail within a vast sphere, ever drifting in uncertainty, driven from end to end." – Blaise Paschal

DRIVE

Drive is both a verb and a noun. I can drive my car or take a drive in the country. I can be a driven person, and I can be hit with a golf ball from someone's driver. To drive carries the connotation of seeking to arrive. Rarely do we drive without a predetermined destination in mind, whether it is a store, a friend's home, work, vacation, or the center of a fairway.

Are you driven? I mean, do you work hard with determination? Is there purpose to your pace?

The Bible tells us that God "made known to us the mystery of his will according to his good pleasure, which he purposed in Christ" (Ephesians 1:9). In other words, the driving force of our lives should be to follow the divine destiny that God has revealed to us through sending His Son who will show us how and save us for the hereafter.

Our drive is determined by our focus and our faith in God's plan. What we do with what we know will drive us closer to Christ or create chaos.

KeyPoints to ponder:
- What or who drives your life?
- Are you driven by faith or by fear?
- How will you get to your determined destination today by pleasing Jesus Christ?

"Nobody ever drowned in his own sweat." – Ann Landers

DRIVER

A driver is someone who drives. It could be a car, a boat, a go-cart, or a float. A driver could also be a golf club with a big face that is supposed to hit a ball hard and long. Whatever you define as a driver, one fact is always true – a driver is someone or something that represents control.

Who or what is driving your life right now? Maybe it's your boss, brother, mother or another. Whoever and whatever it may be – you are under their control.

You might want to relegate this person to the backseat of your life as a sort of "backseat driver." However, use caution with this action, as the original backseat drivers weren't complainers. They were watchful and actually could see better than those in front.

In the early days of fire engines, those backseat drivers were vital to the quick turns of the track and for equipment safety. Today we want to control our lives and our legacies. We believe there is no one more capable than our own selves. Not so!

We need to let go of the driving and let God steer our souls. "My soul finds rest in God alone ... He alone is my rock and my salvation ... I will never be shaken" (Psalm 62:1-2).

KeyPoints to ponder:
- Who controls your life?
- Who are you helping to steer away from sin and suffering?
- Are you willing to let God be your driver? How?

"No detail of your life is too insignificant for your heavenly Father's attention; no circumstance is so big that He cannot control it." – Jerry Bridges

DRUGS

Drugs are classified as either legal or illegal. They are actualized as either helpful or harmful. Drug dependence becomes a problem when it leads to addiction, which leads to decline and sometimes death. Yet, medicinal drugs are a part of our pharmaceutical society, and we are indebted to their prescriptive care when ordered by qualified physicians.

Drugs have sometimes shown up in weird places. Coca-Cola once contained cocaine and the formula for 7-Up included lithium. Around the turn of the twentieth century, Bayer marketed heroin as a cough suppressant alongside its other new "miracle drug" called aspirin.

Whether for healing or for escape, drugs have been available for our use or abuse. Jesus Christ came to take us on a spiritual high that brings us to wholeness and healing. You might say that the Savior is a divine drug of choice; His choice is for you as He waits for your choice of Him.

Jesus said, "I have chosen you out of the world" (John 15:19).

KeyPoints to ponder:
- To what are you addicted?
- Are you drug-dependent or God-dependent?
- What is your choice concerning Christ? Take Him or leave Him?

"You have only always to do what is right. It will become easier by practice, and you enjoy in the midst of your trials the pleasure of an approving conscience." – Robert E. Lee

E

EARLY

When someone asks me to meet them early, I've discovered that to many people this word has many meanings. To some, early is 5:00 AM; to others, it means 9:00 in the morning. The word "early" is relative to your conditioning and expectation.

All of this to say, God loves to meet with us early in our day. Jesus set the stage as He rose early to pray to God (Mark 1:35). The gospel accounts of Mark, Luke and John all attribute the discovery of His resurrection as "very early" (Mark 16:2; Luke 24:22; John 20:1). Good things happen early to those who are awake and alert to experience them.

How did your day start today? Was it a panic or a pleasure? Was it raucous or refreshing? Was it lonely or were you spending time listening to the Lord?

The great thing about "early" is that it's never too late to be early. Whatever your habit, you can change and rearrange to rise early enough not to miss the best part of your day.

KeyPoints to ponder:
- What time did you get up today?
- Was it early enough to spend time with the Lord?
- What adjustments should you make to be sure you don't short-circuit your day?

"Time is too slow for those who wait, too swift for those who fear, too long for those who grieve, too short for those who rejoice, but for those who love, time is eternity." – Henry Van Dyke

EARSHOT

When you're close enough to hear something or someone, you are said to be within earshot. This term originated as an offshoot from the term "bowshot." Land was once measured by shooting an arrow as far as possible, with the range varying from 160 to 240 yards. This unit of measurement was somewhat standard until as late as the 11th century.

Today we can hear and measure sound with greater accuracy and from far-reaching distances. Yet the human ear and hearing has its limitations.

Question: How far away from God can you be to hear His voice? Answer: You can never be beyond earshot of the Almighty.

God's voice is rarely audible to our ears but is always available as He speaks to our hearts. Christ invited us into conversation when He said, "Call unto Me and I will show you great and mighty things which you've never seen before" (Jeremiah 33:3).

In the world of sounds in which we live, it is vital to discern what's worth hearing and what's worth heeding. Listen carefully.

KeyPoints to ponder:
- Are you listening for God's voice in your life?
- Would you recognize it if you heard Him?
- Are you willing to ask Jesus to speak to you now?

"We do not believe in ourselves until someone reveals that deep inside us something is valuable, worth listening to."
                                         – e.e. cummings

ECCENTRIC

Think of the most eccentric person you know, and I'm certain you're thinking, "Strange!" By definition, the eccentric personality is one that falls "outside the normal pattern of behavior."

More specifically, the word eccentric is a geometric one. Its derivation is from a Greek word "*ekkentros*," meaning ex (out of) and kentron (center). The precise translation is "off center" or a bit off balance.

Eccentric actually could describe any one of us because none of us has perfect balance in personality, performance, or popularity. We're all off center if we understand God as the bull's-eye. We've missed the mark by sinning, and that's not altogether bad. The good news is that we have a Helper and a Healer to forgive our sin and help us return to God as the center of our lives.

The Bible says, "All have sinned and fall short of the glory of God ...but the gift of God is eternal life in Christ Jesus our Lord" (Romans 3:23; 6:23b).

All Christians must be strange enough to believe that Jesus saves.

KeyPoints to ponder:
- Are you strange to others?
- In what ways?
- How can you center your life to bring back balance?

"Concentrate all your thoughts upon the work at hand. The sun's rays do not burn until brought to a focus."
– Alexander Graham Bell

ECONOMY

Our concerns over our nation's economy are nothing new. Comparisons to the Great Depression are often made, as some say we have weathered a period called the "Great Recession." The word "economics" is derived from the Greek *oikos* ("house") and *nemein* ("manage"). Put the two together and we are driven to manage our households well.

God is the Giver of everything, because He owns it all. His assignment for us is to be stewards or managers of all His stuff. Some do this well; most don't.

The world's most wealthy man at the time of this writing is Warren Buffett. This legendary investor and self-made, multi-billionaire filed his first income tax return at age 13 from earnings as a newspaper boy. He even claimed a $35 deduction for his bicycle.

However, there is a warning to the wealthy. The Bible reminds us that, "where your treasure is, there your heart will be also" (Matthew 6:21). In times like these, we should examine what is true treasure and what is just temporary.

KeyPoints to ponder:
- Where is your heart today?
- Is your wealth based on what you have or who has you?
- What will you decide to give away to bless someone else and God?

"Someone's sitting in the shade today because someone planted a tree a long time ago." – Warren Buffet

EMOTIONS

Our emotions are like roller coasters – up and down and all around. When we're up, we are happy. When we're down, we are depressed. God meets us wherever we are to take us where He wants us to be. Where are you emotionally right now?

Let's take a ride with Christ the Redeemer. The Bible says to some, "You have loved righteousness and hated wickedness; therefore God, your God, has set you above your companions by anointing you with the oil of joy" (Hebrews 1:9). Love and hate are God-given emotions that can make us or break us. When we love, we usually get loved. When we hate, we usually get hurt. It's your choice how you live and what you love. Our emotions can either turn us toward God or away from Him. They can build up our lives or break them down.

Check your heart and your head to be sure you are loving what is right and hating what is wrong. Otherwise, you're set up for an emotional disaster.

KeyPoints to ponder:
- Are you up or down right now?
- Is this based on circumstances of life or Christ as Lord?
- How will you handle your feelings to turn them toward your faith?

"Love in a Scriptural sense is not a soft, sentimental emotion. It is a deliberate act of my will. It means that I am willing to lay down my life, put myself out on behalf of another." – Phillip Keller

EMPTY

There's a sense of panic whenever we glance at our car's gas gauge and it reads "empty." The glowing "E" has been flashing for many miles, but for some reason, we either ignore it or we have been preoccupied with getting where we are going. What a relief it is when we find a gas station before our car begins to sputter to a stop! It is so embarrassing trying to get someone to help, and even worse to wait on a roadside rescue.

When you look around these days, you see a lot of motion without meaning. Our lives are going full speed with activity, but many of us are running on yesterday's fumes. We're so close to empty and yet we ignore the warnings which remind us to respond.

Jesus said, "... I have come that they may have life, and have it to the full" (John 10:10b). That's good news. No – that's great news!

Instead of trying to squeeze out one more mile out of each day, why not take time – right now – to ask God to fill you with His love, flood you with His power, and help you to find His purpose for your life.

KeyPoints to ponder:
- Are you on empty?
- How long have you known that you need to get your life filled?
- What specific plan will you develop to be sure you don't sputter to a complete stop?

"The best use of life is to invest it in something which will outlast life." – William James

ESCAPE

An escape is a way out. This assumes that you are somewhere you'd rather come from. The famous Alcatraz prison break in 1962 was immortalized by Clint Eastwood in the film depicting three prisoners who cut a hole in the wall and made their way into the San Francisco Bay. Their escape was made on a raft made from raincoats, but they were never to be found again. There's even an automobile named Escape, giving the impression that freedom is only as far as the next highway.

We all want to be free, but at what price? Jesus came to set us free – forever. The Bible reminds us that those who trust Him are free indeed (John 8:32). This escape is not from yourself or your circumstances; it's from your sin.

No one is perfect and no place is either, but God's gift to us is the promise of peace. It comes through the price paid by Christ's crucifixion.

This escape is from earth to an eternity in a place of peace and in the presence of the Power who gave you life and offers a new life to those who believe in Him and accept His escape.

KeyPoints to ponder:
- Do you feel like you are in a prison?
- Have you figured out how to escape?
- What's your plan and who is your planner?

"You cannot escape Christ, do what you will." – A. J. Gossip

ESCAPES

As a young boy, I loved reading about and watching film documentaries about Harry Houdini, the greatest escape artist of his day. His daredevil tricks were unparalleled, and his popularity was unprecedented. One of his death-defying acts was being chained with locks in a strait jacket and dangled over a frozen river, upside down. After the crane lowered him through the hole cut in the ice to plunge head first under the freezing water, he almost died before wiggling his way out.

Most of us don't put ourselves into danger demanding dramatic escapes; however, all of us find ourselves there from time to time. It may be relational, financial, marital or spiritual. Some of you are wiggling wildly right now, wondering if you'll ever get free.

The writer of Proverbs proclaims, "Evildoers are trapped by their sinful talk, and so the innocent escape trouble" (Proverbs 12:13). Jesus came to set us free through His sacrifice for our salvation. But the Bible poses a poignant question when it asks, "How shall we escape if we ignore such a great salvation?" (Hebrews 2:3a). If you're like most others, you need a life-saving escape right now. Quit trying on your own – it's time to trust God!

KeyPoints to ponder:
- What's your biggest trap in life?
- Are you there now?
- Have you ignored the great escape through salvation?

"Sorrow is a fruit. God does not allow it to grow on a branch that is too weak to bear it." – Victor Hugo

EXCHANGE

Following the Christmas gift-giving season each year comes the great exchange. The average person exchanges twenty-five percent of what they received. This makes the week following Christmas Day the busiest retail revenue time of the year. Of course, the After-Christmas Sales lure many more as well.

Exchanges can be good or bad. The Bible warns about those who profess to be wise, but they become fools because, "They exchanged the truth of God for a lie ..." (Romans 1:25). It happened in Jesus' time, and it's happening today. Those who allow creation to take the place of the Creator have exchanged the substance of materialism for the Source of the Maker.

Jesus asked a penetrating question of His disciples: "What good will it be for someone to gain the whole world, yet forfeit their soul? Or what can anyone give in exchange for their soul?" (Matthew 16:26).

Have we not gained the greatest gift of God when He sent us a Savior? Yet, many have exchanged this Gift for their own glory. Jesus offers a no-return guarantee; it's up to you to claim it.

KeyPoints to ponder:
- Have you received the greatest gift from God?
- Can you name times in your life when you regretted trying to exchange it?
- Will you plan today to give others the Gift with an eternal guarantee?

"We make a living by what we get. We make a life by what we give." – Winston Churchill

EXPECTANCY

I grew up in a family of five children, and Christmas morning was always a time of expectancy. Though we were separated as siblings by 14 years, there was always a childlike charge in the air, especially when it came to unwrapping the long-awaited gifts tucked under the tree.

Life brings different levels of expectancy as we age and mature. As a teenager, I wanted and expected acceptance in school and on the football field. As a college grad, I expected my education to pay powerful dividends for my future. As a husband, I expected more than a social spouse. As a father, I expected offspring who would be pleasing to us as parents. As a minister, my expectations have led me not to waste my life on minutia and mediocrity.

As King David declared, "I wait for the Lord, my whole being waits, and in his word I put my hope" (Psalm 130:5). He expected God to meet his need and to renew his heart.

You'll rarely get more than you expect, but you will always get less without waiting.

KeyPoints to ponder:
- What are you expecting in your life today? In a year? In the next decade?
- Is it worth waiting for?
- Do you really expect God to meet your need or are you anxious?

"When you stop expecting people to be perfect, you can like them for who they are." – Donald Miller

EXPECTANT

Looking forward is much more fun than pondering your past. It creates a sense of expectancy and anticipation. I expect the sun will rise from the east, the earth to turn on its axis giving us day and night, and I expect Jesus to return to this world again – just as He promised.

Are you expectant today? Much of what will happen has much to do with what you expect. Some look for the worst; some the best. I'm not proposing that all you expect or wish will come true. It's just that many of us have less-than-the-best of an expectant spirit and that's exactly what we get – less than the best.

"Ask and it will be given to you; seek and you will find; knock and the door will be opened to you" (Matthew 7:7). The Bible further states, "... You do not have because you do not ask God" (James 4:2). It's not a matter of, "Do you have faith?" – we all do. It's a matter of whether faith has you. If your faith is in the one true God, then your level of expectancy should be high and holy. If you have faith in yourself only, then you'll always run on empty.

KeyPoints to ponder:
- Is your gaze on God and your glance on your problems?
- Are you looking forward or stuck in rear-view vision?
- What will you ask God to give you that you've been unable to gain on your own?

"Expectancy is the atmosphere for miracles." – Edwin Louis Cole

EXPECTATION

Have you ever been through a season of uncertainty? Anxious thoughts race through your mind, and uneasiness permeates your actions. You fear the unknown, and you flee because of your indecision. Questions abound!

That's exactly what God's people of Israel experienced when exiled to Babylon. They were displaced, discouraged, and dismayed. Yet, in just the right moment, God met them at their point of need.

Here is a powerful prescription – "For I know the plans I have for you, declares the Lord, plans to prosper you and not to harm you, plans to give you hope and a future" (Jeremiah 29:11).

We serve an "on-time God." He is never too late, and He always knows your needs. Therefore, you can trust Him to prove His perfect plan through you, if you'll invite Him and then allow Him to work. He knows you by name, "And even the very hairs of your head are all numbered ..." (Matthew 10:30). That's a great God! Expect Him to love you, listen to you, and lead you.

KeyPoints to ponder:
- Are you certain that you are uncertain?
- Are you ready for a proven plan to follow?
- How will you allow God to meet your expectation for your future?

"If you expect nothing from anybody, you're never disappointed."
– Sylvia Plath, The Bell Jar

EXTRA

If you have ever ordered a dozen donuts and gotten 13 then you know what it is to get extra. It's known as a baker's dozen. The term probably dates back to 15th century England where strict laws were passed to prohibit bakers from under-weighing their bread. Since weights could not be precise, bakers adjusted the practice by giving 13 loaves for every order of 12. Such a deal!

Getting extra is extraordinary in today's world of shortcuts and profiteering. When someone does something extra for us, we consider it rare rather than routine. In fact, we are often in shock and suspicious when this happens.

Not so with God. He went the extra mile for you and me. The Bible says that He gave His one and only Son to show His love for all mankind (John 3:16). Jesus is the extra chance we all have to live extraordinary lives with exceptional spiritual significance. Little becomes much when you put it in the hands of the Lord.

When the Good Samaritan took care of the beaten and bandaged man, he paid his bill in advance at the inn and told the innkeeper, "Look after him ... and when I return I will reimburse you for any extra expense you may have" (Luke 10:35).

KeyPoints to ponder:
- What have you done lately to go the extra mile for someone else?
- Would you be willing to reach out to a stranger in need?
- Will you pause to rescue yourself from giving less to giving more?

"We don't get a chance to do that many things, and everyone should be really excellent. Because this is our life." – Steve Jobs

EXTREMES

By definition, going to extremes means going way out of range or going out of bounds. The original extremes were places in the early Middle Ages. The Latin word "*extremus*" meant an area of land set beyond the town boundary which was designated for the socially outcast.

I am glad that God does not avoid any of us because of our social system. In fact, He proved through Christ that He would come to us in an extreme way to prove His extreme love.

He left the comfort zone of heaven and pierced the boundaries of earth to show how much He cared. He is not looking for perfect people; rather, He is ready to interrupt our prejudice and heal our pride. God went to the extremes for all mankind when He commanded Jesus Christ to be crucified – giving His life for ours. This supreme sacrifice of His Son was an extreme expression of love for us.

"But God demonstrates his own love for us in this: While we were still sinners, Christ died for us" (Romans 5:8). Now it's our turn to live for Him!

KeyPoints to ponder:
- What have you done recently that proves your extreme love for Christ?
- Who has gone to the extreme in showing you love, compassion and kindness?
- Where are the extreme places where God alone would have to take you?

"Though our feelings come and go, God's love for us does not."
– C.S. Lewis

F

FAITH

When someone asks, "Do you have faith?" what comes to mind? One person thinks about religion; another thinks determination. It all depends upon your perspective and your persuasion.

Growing up in Atlanta, I remember times of racial tension. One group would shout encouragement among themselves by chanting, "Keep the faith, baby." Faith has always been a sign of strength no matter who you ask.

Faith is akin to belief, and belief is determined by trust. Jesus said that if you have the faith of a mustard seed, you can move mountains and nothing will be impossible for you (Matthew 17:20). Can this be true? Of course!

What mountain in your life seems impossible to move? Is it a broken relationship, financial disaster, or grief over the death of a loved one?

We are tempted to fake our way through the mountainous obstacles of life. God's way is to exercise faith. God's desire is that, "the righteous will live by faith"
(Galatians 3:11). As you face a mountain today, trust God with the problem. Faith it – don't fake it!

KeyPoints to ponder:
- Are you faking faith sometimes?
- What's your weakest area of faith?
- Would you ask Jesus to show you what's really real and do it?

"Faith isn't the ability to believe long and far into the misty future. It's simply taking God at His Word and taking the next step."
– Joni Erickson Tada

FALSEHOOD

In the Middle Ages, it was customary for men to wear cloaks with hoods indicating their professions. Doctors were known by one style of hood, clergymen another, artists and musicians yet another. One could tell at a glance what business a man was in.

The unfortunate downside of this practice came when someone attempted to pass himself off as a professional in a field in which he had no background. In such a case the false hood worn gave meaning to the deception attempted.

What happened in yesteryear still happens today. Many people pretend to be who they are not. We live in a world of false hoods. God gave each person a unique personality and skill set. Made in His image, we were created to live up to our potential and not to lie our way through life.

The Bible says that it is impossible for God to lie, but not so for us. We are admonished, "Do not lie. Do not decieve one another" (Leviticus 19:11). Don't try so hard to be someone you cannot be, when it would be so easy to be the "me" which God intended you to be.

KeyPoints to ponder:
- Are you living a lie?
- Do you know someone who is?
- Are you willing to tell them the truth with the intent to offer help, not harm?

"It is better to offer no excuse, than to offer a bad one."
– George Washington

FAMILY

Everybody has a family. You may not know them as you wish or maybe you know them more than you want, but family is familiar to all, and experienced by few.

Here's what I mean. A real family functions in love, rather than laboring through life. A family who cares and shares together is one that lasts. The tragedy today is that far too few learn to love each other in time to make it matter.

Whether you have a mother or father who is still alive is not nearly as important as what you *share of yourselves while alive*. Maybe you grew up knowing little about your parents or even less of some sibling, but today I have a word of hope.

God becomes your Father when you accept His Son as your Savior. Jesus said, "No one knows the Son except the Father, and no one knows the Father except the Son and those to whom the Son chooses to reveal him" (Matthew 11:27). He also declared, "I am the way and the truth and the life. No one comes to the Father but by me" (John 14:6).

So why hesitate? When God gives you a gift, He expects you to open it! Your Father is waiting if you're willing.

KeyPoints to ponder:
- Who's your daddy?
- Is he the Forever Father who will never leave you?
- What are you determined to do to make a difference in God's family?

"The greatest gift I ever had came from God; I call him Dad."
– Anonymous

FARE

When I say the word fare, some think of a term of equity ("that's fair"), other minds move toward the thought of a carnival; but for now, let's focus on a fare as a payment for services rendered. You have to reach in your pocket for this kind of fare. It comes from an Old English word meaning "to travel." So, when you say, "farewell," you are bidding another to have a good trip. For centuries, it has become the fee we pay to take a trouble-free trip.

How much do you think it costs to travel to heaven? What kind of fare would be fair to get with God, the Father? In this, there is good news and bad news – the price paid was enormous, but the gift given from God is free to all who believe.

Jesus paid the fare for your journey through His suffering, crucifixion, and death. God marked your bill "paid in full" at the resurrection of Christ from the dead. He is still alive and praying for you to respond by faith in Him.

Someday, every one of us will bid farewell to this life. If you die in Christ, you will yet live with God in glory. The Father has paid your fare! (Philippians 1:21)

KeyPoints to ponder:
- Do you think faith is a fair fare for you to pay for God's peace?
- Have you paid the price?
- To whom will you share your faith today so they can join you on God's journey?

"Suppose one of you wants to build a tower. Will he not first sit down and estimate the cost to see if he has enough money to complete it?" (Luke 14:28)

FEET

Feet are funny. They come in all sizes, shapes, and smells. They are the pedestals for our posture and the launchers for our locomotion. Feet aren't overly fancy in themselves until adorned with shoes. Once shod, they become a fashion statement for the body.

The tarsus, metatarsus, and toe bones provide the inner structure of our feet that support the heel, instep, sole, ball, toes, and even toenails. The foot is truly a complex creation.

God has much to say about our feet. He called them "beautiful" when we are faithful to share the gospel (Romans 10:15). He called them peaceful when guiding us on His "path of peace." (Luke 1:79). They are defined as dusty when encountering unbelievers who reject His message of salvation (Matthew 10:14). Even the feet of Jesus are described "like bronze glowing in a furnace" as the Apostle John saw Him revealed (Revelation 1:15).

God gave us feet for a powerful purpose. We are not to sit in a satisfied state. Rather, we are to "run and not grow weary" and "walk and not be faint" (Isaiah 40:31).

KeyPoints to ponder:
- Where will your feet take you today?
- Are your feet beautiful to our Lord?
- Are you willing to wash some feet today in service of our Savior? Whose?

"When you serve, you discover that often the most important things you have to offer are not things at all." – Anonymous

FIASCO

By definition, a fiasco is a total foolish failure, but for its origin you'll have to go back to the glassblowers of Italy. As they were creating beautiful bottles, the story has it that if a bottle was noted to have a flaw, it was set aside and reworked into a flask or "fiasco" as the word is pronounced in Italian.

Maybe your life feels like a fiasco. Good! Then you are ready for God to rework you. His desire is to take who you are and to make you better than you could ever be on your own.

You are a creation of the Creator, and He is not finished with you yet. It may be that He has allowed flaws in your life so that you would not think too highly of who you are. The Bible says, "For everything God created is good ..." (1 Timothy 4:4). "For by him all things were created ..." (Colossians 1:16).

Jesus came to live, to die, and to live again so that we might be re-created. "Therefore, if anyone is in Christ, he is a new creation; the old has gone, the new has come!" (2 Corinthians 5:17)

Just think – your fiasco can become your key to being formed again for God's glory.

KeyPoints to ponder:
- What kind of fiasco is frustrating you?
- Can you see it as a good thing?
- What will you do to let the Lord show you how He is re-creating a new you?

"Isn't it nice to think that tomorrow is a new day with no mistakes in it yet?" – L.M. Montgomery

FIGHT

In the early 1700s, Jack Broughton of Great Britain was the knuckle fighting champion for many years. He actually invented and used the first set of boxing gloves. Well, no wonder. Later he was the original author of the first set of boxing rules. Smart guy!

When people say, "fight fair," what do you think they mean? I don't know all the possible answers to that question, but I do know that it's wise to pick your fights carefully. Some things just aren't worth the fuss and harm they bring.

The Bible reminds us to "Bear with each other and forgive whatever grievances you may have against one another. Forgive as the Lord forgave you" (Colossians 3:13).

Whatever fight you're having, wouldn't it be better resolved by forgiveness? Jesus died for our hurts and is alive for our healing. Rather than fighting, let's look to Him for peace and prosperity.

KeyPoints to ponder:
- Are you in a fight right now?
- Is someone fighting against you? Who?
- What steps will you take to forgive them to stop the struggle?

"To forgive is to set a prisoner free, and then discover that prisoner was you."– Anonymous

FIGHTING

Since the first squabble between Cain and Abel, two biblical brothers, there has been tension that leads to fighting. It's a cruel contest of the wills, usually produced by pride. But most fighting brings only further frustration.

The first known gladiatorial contest took place in Rome in 264 B.C., featuring three pairs of armed fighters. The last historical clash was supposedly when Constantine abolished the gladiator shows in A.D. 325. However, fighting among families, nations, employers, and persons has never ceased.

The Bible tells us to, "Bear with each other and forgive whatever grievances you may have against one another. Forgive as the Lord forgave you" (Colossians 3:13). Do we do this? No! Must we do this? Yes!

Our lack of love and our fear of failure lead us to fight for our rights. To trust means that we have to surrender our rights to Christ who gave His life to replace our strife.

KeyPoints to ponder:
- Are you fighting against pride or because of pride in your life?
- Who are the ones fighting against you?
- Will you forgive them even if they won't forgive you?

"You never really understand a person until you consider things from his point of view--until you climb into his skin and walk around in it." – Harper Lee, To Kill a Mockingbird

FIGS

I love figs. I guess it's because of my childhood memories of my grandmother's home in South Georgia. She had huge fig trees outside her kitchen which sent their scent drifting into the open screen windows day and night. My grandmother routinely picked, washed, blanched, canned, and served her famous fig preserves.

Jesus loved figs also. One day He was traveling the road between Jerusalem and Bethany and was hungry for breakfast. He saw a fig tree which had nothing but leaves. It's then that He did something strange. He cursed it and it withered immediately (Mark 11:21).

The reasons for Christ's actions are simple. He saw a picture of people in the fig tree. Many of our lives look lush outside with green leaves, but they have no fruit. We talk the talk, but we don't walk the walk. We waver, compromise and even condescend. Just as the fig trees are expected to produce fruit, so are we.

Check yourself today to be certain that you are more than leaves alone.

KeyPoints to ponder:
- Is there spiritual fruit in your life?
- Is it ripe or rotten?
- What will you do to help others bear beautiful fruit?

"All the energies generated in the soul including talent, gift, knowledge, and wisdom cannot enable believers to bear spiritual fruit." – Watchman Nee

FINAL

Final sounds so permanent. It's an idea meaning last, and usually not subject to change. If you add an "e" to final you get a different, more positive twist with the word – finale. A finale is akin to a closing grand display like fireworks on the Fourth of July. Instead of something to dread, we are drawn to it with great expectation.

The final words from anyone carry importance and urgency. Your last words should be lasting – they certainly were for Jesus. He told us to, "Go, therefore, and make disciples of all nations, baptizing ... and teaching them to obey everything I have commanded you" (Matthew 28:19-20). His closest friends took His final words seriously and so should we.

However, God still speaks, and His final finale is yet to be. The Bible says we are living in the last days (2 Peter 3:3; Jude 18). The strangeness of the times in which we live is not so strange to God. Christ foretold that, "The first will be last, and the last will be first" (Mark 10:31).

God's great and final days for us are yet to be. The Apostle Paul said that someday a grand finale will be preceded by the sound of God's trumpet, His angels' voices and the raising of the dead (1 Thessalonians 4:16-18). Wow! This final shout will be a finale which will last forever.

KeyPoints to ponder:
- Do you expect your finale to be grand or gruesome?
- Why?
- What would you do differently if you knew this was your final day?

"So how do you make each day count? You learn from God about what's worth your time. Then you make sure you do it. You live with purpose." – Clarence Peters

FIRE

Fire is hot, and it burns. Fires are both destructive and delightful. When under control, they can be a cure for the cold weather; when they blaze without boundary, they can create chaos.

Some people say we should fight fire with fire, and it's true. To put out great prairie fires, early American settlers learned that by setting ablaze a circle or strip of land in the path of a fire, they could lessen its impact. The errant fire spread to brush already burned and became controllable. It was a dangerous measure to solve a dangerous problem.

There is a kind of fire that the Bible says should burn brightly. We are admonished, "Do not put out the Spirit's fire" (1 Thessalonians 5:19). We are also reminded of the character of Christ as the scripture speaks that, "our God is a consuming fire" (Hebrews 12:29).

Don't be burned by fake fire. Go to God and ask Him to keep you burning with a love for Him and a heart for hearing how He can fan your flames forever.

KeyPoints to ponder:
- How hot is your fire for the Lord today?
- Is God burning a particular project in your heart?
- What's your plan to fan the flame of God to others?

"When you set yourself on fire, people love to come and see you burn." – John Wesley

FIRST

Everybody wants to be "first," or so it seems. Athletes point one finger to the sky stating they are #1, or least they want to be. Drivers race around interstate highways pushing to be first in a long line of never-ending traffic. It's a fact – first is famous!

But what does it really mean to be at the head of the class or above the rest? Is it really for the best? Jesus said, "The first shall be last, and the last shall be first" (Matthew 20:16). This divine paradox denies our reasoning and rational thought. Why would He make such a statement to a get-ahead group such as us?

I believe it's because Christ knows that when we score more, run faster, brag better, or push others aside for our benefit, it becomes prideful digression that leads to a dead-end. He wants us humble, not like a loser, but humble as a person whose power comes from above and not from within.

KeyPoints to ponder:
- Who's first in your life today?
- Is it God or your goals?
- What steps will you take to put first things first?

"I don't know what your destiny will be, but one thing I know: The ones among you who will be really happy are those who have sought and found how to serve." – Albert Schweitzer

FISH

Since the beginning of time, fish have been slippery and sought-after. Men have used spears, nets, hooks, and bait to get fish for food. One of the problems is that they are elusive. Since fish don't sleep, they are constantly in motion – mostly away from my line and lures. Some fish are ferocious. A school of 10-inch piranhas, which inhabit the fresh water rivers of South America, have been observed gnawing a 400-pound hog.

God gave us "rule over the fish of the sea," though we may not always know where to find them (Genesis 1:26). A huge fish once became the home for Jonah when he ran from God's assignment to preach (Jonah 1:17). Jesus used two fish to show a willing boy and a wayward crowd how little can become much in the miraculous hands of God (Mark 6:38). More than 5,000 people were fed.

Inside every person is a hunger for what seems hard to catch. God has an incredible opportunity for you to find favor with Him. All you have to do is believe to receive
(1 John 5:10).

KeyPoints to ponder:
- What are you fishing for?
- Would you be willing to share your fish and food with others?
- Will you make a list of those who Christ would like to call His catch?

"Progress always involves risk; you can't steal second base and keep your foot on first."– Frederick Wilcox

FLIGHT

As I write this devotional, I'm aboard a Boeing 767, 30,000 feet above earth, cruising at 587 miles per hour. It's quite a sight, making for a memorable flight.

To fly has always been man's dream until it became reality in Kitty Hawk, N.C., under the inventive actions of Orville and Wilbur Wright. Flight brings a sense of might, along with wonder, awe and inspiration. Did you know that the Bible teaches that someday every believer in Christ will have an appointment with flight? When Jesus comes back to earth, we get to go.

The Bible says, "The Lord himself will come down from heaven, with a loud command, with the voice of the archangel and with the trumpet call of God, and the dead in Christ will rise first" (1 Thessalonians 4:16). Wow, that's wonderful! Are you ready to fly? If you'll let God guide your life, there's a life and a land of promise waiting for you. So, let's fly high!

KeyPoints to ponder:
- How high do you want to fly today?
- What would you want to see if you could fly anywhere in the world?
- What needs to change as you prepare to take the ultimate flight to your heavenly home?

"Courage is being scared to death -- but saddling up anyway."
– John Wayne

FLYING

Have you ever wanted to fly? I have! I've had multiple dreams of being able to fly. I guess it goes back to my boyhood days of fascination with Superman. Spine-tailed swifts can fly 220 miles per hour. Peregrine falcons have gone 217, racing pigeons about 100 miles per hour and migrating ducks average about 60 miles per hour.

Someday we will all fly. That's right! The Bible says if you are a believer in Christ when the final trumpet of God blows and the angel's call is given, then those who are still alive as faithful followers will meet together in the air to meet the Lord (1 Thessalonians 4:17). Wow, what a flight! Orville and Wilbur Wright would never have imagined that.

Whether you live in Kitty Hawk or Kalamazoo, God's call will signal your flight to be with Him forever. Our souls join our bodies and remain to celebrate the fulfillment of God's promise for a forever in His presence. Up, up and away!

KeyPoints to ponder:
- Does flying scare you?
- Has there ever been a time when you wanted to fly away?
- Are you ready for the final flight with Jesus?

"To the person who does not know where he wants to go, there is no favorable wind."– Seneca

FLOOR

A floor is always on the bottom, whether it is below your feet, your office, your home, your school or even your life. Being on the bottom is never easy, but it is often experienced. When you are down, it always brings a frown.

So, how's your life today – up, around, sideways or down? If you are down, there's no need for you to drown. God still has a plan for you. He wants to take away your hurt and bring you help. Really? Yes! A hopeless feeling is never a helpless future.

God said to the prophet Jeremiah, "For I know the plans I have for you," declares the Lord, "plans to prosper you and not to harm you, plans to give you hope and a future" (Jeremiah 29:11). So, no matter how you may feel and how low you may go, it's time to get up and get on with life.

Talk to Jesus, tell Him your trouble, confess your need, and the comfort that God has for you will come to you.

If you are on the bottom floor, realize that this is not God's forever plan. Build on it.

KeyPoints to ponder:
- Have you hit bottom yet?
- Are you ready to get up?
- Will you ask Jesus for a lift?

"Everything can be taken from a man or a woman but one thing: the last of human freedoms – to choose one's attitude in any given set of circumstances, to choose one's own way." – Victor Frankl

FLOWERS

February is a month for flowers. At least the market moguls tell us so. Valentine's Day sales of flowers are the largest of the year because many believe that love comes on a stem.

As beautiful as flowers appear, did you know that there are some flowers that also appeal to the appetite? Chrysanthemums and marigolds have a spicy flavor, nasturtiums resemble radishes in taste, and rose petals are slightly sweet. The problem with flowers is that they fade. Their look and their taste just don't linger forever.

The Bible says, "Grass withers and the flowers fall, but the word of God stands forever" (Isaiah 40:8). The sight and smell of flowers soon sours, but life with God never does.

When you buy your next bouquet to express your love for someone, don't fail to remember the greater gift of God's love given to you through His one and only Son, Jesus Christ. He is the living Word of God whose beauty and fragrance will never fade.

KeyPoints to ponder:
- In what ways do you share your love with others?
- Is it based on their outer or inner beauty or both?
- Do others see you blossoming for Christ and how?

"To love another person is to see the face of God."
– Victor Hugo, Les Miserables

FOG

Fog is funny – it's neither rain nor sun; it's a milky mixture of both. Apparently, it happens when extreme humidity is in the air along with a cloud cover to keep it trapped.

On a recent foggy drive from my home to my office I could barely see ten feet in front of my car, but no other cars had their lights on because it seemed too bright. To me fog is a meteorological picture of confusion where rain meets sun but neither backs off.

Jesus labeled a church in Laodicea likewise. He called it lukewarm – neither hot, nor cold (Revelation 3:16). They were in a spiritual fog. The problem is that they were stuck in the middle of a theological compromise. Christ condemned them and said he would "spit them out of His mouth."

Is your life a fog right now? Are you confused, or have you compromised your character for the clamor of the crowd? Ask God to help your confusion and to bring you back to clarity.

KeyPoints to ponder:
- Do you know any lukewarm Christians?
- Would others label your spiritual life the same?
- How will you clear the fog out of your life today?

"For God is not a God of disorder but of peace."
(1 Corinthians 14:33)

FOOD

Food is the one craving we all have in common. Except for illness, dieting, or while fasting, we all grab forks and go for the food. More than a craving, it's a necessity. But the Bible says, "Man does not live on bread alone, but on every word that comes from the mouth of God" (Deuteronomy 8:3; Matthew 4:4).

Some foods are named for people, like Bob Cobb who invented the Cobb salad at the famous Brown Derby restaurant in Hollywood. Then there's the Caesar salad, not named for the Roman emperor, but instead for Caesar Cardini, a restaurateur in Tijuana, Mexico.

What kind of food does God offer us? It goes far beyond "food for thought" to the nourishment of our souls. His written word dispels worry. His Living Word – Jesus – determines our direction and destiny.

The tragedy comes when we realize that as much as one-quarter of the food produced in America annually is lost to spoilage or nonuse.

KeyPoints to ponder:
- What kind of food do you crave?
- Have you taken a bite of God's Word today and chewed on it for a while?
- What actions will you take to get spiritual food to the hungry around you?

"Crave pure spiritual milk, so that by it you may grow up in your salvation." (1 Peter 2:2)

FORMULA

The word formula finds its origin from the early Roman culture. Romans were precise and exact in religious and political practices. Any pattern of words giving specific direction to be undertaken without change was called "*forma*," meaning form. Short passages became "*formula*," or little form. Today we think of formulas for physics, medicine, recipes, chemical calculations, or even a baby's bottle. Following precise instruction can prevent one's sure destruction.

Since this is true physically, it is also true spiritually. Some would say we are free to follow any formula we choose as long as we are sincere. This would prove to be sincerely wrong. Just as you cannot mix chemicals or foods any way you choose and expect a given result, you cannot blend your beliefs without blunder.

Jesus said, "I am the way and the truth and the life. No one can come to the Father except through me" (John 14:6). His formula is clear, precise, and pure. It's not just a good way; it's God's way. He meant what He said and He said what He meant.

If you want to have a secure future, you must follow our Savior's formula. He's not just a good way; He's the only way.

KeyPoints to ponder:
- What's your formula for spiritual success?
- Is it a secret you hold closely or share freely?
- Is the image of Christ being formed in you daily? How?

"I must take care above all that I cultivate communion with Christ, for though that can never be the basis of my peace, it will be the channel of it." – Charles H. Spurgeon

FORTRESS

A fortress is best defined as a place of protection. We may picture it as a high-walled stockade. We often abbreviate the term with the word "fort." However you say it, it still means the same thing – reminding us that when we are under attack, we need a safe place to retreat.

The Psalmist said repeatedly, "the Lord is my rock, my fortress" (Psalm 18:2; Psalm 31:2; Psalm 71:3). We need to know this. We need a place of protection, security, safety, and solace.

The threat of terrorist invasion is nothing new. Our world has been under attack from the time that the serpent enticed Adam and Eve to disobey God's promise of protection in the Garden of Eden. Jesus said, "The thief comes only to steal and kill and destroy …" (John 10:10a). However, His warning against the devil's delight is backed by His promise of power as He went on to say, "I have come that they may have life and have it to the full" (John 10:10b).

When Martin Luther wrote "A Mighty Fortress Is Our God," he knew our need and the One who can meet it. So should we.

KeyPoints to ponder:
- What's the most vulnerable part of your life?
- Have you asked for God's protection?
- Who are others around you to whom you can offer God's security?

"If we follow Jesus and look only to His righteousness, we are in his hands and under the protection of Him and His Father. And if we are in communion with the Father, nought can harm us."
– Dietrich Bonhoeffer

FREEDOM

Today there is a straining and a searching for the next big thrill – the immediate rush and the secret to instant success. We act as if that will make us free. We forget the price that was paid in the past for what we have in the present. Somehow it seems so irrelevant and unnecessary to look backward, but in order to see more clearly in the now, we must.

Each July 4 we celebrate our nation's freedom. The liberty that we enjoy was blood-bought, life-given, and a product of the prowess of the saints and heroes from the past. Our glibness and apathy are no match for the courage displayed by those who fought for our freedom.

We need to remember. We must reflect, and we cannot reject, the incredible sacrifice paid for the privileges which we enjoy in America today. God forgive our superficial selfishness when we fail to be grateful to our forefathers.

Let's do what the Bible says, "Live as free men, but do not use your freedom as a cover-up for evil; live as servants of God" (I Peter 2:16).

KeyPoints to ponder:
- Do you feel free today?
- What or who has you in bondage?
- In what ways has God set you free?

"History does not long entrust the care of freedom to the weak or the timid." – Dwight D. Eisenhower

FRESH

Did you know that the color of the plastic tab used to close a loaf of bread indicates the day it was delivered fresh to the store? It's a funny fact, but it's true. While the colors can vary regionally, traditionally they run alphabetically to indicate what's fresh and what needs to be frozen. Blue means delivered on Monday, green on Tuesday, orange on Wednesday, red on Thursday, white on Friday and yellow on Saturday. When what you eat is fresh, its taste is at the top, and if it's not, the risk is rot.

Jesus taught us to pray, "Give us each day our daily bread" (Luke 11:3). One translation states it this way, "Give us our food day by day." Christ knew that each day we need something fresh both physically and spiritually. God never intends for us to survive from stale bread, but to fulfill our spiritual hunger each day from His word.

As you spend time in prayer and Bible study today, you'll experience a bite of fresh faith. Jesus said, "I am the bread of life." Take a slice. It's nice!

KeyPoints to ponder:
- Is your faith stale or fresh?
- How hungry are you for a fresh word from the Lord?
- Would you be willing to share your spiritual food with others whose has gone stale?

"Blessed are those who hunger and thirst for righteousness, for they will be filled." (Matthew 5:6)

FRUIT

A stroll down the produce aisle at your favorite grocery store will inevitably lead you to displays of fruit awaiting your selection and sale. The beauty and bounty of these choices came with lots of labor. First the seed, then the soil, followed by planting, watering, cultivation, and crating. It's a carefully planned process.

Jesus said, "By their fruit your will recognize them" (Matthew 7:16). He was warning His disciples against false prophets whose personal lives were like rotten fruit.

We would do well not only to check out the lives of others, but especially examine our own. Is your life fruitful for God? Do you find yourself driven to success more than significance? Like cranberries which don't show their ripeness by color, but by bounce, what we see on the outside may not be how sweet we are on the inside.

If God were to check your bounce as well as your beauty, would He pick you for His garden?

KeyPoints to ponder:
- Who is the fruit inspector in your Christian life?
- Is your fruit sweet or sour?
- What are you doing to keep your fruit from rotting?

"My philosophy of life is that if we make up our mind what we are going to make of our lives, then work hard toward that goal, we never lose, somehow we win out." – Ronald Reagan

FRUITFUL

Christmas is a time of giving, getting, eating, and indulging. It's not the bad stuff we run from, but the good. The desserts are delightful, but they put pounds on us that are frightful! What's a person to do?

The sweetest delights come in God's wrappings – like fruit. The apple has skin, the orange has a peel, and the banana has a yellow jacket. We know they're good for us, but still we go with the ooey-gooey, calorie-filled confections.

The same is true spiritually. The sweeter and easier it is to eat, we go for it. But the real nourishment comes when we unpeel the truths that are God-given, when we seek what is fruitful from God our Father.

The Bible tells us that if we delight in the Lord we will be like a fruit-yielding tree
(Psalm 1:2-3). Jesus scolded the religious do-gooders of His day, admonishing them to "produce fruit in keeping with your repentance" (Matthew 3:8). The Apostle Paul wrote that we were made to "bear fruit for God" (Romans 7:4).

Check your appetite for fruit during this season; refuse to race to what's sweet, easy, and empty. Be fruitful in blessing God, others, and yourself.

KeyPoints to ponder:
- What is the evidence that you are fruitful in God's service?
- Have you fallen recently to fruitlessness?
- How will you get up and get going to bear spiritual fruit for God's glory?

"Every day that we're not practicing godliness we're being conformed to the world of ungodliness around us." – Jerry Bridges

FULFILL

The word "fulfill" is actually two words that work as one – full and fill. Actually, its meaning is better understood when you transpose the words for a clear descriptive. Fulfill means to fill full. Even when you understand it, you may not be experiencing it. Most of us live lives that are full, but few of us can say we are completely fulfilled. The wise writer of Proverbs reminds us, "A longing fulfilled is sweet to the soul ..." (Proverbs 13:19).

"The Lord is not slow in keeping his promise ... He is patient with you, not wanting any to perish ..." (2 Peter 3:9). We serve no slack Savior. He wants us to live fulfilled lives and created us to hunger for that which is holy.

Our problem persists in that we want the quick and easy solutions, rather than the tough and difficult struggles. But you cannot grow to fulfillment until you understand your weaknesses and flaws. Every marble statue is a product of pressure from the chisel and hammer blows of the artist.

Before our lives become truly fulfilled, we must also feel the pains that will ultimately lead to life's gains.

KeyPoints to ponder:
- Do you feel fulfilled?
- What would it take to get you to a place of purpose in life?
- Will you allow today's pressures and pains to bring you ultimate peace?

"Life is not easy for any of us. We must have perseverance and, above all, confidence in ourselves. We must believe that we are gifted for something, and that this something, at whatever cost, must be attained." – Marie Curie

FULL

If someone says "I'm full," it obviously means the opposite of empty. It may be full of food or full of joy or full of life. Whatever the state of fullness, it usually becomes a statement of satisfaction.

However, the antithesis can also be anticipated. For instance, you can be full of anger, full of sorrow, or full of greed. It is vital that our fullness be favorable and not foolish to God and to ourselves.

The Bible tells us, "Do not hate your brother" (Leviticus 19:17) and to "be on your guard against all kinds of greed ..." (Luke 12:15). Instead, we are admonished to be "full of faith and of the Holy Spirit" as was Stephen, who was chosen as an early church leader (Acts 6:5).

What fills your day? Idle clutter and senseless searching are not signs of security. Our Savior has a plan for your life that includes fulfillment and joy. If you'll turn from what seems so right in your life to the One who knows what's right for your life, you can be full – forever!

KeyPoints to ponder:
- Do you feel full?
- Is it a fullness which brings you satisfaction or sadness?
- What will you plan today which will clear your clutter for Christ's sake?

"The biggest mistake people make in life is not making a living at doing what they most enjoy." – Malcolm S. Forbes

G

GAMBLE

In 1932, Werner Heisenberg was awarded the Nobel Prize in physics for his uncertainty principle. In response, Albert Einstein remarked, "I shall never believe that God plays dice with the universe." He said such a statement because he believed the principle made a mockery of cause and effect.

Have you ever accused God of gambling with your life? He is a God of order and creation, not confusion. The Bible reminds us, "In the beginning you (God) laid the foundations of the earth, and the heavens are a work of your hands" (Psalm 102:25).

What Einstein knew is that God is the cause of all matter, and we are the product or the effect. Our problem comes when we insist on leaning on our luck in life, rather than leaning on the Lord.

We make a mockery of our Maker when we act as if we are put on earth by chance, rather than by divine choice. Don't gamble with God.

KeyPoints to ponder:
- Are you leaning on luck or the Lord to guide you?
- Do you believe God made you for a divine purpose?
- What will you do to discover His purposes for your life?

"What is my vision of God's purpose for me? Whatever it may be, His purpose is for me to depend on Him and on His power now."
– Oswald Chambers

GARBAGE

On average, more than 1,500 pounds of garbage is generated annually by every man, woman, and child in the United States. In fact, this discarded trash includes up to 20 billion disposable diapers. Yuck!

There's a well-known computer adage that was popular in earlier days which proclaimed, "Garbage in – garbage out." In other words, what is programmed into the computer is what will be delivered as the product from the computer.

The same is true of our hearts and heads. What we put into them will also come out. Sometimes it spills out, depending on how hard we are pushed. Have you ever said something that surprised you, wishing you could take it back? Sure, we all have. The truth is that what we say or spill comes from the information we have stored.

The Psalmist said, "Your word have I hidden in my heart, that I may not sin against you (God)" (Psalm 119:11). Storing up wise words will help you later to spill them out on others.

KeyPoints to ponder:
- Is there any garbage in your life right now?
- Have you given it to God to dispose of it?
- Do you find yourself going back to it even if you've thrown it away?

"A wise man's heart guides his mouth, and his lips promote instruction." (Proverbs 16:23)

GARDEN

Several years ago, I traded my pastureland attached to my former house for a small garden that now takes my time. I went from eight acres of land to one-third of an acre that is mostly house. But I love my garden.

The word's origin is interesting, as it was first spelled "gardin" in the Old English and was a sacred place. Containing the substance of life, gardens in medieval times were the responsibility of monks; as a result, you could find one near every monastery and abbey. Before long, the monks devised walls and fences to protect these sacred plots, areas referred to as the "guarded" lands. Later translated as garden, that came to stand for any amount of land set aside for growing, guarded with walls or not.

God gave man his first home in the Garden of Eden (Genesis 2:8). It was in a garden that Judas betrayed Jesus (John 18:1-2). The Christ was crucified near a garden and placed in a new tomb nearby (John 19:41). Just as plants come alive from seeds that appear dead, so Christ arose to invite us into His garden of life. Our need is to plant this truth deep into the soil of our souls.

KeyPoints to ponder:
- Does your life garden have weeds in it?
- Are you in dire need of being watered with God's Word?
- How are you planning to bear spiritual fruit to share with others today?

"God Almighty first planted a garden. And indeed, it is the purest of human pleasures."—Francis Bacon

GIFTS

'Tis the season to give and get. Gifts are the name of the game. What you get is supposed to represent your value; what you give is sure to prove your love. Oh, if it were really so simple.

Think of the gifts brought to Jesus to celebrate His birth. The Magi opened their treasures and presented Christ with gifts of gold, incense and myrrh (Matthew 2:1-2, 11). Today's shoppers spend more than $4 billion per Christmas shopping day or about $2.8 million each minute during the holiday season in the United States alone. The average person will spend more than $1,000 on Christmas gifts this year.

God's gift to us was priceless. He sacrificed His Son to give us eternity and a powerful promise of His presence. We have the best-ever as believers, and yet we crave more. We look to get, rather than give because our selfishness precedes our selflessness.

The Magi brought valuable gold, incense and myrrh – all three of which were incredibly valuable.

KeyPoints to ponder:
- What gift do you bring to Jesus this year?
- Will it be simple or sacrificial?
- Have you accepted God's greatest gift of Jesus Christ as your personal Savior?

"Relationships with people, not things, are the best gifts of all."
– Anonymous

GIVING

Giving is a generous term. It encompasses what we share with others, as well as how much of ourselves we offer. We cannot determine the response to our giving, and we really shouldn't demand it. Giving is at its best unselfish, and at its worst self-serving.

What kind of giver are you? I like what the Apostle Paul proclaimed, "Each man should give what he has decided in his heart to give, not reluctantly or under compulsion, for God loves a cheerful giver" (2 Corinthians 9:7). Your heart should guide your hand in giving so the question is "How's your heart?" A good guideline is to understand that we are to "Give, and it will be given to you ... For with the measure you use, it will be measured to you" (Luke 6:38).

Since God is so generous in giving us all we have, why then do we hoard so much? Why do we hold on to what we have when it's all on loan anyway? The more we let loose of what we hold, the freer we can become to receive what God is willing to give. Today is a great time for a heart check.

KeyPoints to ponder:
- Is your heart generous or greedy?
- Do you honestly believe it is more blessed to give than to receive?
- How will you prove your love for God and others today through giving?

"Giving frees us from the familiar territory of our own needs by opening our mind to the unexplained worlds occupied by the needs of others." – Barbara Bush

GLASS

Did you know that glass is made up of three components: silica, or sand; an alkali flux, such as soda or potash; and lye, which stabilizes the mixture? We say statements like "clear as glass," "slick as glass," and "clean as glass." Some say the glass is half-empty; to others, the glass is half-full. What do you say?

Glass is used as a container to hold what we want. A problem occurs when we drop it. It shatters because it is fragile. Like life, a glass can offer nourishment or become a nuisance if its sharp edges cut into our routines.

The Bible tells us that, "Now we see but a poor reflection as in a mirror ..." here on earth (1 Corinthians 13:12). But someday we will see God as through a clear glass, face-to-face. What will you do when that day arrives? Will you be prepared by faith or petrified in fear?

God's offer for a clear view of life is available to all. He wants to fill your glass and your life with His love and His luster. When your glass seems half-empty, it's time to turn to Jesus who fills it full.

KeyPoints to ponder:
- Does your life feel shattered?
- Will you ask God to give you a clear view of what's going on?
- Whose glass do you need to clean today?

"Vision is the art of seeing the invisible." – Jonathan Swift

GO

"Go" is an action word! Green means go; horn-honking means go; a wave of a hand can mean go.

When Jesus said, "Go and make disciples of all nations" (Matthew 28:19), it was not a soft suggestion, but a solid command. He knew that God's message of hope needed our initiative to be complete. Actually, the literal rendering of his command is better understood "as you go."

God knows we are people on the go as we go, day and night, week by week, and year after year. Our going can be filled with purpose and power or it can be idle and useless. He wants our going to have a meaning and a message. Does yours?

If you journaled your goings today, what would they offer in return? Was someone's life encouraged? Was there a conversation which brought healing? Did you challenge someone to become a stronger disciple of God? As you go about your activities today, determine to make a difference to please God in all you do, wherever you go.

KeyPoints to ponder:
- Are you ready to go?
- If you are, then where are you going to go?
- How can you support and help others to go and share the Good News of Jesus?

"If your actions inspire others to dream more, learn more, do more and become more, you are a leader." – John Quincy Adams

GOAL

When I say the word "goal," the athlete thinks of scoring. To the student it means achievement. To the business person it proclaims productivity. Just because you score more does not necessarily mean you've reached your goal. The highest scoring pro basketball game to date was played in 1983 when the Detroit Pistons beat the Denver Nuggets 186-183. Gordie Howe holds the lifetime record for hockey goals with 801 in his 25-year career, ending with the Detroit Red Wings. Are these records really revealing of a deeper goal? Maybe not.

The highest goal is to please God. The Apostle Paul said, "I press on toward the goal to win the prize for which God has called me heavenward in Christ Jesus" (Philippians 3:14).

Our great goal is accomplished when we discover who we are, decide where we need to go in our lives, determine to gain God's help to get there, and ultimately bring delight to our Creator and his creation.

KeyPoints to ponder:
- What's your goal going to be?
- Are you scoring for self-gain or God's glory?
- Who's keeping score on your life and why?

"If you don't know where you are going, you might wind up someplace else."– Yogi Berra

GOBLIN

Spooks, spirits, ghosts, and goblins are more than a Halloween haunting; they are an everyday fear for many people.

While several accounts exist for the origin of the word "goblin," perhaps the most popular dates back to the early 1400s. At the time, a beautiful red fabric came out of Paris, created by Gilles and Jehan Gobelin. So stunning was this cloth that Louis XIV declared their factory a royal business.

With this, the superstitious and jealous locals of the day started rumors suggesting that the brothers must have sold their souls to the devil in exchange for the sudden fortune. As a result, the Gobelins were ostracized, and their names were made synonymous with the word we now associate with evil and mischief.

But God's Spirit is the opposite of evil. Jesus said, "The Spirit of the Lord is on me ..." (Luke 4:18). We are told that, "God is Spirit ..." (Luke 4:24), and we are commanded to live lives that are filled with God's Spirit, led by His Spirit, and producing the fruit of His Spirit (Galatians 5:18-23).

KeyPoints to ponder:
- Which spirit are you following?
- Is it holy or haunting?
- Where is God guiding you to amplify His Spirit's affect in your community?

"A sinner can no more repent and believe without the Holy Spirit's aid than he can create a world." – Charles Spurgeon

GOOD

When someone asks you, "How are you today?" most people respond, "Good" whether it's the truth or not. I've changed my answer to "I'm well – thank you." The reason is personal, but it's also biblical. Scripture teaches us that, "No one is good – except God alone" (Luke 18:19), though we are continually admonished to do good.

Isaiah tells us to "learn to do good" (Isaiah 1:17), and the gospel of Luke reminds us to "do good to those who hate you" (Luke 6:27). Jesus defined Himself as the "good shepherd" (John 10:14), and we are commanded to "fight the good fight of the faith" (1 Timothy 6:12).

So, what's good about your day so far? Did it start right? Will it end right? What good will occur for you in the next twenty-four hours, week, month, and year?

Much good depends on you and your connection to Christ. Since God alone is truly good, then we would do well to listen to His wise words, learn from His godly guidelines, and lean on His holiness.

KeyPoints to ponder:
- Getting back to where we started, "How are you today?"
- Can you really say, "good"?
- What will it take for you to make it better than a good day?

"Do all the good you can. By all the means you can. In all the ways you can. In all the places you can. At all the times you can. To all the people you can. As long as ever you can." – John Wesley

GOSSIP

Do you notice that many people love to whisper a bit of juicy gossip to their friends? This isn't a twenty-first century invention. It links itself to ancient Greece where the retelling of gossip became a favorite pastime.

Such confidential tidbits were termed anecdotes, from the two words "*an*" (not) and "*ekdotos*" (published). Though most good gossip seems to quickly find itself into media publications today, still the unpublished anecdotes remain extremely popular and ever-dangerous.

The Bible warns against idle gossip because of the hurt it brings to our character and even to the church. We are told, "a gossip betrays a confidence" and thereby distorts the truth (Proverbs 20:19). "Gossip separates close friends" according to one wise proverb (Proverbs 16:28) and we are given a long list of destructive disorders such as quarreling, jealousy, anger, factions, slander, and arrogance, including gossip, as ways which deny and delay the power of God.

KeyPoints to ponder:
- What is your tongue telling others which should be kept to yourself?
- Have you hurt the heart of another or bruised a reputation recently?
- Are you willing to ask for forgiveness from them and from God?

"Notice, we never pray for folks we gossip about, and we never gossip about the folk for whom we pray! For prayer is a great deterrent." – Leonard Ravenhill

GRASS

I love the smell of freshly-cut grass. It brings a memory back to my days of playing football every fall. Grass is green and grows so quickly that it demands constant attention lest it look unkempt.

Wintertime is a reminder that the green, lush grass of spring and summer quickly withers with the weather. As this is true in the life cycle of grass, so it is true of our lives. We will not last.

It's a sad fact that degeneration begins at birth. Though our bodies build up through the years, they also break down. Isaiah the prophet, once wrote, "All men are like grass and all their glory is like the flowers of the field. The grass withers, and the flowers fall ..." (Isaiah 40:6-7). By itself, this statement would be depressing, but he continued in his truth-telling saying, "the word of our God stands forever" (Isaiah 40:8).

This is great news! In our times of sorrow, God becomes our strength. Though nothing seems to last, God does, and He will not forget or forsake you (Hebrews 13:5).

KeyPoints to ponder:
- What is fading fast for you today?
- Have you made the Word of God your greatest source of strength?
- What actions will you take to leave a legacy of love after you go?

"Spiritual seasons are not spiritual conditions of the saint nor a way of measuring Godliness. God ordains spiritual seasons to provide the greatest spiritual fruit bearing and the greatest spiritual growth."– Dennis Mutumma

GRAVE

When thinking about the word "grave," most minds race to several thoughts. One is a burial spot; another is a condition of great or serious concern – like, "He has a grave medical condition." The more popular thought of a grave invokes a cemetery setting.

Did you know that it was Hubert Eaton who came up with the idea of having grave markers flush with the ground in order to give cemeteries a more "park-like" feel? He also knew that it was easier to cut grass this way. No wonder, he's the founder of Forest Lawn Memorial Parks!

Jesus had both a grave condition and a burial grave. His condition was one that led Him to a crucifixion cross (John 19:16). His grave was a borrowed tomb in the side of a cliff (John 19:41). His condition was one of love for all mankind. Though He died for love, He lives today because the grave could not hold Him. His resurrection from the dead proved His divine nature and the power of God.

Just remember, where you may be buried someday is of little significance in comparison to what you do to prepare for that grave.

KeyPoints to ponder:
- Are you ready for your grave?
- Do you believe that your grave will not be your final resting place?
- Is the resurrection of Jesus Christ a life-changing reality for you?

"We may speak about a place where there are no tears, no death, no fear, no night; but those are just the benefits of heaven. The beauty of heaven is seeing God." – Max Lucado

GREAT

"Great" is a comparative term. Great is better than good, but not as good as perfect. "Great" is a word meaning excellence or bigness. It is also a way to express approval and appreciation – like, "That's great!"

Is there anything great going on in your life right now? Are things better than good? Are they moving toward God and excellence and gaining the approval of God and others? If not, you're not alone.

God's got a plan of greatness for you. The Psalmist declared, "Great is the Lord and most worthy of praise" (Psalm 48:1). He wants us to reflect His greatness to others and gives us ways to do this.

Jesus said, "Greater love has no one than this, that one lay down his life for his friends" (John 15:13). Does this mean we'll not have great love unless we die for someone? Of course not. Christ is telling us that we must be willing to sacrifice to save a friend. That's exactly what He did for us. The greatest message of love was given when Jesus Christ died for our sins and rose for God's glory.

KeyPoints to ponder:
- Have you accepted this great news?
- Is God truly being made great through your life?
- Who will you tell today about our great God?

"Great is thy faithfulness! Great is thy faithfulness! Morning by morning new mercies I see; all I have needed thy hand hath provided; great is thy faithfulness, Lord, unto me!"
                    – Thomas O. Chisolm

GROWTH

Growth is an essential element of life. Nothing is supposed to stay stagnant. We were created to grow and develop, and the challenge comes when we substitute mediocrity for maturity and refuse to grow at a reasonable rate.

What we do with what we have is not just important, it's essential. How well are you growing these days? The rapidity of your growth is not as important as the quality of your growth. To grow well is to be well. God gave you life for you to enjoy and to advance. The Bible admonishes us to "grow in the grace and knowledge of our Lord and Savior Jesus Christ" (2 Peter 3:18).

The sad part is that many consider growth in God as their last concern instead of their first. We work to build up our budgets, buildings, and even our bodies, but we leave our beliefs behind.

If you were to get a grade from the Lord as to how well you live, what tale would it tell about your advance or decline? We don't need to wonder or worry about it. We just need to work on it.

KeyPoints to ponder:
- Are you spiritually stunted in your growth for God?
- Would you say you have grown in Christ from this time last year?
- What will you begin to do to be certain that you have grown by this time next year?

"Like newborn babies, crave pure spiritual milk, so that by it you may grow up in your salvation." (1 Peter 2:2)

GUM

The first chewing gum was the flavorless. Adams New York Chewing Gum was developed by Thomas Adams and introduced in 1871. Flavored gum followed in 1875, and bubble gum came a decade after that.

Gum is chewed by our teeth and gums. Our mouths become the motors that make the action work. What we do with our mouths really does matter, whether we use them to chew gum or "chew out" someone we dislike. Both can make a difference.

God intended us to use our mouths for more than eating. They are the megaphones for expression and the multipliers of our thoughts. The Psalmist pled, "May the words of my mouth and the meditation of my heart be pleasing in thy sight, O Lord ..." (Psalm 19:14). The wisdom of Solomon stated that, "He who guards his lips guards his life" (Proverbs 13:3).

If your mouth is nothing more than a feeding trough or a chewing machine, you're not reaching your potential. God gave it for your good and to bring Him glory.

KeyPoints to ponder:
- How well would you say you use your mouth for God's good?
- Does it need cleaning?
- What ways will you use your mouth to share good news and encouragement for others?

"Words have incredible power. They can make people's hearts soar, or they can make people's hearts sore." – Dr. Mardy Grothe

GUTTERS

Not long ago I hired two men to unclog my gutters. Gutters are great until filled with leaves where the flow gets slow. These amazing gutter guys were the perfect picture of trust. They both used rope repelling belts as one anchored himself to the roof ridge, while the other leaned over the roof's edge to clear the gutter clutter with a backpack blower. One slight slip of the rope between them would have sent both sliding to danger and possible death.

As go gutters, so goes life. When clear and clean, it works well. When filled with trash and debris, it can be a disaster. What's clogging up your life right now? Is it an unholy habit, an untamed tongue, or an angry attitude? Do you need someone to blow out your troubles and help you get away from a slow spiritual flow?

Jesus called Himself "Living Water" to a woman whose life was lost (John 4:10). We need to invite Christ to clean us out so we can perform the purpose for which we were born.

KeyPoints to ponder:
- Is your life clogged up or free flowing?
- Who have you asked to help you to stay clean?
- Are you willing to help others do the same?

"Only when we treat others the way Jesus treats us will we demonstrate the kind of love he wants us to have." – Jack Zavada

H

HAIR

The average human head has about 100,000 hairs that grow at the rate of 0.01 inch every day. Whether male or female, we all lose between 25 to 125 hairs every 24 hours, which thankfully are replaced unless we are going bald – ouch!

The aging and genetic process seems to determine the direction of our hair. Most people cut their hair, all of us comb it (at one time or another), and some color it. The Bible says, "Gray hair is a crown of splendor," although most of us try to cover it (Proverbs 16:31).

One woman once came to Jesus and used her hair to wipe his feet with her tears and expensive perfume. Her expression of love was a signal for our Savior to forgive her sins (Luke 7:44-48).

Are you having a "bad hair day"? Remember that your outer look is not nearly as important as your inner longings. If you long to love the Lord, it doesn't matter if your hair is long or short, clean or dirty, combed or messy, straight or curly. What matters most is how you wear your willingness to care – even more than how you wear your hair.

KeyPoints to ponder:
- Are you spiritually groomed to meet with God today?
- What's messed up that needs fixing up in your life?
- Would you have been willing to clean the fee of Jesus if opportunity arose?

"It is amazing how complete is the delusion that beauty is goodness." – Leo Tolstoy

HAPPY

On January 1 of each year we shout, Happy New Year! At that time our world celebrates the promise of new beginnings. We have 365 days to design what we hope will be happy in this new year.

Is happiness really enough? Jesus said, "I have come that they may have life, and have it to the full" (John 10:10b). Sometimes happiness is empty. A full life is one of joy. Joy is a prominent piece of the fruit of God's Spirit (Galatians 5:22). "Joy comes in the morning" (Psalm 30:5) the Bible tells us, meaning that God gives a new opportunity to make the wrong become right.

A new year allows us to move beyond our quest for happiness to discover the deeper delight found in God's joy. Maybe we should change our saying to "Joyous New Year." We usually live up to what we say, or at least we try to.

A new year is an opportunity to create a new you. It's God's gift of starting over – enjoy it!

KeyPoints to ponder:
- Are you happy?
- Do you need more joy?
- How will you determine to make improvements this new year?

"Resolve to keep happy, and your joy and you shall form an invincible host against difficulties." –Helen Keller

HEAR

To hear is to process sounds through the filter of your objectivity. To really hear is to have some semblance that sounds make sense. It's what you hear, not just with your ears, but with your heart.

On several occasions, Jesus said, "He who has ears, let him hear" (Matthew 11:15) and blessed are "your ears because they hear" (Matthew 13:16). In other words, there were some people then as there are now who hear truth, but only those who heed the truth really hear it.

Our world is filled with sound – some we need, much we don't. We need a spiritual filter to separate sacred sounds from nonsense noise.

The early church was warned that there would be those who speak what others want to hear; yet it would have no lasting value. The Apostle Paul foresaw a time that would come when teachers would "say what their itching ears want to hear" (2 Timothy 4:3).

Shhhh...be quiet. What do you hear? If it's a word from God, follow it. If not, forget it.

KeyPoints to ponder:
- Has it been a while since you've heard from God?
- When you do hear from Him, do you follow Him?
- What kind of noise in your life needs to be turned down to hear more clearly?

"Most of us have been gifted with the ability to hear, but few of us have taken hearing and refined it into the art of listening."
– Don Anderson

HEART

Assuming that your heart beats at least once a second, by the time you are 70, your heart will have beaten 2.8 billion times. It all began at age three weeks in your mother's womb. That's a lot of rhythm!

What is your heart condition today? Maybe you're taking a blood thinner or cholesterol-clearing medication to help remedy your doctor's diagnosis. Maybe you're in great shape, and your workout routine keeps you accountable to good health. I don't know, but God does. He gauges your heart not by its performance inside your chest, but by its purpose through your charity. As the Divine Physician, he reads your heart from a spiritual perspective. He diagnoses our diseases of sin.

The Psalmist cried, "Search me, O God, and know my heart ... see if there is any offensive way in me" (Psalm 139:23-24). This plea for God's pardon was reinforced by Jesus himself when he proclaimed, "Blessed (or happy) are the pure in heart, for they will see God" (Matthew 5:8).

Check your heart and give it to God today.

KeyPoints to ponder:
- Is it time for a heart check-up?
- Would you let the Great Physician do it?
- If He diagnoses you with spiritual heart disease, will you follow His divine directions for a cure?

"Among the things you can give and still keep are your word, a smile, and a grateful heart." – Zig Ziglar

HECKLE

Everybody has an opinion and most people have no problem in expressing theirs. Some are encouragers; others use their voices to heckle. One leads to help; the latter usually hinders. The word heckle actually comes from a verb meaning "to scratch with a steel brush" or "to look for weak points." The instrument used to comb materials for medieval cloth making was a heckle comb, which separated the good cloth fiber from the bad.

Jesus had His share of hecklers who wanted to comb Him away from their exclusive religious communities. You probably have people who do the same to you. Our society doesn't like change, especially if it violates well-worn traditions. No wonder Christ brought chaos into the lives of those who served routine.

"Blessed are you when people insult you, persecute you and falsely say all kinds of evil against you because of me" (Matthew 5:11). When Jesus spoke these words, He knew from personal experience how it hurts to be heckled. Next time someone says something to you which stings, thank God that He will never condemn those who trust in Him.

KeyPoints to ponder:
- Who has been heckling you recently?
- Would you say you are more of an encourager or analyst for others?
- What steps will you take to give the insults from others over to Jesus?

"He who wishes to exert a useful influence must be careful to insult nothing."– Johann Wolfgang von Goethe

HELMET

A helmet is designed and intended to protect. I have several. There's an old football helmet I have from my high school playing days – it kept me safe through fourteen straight victories my senior year. Then there's my motorcycle helmet. It keeps me safe each time I get on the battlefields of Atlanta's roads and highways.

However, the most important helmet I wear is one for spiritual protection. God wore it first and called it a "helmet of salvation" when the prophet Isaiah recounted a time when no justice was to be found (Isaiah 59:15-17).

Our world is at war, and it's a battle that has been waging since sin entered our existence. We are admonished to fight against wickedness. One way is for us to follow the Apostle Paul's teaching to "take the helmet of salvation" (Ephesians 6:17). The purpose is one of protection. If we're to keep our heads and protect our minds, we must daily don this sacred hat.

KeyPoints to ponder:
- Are you wearing your helmet today?
- Do you feel protected?
- Will you be willing to put it on every day and not just when you think you need to?

"I now make it my earnest prayer that God would have you, and the State over which you preside, in his holy protection."
– George Washington

HEYDAY

Heydays of yesteryear were literally feast days. In medieval times, a serf who tended his lord's manor was entitled to a portion of the harvest. Besides the produce, he was given one day each year to store up complimentary hay for his livestock. It was pay day accompanied by great celebration and feasting – thus giving us our modern day meaning of heyday.

We all love pay days, don't we? We work hard and long to get support for our labors. A 40+ hour work week is wearisome but made wonderful when we get the "hay" for our day. The difference between then (the past) and now (the present) is minimal regarding expected returns and rewards.

What are you expecting for your labors in life? The Bible states that we are saved by grace and not by works, lest any of us should boast (Ephesians 2:8-9). It's a twist from the norm of "no work – no pay." It's a gift from God, not payment for our pursuits.

You can experience a heyday someday if you believe in Someone bigger than yourself. Jesus offers the final pay to each of us based upon our belief in Him, not just our behavior.

KeyPoints to ponder:
- Will you experience the biggest payday of heaven one day?
- Do you know that you know or are you just hoping?
- How will you help others to get God's gift of forever forgiveness?

"Hard work is the price we must pay for success. I think you can accomplish anything if you're willing to pay the price."
  – Vince Lombardi

HOG

Okay, here's a course you never took in college: Pig Anatomy 101. Parts high on the hog include: tenderloin, bacon, pork chops, spare ribs, and ham – the better parts. Low on the hog would be like pig's feet, knuckles, and jowls. Hogs or pigs have never been especially popular. They roll in mud, snort around for food, make funny sounds, and don't smell so sweet.

Once, Jesus was instructing His disciples about judging others and having proper priorities. He admonished them, "do not throw your pearls to pigs. If you do, they may trample them under their feet, and turn and tear you to pieces" (Matthew 7:6).

The problem is that hogs have bad habits, but then again, so do we. Today, why don't you turn over your hog-like habits to the Holy God who can make you clean?

His priorities are always perfect, and His intent is to offer you instruction as to how to live a life of peace and prosperity. He will never turn on you if you will turn to Him.

KeyPoints to ponder:
- Is your life sometimes slipping into slop?
- Are you snorting around in unholy habits?
- What will you do to get out of the sty and clean up for Christ?

"I have been all things unholy. If God can work through me, He can work through anyone." – St. Francis of Assisi

HOLE

Hole is a two-way word. If spelled with a "w" it means complete or solid. If you drop the "w," it refers to a crevice or a hollowed-out spot.

Historically, to be "in the hole" refers to being in debt, originating from the gambling houses of old. Part of each game was stuffed in a slot or a hole in the center of the table, secured by a hidden box below. The losers obviously wound up with more money in the hole than they did in their own pockets.

What's your deepest hole in life right now? Is it economic, intellectual, social, or spiritual? The good news is that – with God – you can never get too deep to be received and to be recovered. He cares for you, because He created you. He said, "I have loved you with an everlasting love ..." (Jeremiah 31:3), even when it seems that no one else does.

Jesus Christ came to make us whole with a "w" to get us out of the hole (no "w") of selfishness, suffering and sin.

KeyPoints to ponder:
- How deep is your hole today?
- Do you need a hand up?
- Who will you call on to help you?

"What can make me whole again? Nothing but the blood of Jesus."
– Robert Lowry

HOLLY

"Deck the halls with boughs of holly, fa la la la la – la la la la; 'tis the season to be jolly, fa la la la la – la la la la." The plants of holly can remind us of our place of being holy. Thanks to the Christian symbolism passed on by the host of early church missionaries and clerics in Germany, holly was called "*Christdorn*." According to legend, actual holly branches were woven into the painful crown on Christ's head.

Germans even taught that holly berries had once been white until the crown of thorns cut into Jesus' brow. His blood was so powerful that it turned the crown's berries crimson, and suddenly every holly berry in the world turned red. Another legend claimed that the wood of the holly tree was used to construct the crucifixion cross of Christ. The green of the leaves remains vibrant throughout all of winter to remind us that eternity never dims.

Jesus said, "I have come that you may have life (eternal) and have it to the full (abundant)" (John 10:10b). So, when you see holly this Christmas, remember the Christ who gave us His holy self to become our eternal Savior.

KeyPoints to ponder:
- Do you understand that Jesus was born to die?
- Are you experiencing His offer of abundant life?
- Do you know for certain that you will spend an eternity with Him?

"Everything that sustains and enriches life, is a divine gift. And how abundant these gifts are!" – J. I. Packer

HOT

When I say, "hot," most minds move in several directions. I could be expressing either temperature or temperament. The water is hot if it burns you, but an angry attitude could be someone who gets hot. Then, there's another angle of hot meaning attractiveness. You could say, "That's a hot car," or "a hot item," which means it looks great. Of course, another approach would be concerning something stolen. Hot can mean a lot!

God's Word warns churches today, "I know your deeds that you are neither cold nor hot. I wish you were either one or the other!" (Revelation 3:15). Jesus was giving advice about our need for spiritual passion. Christ's desire is that we be hot for God.

If you are a believer in God's ways, then your behavior needs to follow a path of passion toward God's will. A lukewarm disciple simply will not do. God is searching for souls who want to join Him as He takes us from cold-heartedness to a passionate pursuit.

KeyPoints to ponder:
- Are you hot for God today?
- Are you living some days as a lukewarm believer in Christ?
- What will it take to warm your heart for Jesus?

"Lukewarm people don't really want to be saved from their sin; they want only to be saved from the penalty of their sin."
– Francis Chan

HOUR

There are sixty seconds in each minute and sixty minutes in each hour. It takes 24 hours to complete a day and 365 days to fill a year. Time is ticking, minute by minute, reminding each of us of the brevity of life.

To some, the word "minutes" refers to the notes taken at a meeting. The term comes from a Latin word meaning small. It's a reminder that the occurrences of the meeting are meant to be noted shortly or quickly, not indicating that the events are unimportant. In much the same manner, life is short and quick. Time truly flies by (*tempus fugit!*). Every hour we lose power to beat the clock.

Jesus understood the brevity of life and the power of the hour. Before his death, he prayed, "Father, the hour has come ..." (John 17:1). When the disciples wanted to know about His earthly return, He warned them saying, "No one knows about that day or hour..." (Matthew 24:36). How you use or abuse your hours will bring you either fulfillment or folly.

KeyPoints to ponder:
- What will you do with your time today?
- How can you redeem the time?
- Can you name three personal ministries you can fulfill before next week?

"Time is short – but grace is forever." – Unknown

HOUSE

Perhaps the most well-known house in America is the White House. Initial construction for this palatial estate was completed in 1800 and did not include indoor plumbing. During World War I, President Woodrow Wilson secured sheep to graze the grass since the grounds-keeping staff were off fighting for our freedom. Even the wool was sold to help the soldiers by donating the proceeds to the Red Cross.

Houses come in all sizes and shapes. The housing market goes up and down, depending on consumer cash. Yet it's still a matter that you get what you pay for. Not so with God's house. Jesus promised a provision for every believer. He said, "In my Father's house are many rooms (or dwelling places); if it were not so I would have told you. I am going to prepare a place for you" (John 14:2).

Imagine a heavenly home built to stand the test of time through eternity. No mortgage, no peeling paint, no lack of rooms, and probably no need for plumbing!

What you do here determines whether you'll be there.

KeyPoints to ponder:
- Is your house in order to go to His house someday?
- What steps will you take to prepare for going to your heavenly home?
- Since there is plenty of room(s) there, who will you invite today?

"It is not the jasper walls and the pearly gates that are going to make heaven attractive. It is the being with God."
– Dwight L. Moody

HURT

Sometimes the best time of healing in our lives follows the worst hurt. Whether the hurt is physical, emotional, mental, or spiritual, it creates an opportunity for healing.

We usually run from hurt because it hurts! Easy and comfortable seem to be more attractive to our lives, but these standards will never leave us stronger.

Life has a way of running "roughshod" over us. This concept originates from horses whose shoes had nails protruding through. They were designed to keep the animal from slipping; however, it was discovered that the shoe could also serve to do damage to any fallen enemy as the horse ran over the body.

Perhaps you feel trampled today. Someone or something has run over you recently, and your hurt needs healing. Good! Jesus said, "It is not the healthy who need a doctor, but the sick" (Matthew 9:12). Let Him heal your hurt and help you become healthy. The Divine Physician has a cure for you.

KeyPoints to ponder:
- Who has stepped on you recently?
- Who have you stepped on recently?
- How will you help to heal someone who is hurting today?

"Comfort and prosperity have never enriched the world as much as adversity has." – Billy Graham

I

IDENTITY

Identity theft is a huge problem and increasingly difficult to deflect and detect. We work all our lives to protect our reputation and build up our credit rating only to have a thief steal our sense of stability.

Though you may be robbed of your bank holdings, no one can truly take your inner identity. You are unique and identified as a creature made in the image of God (Genesis 1:27). The Bible says, "We are God's workmanship, created in Christ Jesus to do good works, which God prepared in advance for us to do" (Ephesians 2:10).

How well are you using your works for good? We have an assigned role in life as well as a name. Our greatest success comes when we learn to put our purpose into practice and clearly identify ourselves with the One who gave us life and who offers an extended life worth living.

As we learn to understand that we are who we are, instead of identifying ourselves with what we have, we are coming closer to fulfilling our true identity.

KeyPoints to ponder:
- Have you discovered your true identity in Christ yet?
- Do you have a false ID, or one based on faith?
- How will you keep your identity safe and secure?

"If you are what you've always been, you are not a Christian. A Christian is a new creation." – Vance Havner

IDOL

An idol is whatever we choose to worship, place trust in or expect to bring us something better in life. The television version of "American Idol" has become synonymous with stardom. Millions watch weekly to see who will be voted to have the best vocal presentation; but idols are more than people – they also include our property.

In today's world of sinking security, we say, "In God we trust," but we behave altogether differently. We've proven our truer trust to be in cash or commodities, in alarm systems and solar systems, in the housing market and the supermarket. We've reversed reality by putting our trust in circumstances more than the Sovereign God who gave us everything we have to enjoy – not to idolize.

The writer of the Psalms warned, "Their idols are silver and gold, made by the hands of men. They have mouths, but cannot speak, eyes, but they cannot see ... ears, but cannot hear ... noses, ... hands, ... feet, but they cannot walk ... Those who make them will be like them, and so will all who trust in them" (Psalm 115:4-8).

It is time to turn back to the Creator rather than creating your own superstitious solutions. These times of international uncertainty are calling us to return to "my Rock and my Redeemer" (Psalm 19:14). Instead of hedging your bets on good luck, we need to be holding onto our beliefs in our great God.

KeyPoints to ponder:
- Can you identify idols in society today?
- Are you attracted to any or all of these?
- How will you show honor and tribute to the One true God over all?

"Money promises happiness, and we serve it by believing the promise and walking by that faith." – John Piper

IN

I remember as a teenager how important it was to be "in." This term meant that you were accepted, appreciated and acknowledged. I'm not quite sure what it took to be "in," but there were times when I wish that I hadn't been.

When you're told you're "in," there are expectations, and with expectations comes peer pressure. With peer pressure comes compromise, and with compromise can come sin.

To many, it was "in" to sin. It's not necessary to detail the dirt of disobedience. We all know how it harms; it harms our parents, family, friends, ourselves, and most of all our God.

God put us here for His pleasure, but it seems we often bring Him bruises rather than blessings. The good news is that we can gain his favor through forgiveness. Confess your sins, says the Scripture, and God is faithful and just and will forgive us our sins and purify us (I John 1:9). To be "in" with our friends is fun, but to be "in" with God lasts forever.

KeyPoints to ponder:
- Do you feel accepted by others?
- By God?
- What can you do or say that will gain God's forgiveness and favor?

"If you do what is right, will you not be accepted? But if you do not do what is right, sin is crouching at your door; it desires to have you, but you must master it." (Genesis 4:7)

INFLUENCE

As a child, I was highly influenced by my teachers and coaches. I believed almost all they told me. Peer pressure is a kind of influence that can be positive or poor. In either case, from figures of authority to friends, it is very important to follow only those who know the right way.

Have you ever wondered why some bad children seem to come from some good people? Behavior is not an inherited trait – it's learned. Who we allow to influence our children and ourselves can mean the difference between having a life fulfilled with purpose or a life flooded with problems.

Who is your greatest influencer? Jesus said to His followers, "You are the salt of the earth. But if the salt has lost its saltiness ... it is no longer good for anything ..." (Matthew 5:13). Salt has several qualities: it preserves, it adds flavor, and it can prevent you from slipping on a frozen path.

The influence we have on others can be similar to salt. Determine today to make a difference in the lives of those who are looking at yours.

KeyPoints to ponder:
- Who is the greatest influence in your life?
- Who are you influencing for good and for God?
- What steps can you take to move toward a more positive influence on others?

"The church must encourage Christians to be not merely consumers of culture but makers of culture." – J. Gresham Machen

INTEGRITY

God smiles on people with integrity and he frowns on the foolish. In our homes, schools, businesses, and hearts, we desperately need to be people who live rightly and love richly.

I like God's guarantee which comes from the Psalmist, "For the Lord God is a sun and shield; the Lord bestows favor and honor; no good thing does he withhold from those whose walk is blameless" (Psalm 84:11).

A blameless walk is not a perfect path, but rather living a life devoid of lies and infused with integrity. Our world's ways push us to do more, get more, and demand more. Our great God guides us to "be" more. He reads our hearts, not our resumes, roles, and reputations. He wants you to be all you can be – even more than you want to be the best that you can be.

I like that the Bible says, "The man of integrity walks securely, but he who takes crooked paths will be found out (Proverbs 10:9).

KeyPoints to ponder:
- Are you walking securely in our Savior today?
- If not, why not?
- Who will you help walk on the path of integrity?

"Sincerity is the same in a corner alone, as it is before the face of the world." – John Bunyan

INVENTIONS

Years ago, Richard James was trying to develop a spring to stabilize submarine instruments when he accidentally knocked one off a shelf. It "walked" down to a tabletop that led to his invention of the Slinky.

Another toy that was inadvertently invented was the Hacky Sack. In 1972, John Stalberger made one as a way to rehabilitate his knee that he had injured while playing football.

However, there is no mistake that God invented life as a gift to Himself and us for Him. The creation of the world and life-forms were intentional inventions from a loving Lord Who molded the universe to be a perfect reflection of His very self.

The Bible states, "In the beginning God created the heavens and the earth" (Genesis 1:1). Aren't you glad that you are not a protoplasmic product of happenstance? A generous God placed you here to provide His pleasure and for you to glorify His goodness.

KeyPoints to ponder:
- Do you ever feel like your life was a mistake?
- Have you discovered God's purposes for who you are and what your are to do?
- Will you ask Him again today to show you?

"Thou hast created us for Thyself, and our heart is not quiet until it rests in Thee." – Augustine of Hippo

J

JEWELS

Diamonds were not a standard part of the engagement ring until DeBeers launched an aggressive ad campaign in 1939. In the book <u>The Wonderful Wizard of Oz</u>, the slippers worn by Dorothy were not made of rubies, but of silver. In the 1963 film (and its 2006 remake), the Pink Panther was not a cartoon character, but a rare jewel.

Jewels have always fascinated the minds and eyes of the beholders. We love gems that glitter and stones that sparkle. These images create a sense of wonder and awe.

God has made a city with walls of jasper, streets of gold, and gates of pearl
(Revelation 21:18-21). It's a home waiting for habitation. It's a house that is called heaven, created for all who will believe.

The good news is that there's room for us all; the bad news is that many don't believe. Our faith is the key to this kingdom that God designed. Do you believe? Have you received? Jesus is waiting to welcome all who say, "Yes" to His invitation to His heavenly home.

KeyPoints to ponder:
- Do you feel like a precious jewel or another rock before Jesus?
- How brightly are you shining for Him?
- What ways will you reach out to others to help them to inherit a heavenly home?

"There will be a day, with no more tears, no more pain and no more fears. There will be a day, when the burdens of this day will be no more, and we'll see Jesus face to face." – Jeremy Camp

JOSH

To josh someone is to joke or banter with them. Some say the origin of the word is a combination of "joke" and "bosh," which means "foolish talk." Others would say its derivation is Scottish from the word "joss," meaning to push against or jostle.

Do you think life is a joke? Do you feel like people banter with you more than they share genuine expressions of concern and care? Think about this statement: life is short, sin is serious, and God is sure.

The Bible asks, "What is your life?" Scripture answers this question, "You are a mist that appears for a little while and then vanishes" (James 4:14). What we do in life soon will pass, but what we do for Christ will surely last.

There's no time to waste our lives, we can't josh with Jesus. He knows our needs, cares for our crises, and loves us in spite of our lostness. No joking!

KeyPoints to ponder:
- Who is joshing with you lately?
- Are you joshing others or showing genuine love?
- If you knew this was your last day to live, what would you change?

"I would always be the kid that got in trouble in school, that's for sure, for joking around."—*Matthew Perry*

JOURNEY

The word journey comes from the French *journèe*, which means "a day." Derived from the Middle Ages, a journey was a day spent traveling, which averaged about 20 miles. Today a journey is less literal and more figurative in its usage. We are more interested in finding out what's next, where we're going, and who's coming with us. Our journey may be thought of in daily segments, seasonal chunks, or even the span of a lifetime.

The journey of Jesus was short. In 33 years of life, He transformed religion into relationship and substituted love for legalism. He invited many to join His journey and He still does. Where is your journey in life taking you? Are you closer to the Creator or is there a chasm which needs closure?

Jesus beckons us all to, "Come to me, all you who are weary and burdened, and I will give you rest" (Matthew 11:28). This journey with Christ is not fatal, but it is fulfilling and final.

KeyPoints to ponder:
- What journey are you on right now?
- Is it a dead-end or a long, sweet street?
- Before it ends, will you come to Christ for His direction?

"We may run, walk, stumble, drive, or fly, but let us never lose sight of the reason for the journey or miss a chance to see a rainbow on the way." – Gloria Gaither

JUMBO

In 1881, P.T. Barnum, of Barnum and Bailey Circus fame, purchased a huge 6½ ton elephant discovered in West Africa. He paid $30,000 for Jumbo who had become a favorite of the London Zoological Society. Barnum is reported to have recovered his mammoth investment in Jumbo the elephant tenfold, within six weeks. Thanks to Jumbo's size and Barnum's marketing, "jumbo" became the word for the largest thing going.

What's jumbo in your life these days? Is it your job? Your school work? How about your investments, or even your family? All of these are important and linger as large, but nothing can be bigger than your relationship with God. If Christ is not a priority in your life, then you have lost the biggest, best, and most jumbo opportunity to live an optimum life.

Jesus said, "I have come that they may have life, and have it to the full" (John 10:10b). He also said, "I am the way and the truth and the life" (John 14:6). Wow! That's a jumbo Jesus and Someone who is bigger than any problem you might possess.

KeyPoints to ponder:
- Do you serve our big God with a puny piety?
- What plans will you make that only God could help you accomplish?
- How will Jesus become your biggest event today?

"I can see how it might be possible for a man to look down upon the earth and be an atheist, but I cannot conceive how he could look up into the heavens and say there is no God."
– Abraham Lincoln

K

KEY

Keys are important. With a key, I can unlock my home, my car, my office, my safe deposit box, my gym locker, my gate, my trunk ... well, just about anything that's locked up.

A key is a tool of entry. It allows us to go places and do things that otherwise would be impossible. Types of keys are varied; they come in all shapes and sizes. There are tubular keys, mortise keys, cylinder keys, keys cut by number, and electronic chip keys to name a few of the choices.

When Jesus asked His disciples, "Who do you say I am?" Peter responded correctly and quickly, "You are the Christ, the Son of the living God" (Matthew 16:15-16). Our Lord then went on to reveal that He would give all who believe, "The keys of the kingdom of heaven" (Matthew 16:19). Wow! That's incredible! What a powerful promise this is for you and me.

Today, when you use your keys to unlock a door, think about God's key to heaven, opened by Jesus Christ the Savior.

KeyPoints to ponder:
- What part of your life needs unlocking?
- Are you trying to hide something from God and others?
- Will you allow Jesus to open your heart to all He has for you?

"Christian, that is the secret—you can be so filled with the things of Christ, so enamored with the things of God that you do not have time for the sinful pleasures of the world."– Billy Graham

KINDNESS

To be kind is different from being one of a kind. A kind person is caring and sensitive, where a kind of person is simply a descriptive of type, culture, or creed. You are a kind of person, but you may not be a kind person. You develop character as you age, but you may not develop kindness.

All of this is to say that God offers us great guidance in the matter of kindness. His kindness, as expressed in his character, is expressed throughout the Bible. When the kindness of God appeared through Jesus our Savior, the Scripture says, He saved us not because of righteous things that we've done, but because of His kindness and mercy. "Know that a person is not justified by the works of the law, but by faith in Jesus Christ" (Galatians 2:16).

Our Creator is kind, and he expressed it through our first birth and again in offering us another chance at life that will last forever. Are you willing to accept his kindness?

We create problems when we think that this offer is too kind, and we spend time calculating the risks rather than reaching out for the reward. God has a plan for you today if you care to become one of His kind.

KeyPoints to ponder:
- What kind of believer are you?
- Are you one of a kind or unkind?
- How will you extend Christ's kindness to others today?

"Do something wonderful, people may imitate it."
– Albert Schweitzer

KING

Have you ever met a king? Have you ever wanted to be a king? Kings are known as rulers, those who reign and who carry responsibilities over those they represent.

Pepi II, King of Egypt, was the longest serving potentate, with a 90-year tenure (dating back to 2266 B.C.). King Herod, mentioned in the Bible, was actually one of the reigning Herods (from 41 B.C. to 44 A.D.). Whether known by name or by fame, kings can change the course of history. Their power and decisions have left lasting impressions on every society.

One king stands out above all others. The Psalmist asks, "Who is this King of glory?" (Psalm 24:8). The magi, following the sign of a star asked, "Where is the one who has been born King of the Jews?" (Matthew 2:2).

The Apostle Paul aptly answered these questions by describing Jesus, the Christ, as "the blessed and only Ruler, the King of kings and Lord of lords" (1 Timothy 6:15).

Jesus is the King who can conquer our sins and rule over hearts and lives. He is asking you to serve Him faithfully today.

KeyPoints to ponder:
- Who really rules your life?
- Do you enjoy serving?
- How will you honor and show respect for Christ the King today?

"Nearly all men can stand adversity, but if you want to test a man's character, give him power." – Abraham Lincoln

KINGDOM

A kingdom accurately refers to the domain of a king. All you need to do to derive this definition is to divide the word into "king" and "dom."

The deeper descriptive comes in asking the questions, "Who is your king?" and "What domain have you allowed him to have?" The Bible refers to Jesus Christ as "the Lord of lords and King of kings" (Revelation 17:14). Since He is supreme over all sovereign rulers, we should surely serve Him. We often glibly substitute other kings for The King.

It may be our jobs, schools, reputations, financial holdings, or even our families that take precedent over the true King. God does not want us to ignore those other items of concern, but they are not to take His place.

Ultimately God invites us to join Him in His heavenly kingdom where we will share together. The kingdom of heaven awaits all who will trust Him and obey Him, for He is the only king who will never be dethroned or destroyed.

KeyPoints to ponder:
- What king do you serve today?
- Have you substituted the priority of your family for the family of God?
- What will you do today to show the supremacy of Jesus through how you live?

"As every divided kingdom falls, so every mind divided between many studies confounds and saps itself."—Leonardo da Vinci

KISS

A kiss is usually a sign of affection, but sometimes it spreads an infection. Here's what I mean. If a kiss is shared because of love, it is affection; if it's out of lust, it's infection. A kiss is an expression of emotion between two people who care for each other and are willing to share with each other. In the 1926 film, "Don Juan," Mary Astor and Estelle Taylor received 127 kisses from John Barrymore – a record that has yet to be exceeded.

The problem with this and many films is that they are nothing more than expressions of fantasy, instead of being instigators of integrity.

When Jesus was arrested, it was preceded by a kiss of betrayal from Judas, one of His disciples (Luke 22:47-48). This became a kiss of defiance that ultimately led to his death.

Next time you share a kiss, be sure it is for the right reason, with the right person, at the right time, for the right relationship.

KeyPoints to ponder:
- Are your kisses ones of love or lust?
- Is there ever a time where you wished you hadn't kissed?
- Will you accept the sovereign kiss of God on you for strength today?

"Don't let a kiss fool you, or a fool kiss you." – Joey Adams

KITE

I remember having a kite-flying contest when I was a Cub Scout. Our troop worked for weeks to build our own kites, under the direction of our den mother and parents.

When the big day came to put our wares into the wind, it rained! The disappointment was deep, but made worse when no one took the time to reschedule the event. My kite stayed secure in my closet until years later when I took it out to fly on my own.

Kites come from the word for a British bird. England's most common bird of prey – a kite – can be seen daily riding the wind with its wings, looking for a rodent as its next meal. In the beginning of the seventeenth century, children learned to make wooden frames with tightly-stretched paper. With strings attached, they fluttered and flew much like the bird, thus its name.

The Bible reminds us that, "those who hope in the Lord ... will soar on wings like eagles" (Isaiah 40:31). The key to having a kite-like life is learning to lean on Jesus and to wait for His winds to take you above your world of worries.

If you won't wait on Him, you'll be in a hurry going nowhere. God created you to fly high; so ... soar!

KeyPoints to ponder:
- Has your life's kite crashed?
- Could you use a fresh new wind to help lift you above your circumstances?
- What will you work on to get off the ground and start to soar?

"Every man dies, but not every man really lives."
– William R. Wallace

KNOW

What we know seems to affect how we grow. Knowledge is a powerful tool but should not rule over everything else in our lives.

I have friends who have double master's degrees and even double doctorates. They are the first to admit that their knowledge is no replacement for the greater gift of wisdom.

It's how we handle what we know that makes a difference. Scientists and physicians claim that our brains are capable of storing thousands upon thousands more facts than we claim to know. The capability is there, but our willingness is weak.

The Bible says, "Know that the Lord is God. It is he who made us, and we are his; we are his people, the sheep of his pasture" (Psalm 100:3).

What we know is not nearly as important as Who we know. When we know God, we have enough knowledge to guide us, guard us, and give us all we need, especially in times of turmoil.

KeyPoints to ponder:
- How well do you know Him?
- How can others get to know Him through you?
- Has it been a while since you've prayed for wisdom as well as knowledge?

"It is incomprehensible that God should exist, and it is incomprehensible that he should not exist." – Blaise Pascal

L

LABOR

Work can be wonderful or wearisome. When we labor for a living, it should be for pleasure, not just for a paycheck. Each year, Labor Day is a reminder of the privilege we have to provide for ourselves and our families, but to many, labor is purely painful.

We should thank God for the ability to work. Think of those who are unable to labor because of a loss in their lives whether it be physical, mental, emotional, or spiritual.

Take time to rest and get restored. When God gave us commandments, He did it for our good. "Six days you shall labor and do all your work, but the seventh is a Sabbath to the Lord your God" (Exodus 20:9-10).

God knows we need a break before we have a breakdown. Our temptation is to labor longer to collect more cash or to be lazy in life and let others carry our load. The truth is found in balance. Use today to balance your life and labor for the Lord.

KeyPoints to ponder:
- How well do you work?
- Do you have a passion for what you do and those with whom you do it?
- In what way will you begin your next workday refusing to let routine rule over relationships?

"God sells us all things at the price of labor." – Leonardo da Vinci

LAKE

I've been around lakes all my life. Having grown up in Atlanta, I played in Lake Allatoona for years. I learned to swim in the lake, ski in the lake, laugh at the lake, and once, I almost lost my life at the lake.

Lakes are more than bodies of water; lakes are life. But not all lakes are lovely. In the Scriptures we read that there is a lake of fire. This symbolic sea is a scorching alternative received by those who reject Jesus Christ as God's Redeemer.

The Bible tells us about the Book of Life and warns that those who do not believe will be cast into this lake of fire. That's God's word, not mine. The better alternative is to trust God rather than tempting Him. We tempt our Lord when we refuse to repent and turn our lives over to the only lasting source of security.

God is good and He intends good for all of his creation, but He gives us a choice. He's calling you to take a leap into the lake of life and flee from the lake of fire. Come on, jump in!

KeyPoints to ponder:
- Which lake are you swimming in right now?
- Are you trusting God or tempting Him?
- How can you rescue others who may be drowning in sin and sorrow?

"Young man, young man, your arm's too short to box with God."
– James Weldon Johnson

LAME

A "lame duck" is a term which refers to someone whose authority and influence has been withdrawn, either because of disqualification or shortened tenure. The word's origin dates back to the term for a member of the British Stock Exchange who couldn't meet his liabilities on a settlement date, and thus flew off without settling his account.

The term paints a picture of a wounded bird that can no longer fly. We love to blame others for our lameness in life. We blame them for our insufficiencies and insecurities. Many love to brandish the lame to a lonely corner of culture because we think wholeness equals winning. Conversely, we equate lameness with losing.

Some would say that Jesus was lame. He was born to a common family, provoked riots among the religious, and then was crucified on a criminal's cross. Is that lame? Before you dismiss Christ's claims, consider His continuing authority and His influence. Remember that His lameness brought us wholeness of life through His love.

KeyPoints to ponder:
- Do you consider yourself lame?
- Is it social, spiritual, mental, physical, or all of them?
- What will you do to fly high again for yourself and for your God?

"You may not realize it when it happens, but a kick in the teeth may be the best thing in the world for you." – Walt Disney

LAST

Last means coming after all the others in sequence or chronology. It can also mean to continue or endure. It's a word that worries us. We don't like to be last in line, but we do want to last in life. Endurance is a valuable virtue even if you don't earn a first-place ribbon. The tortoise and the hare become a model story for us as we remember that perseverance pays.

Jesus proclaimed, "I am the First and the Last," meaning He started everything and will end it as well (Revelation 1:17). One day there will be a blaring of the "last trumpet" when those whose lives were committed to God through Christ will be raised from the dead (1 Corinthians 15:52). Wow! What a sight this will be – not one to bring fear, but to usher in God's promise of forever.

Even when this life grows weary, God has a better world prepared for you. Though you may be troubled today, know that God has the last word for your tomorrow.

KeyPoints to ponder:
- Do you really believe the last shall be first and the first shall be last?
- Has your endurance been replaced by your impatience?
- Can you name some steps you can take to keep on keeping on?

"Some people dream of success ... while others wake up and work hard at it."– Author Unknown

LAW

Did you know that in American courtrooms, John Doe is the name used for an anonymous defendant? An unknown plaintiff, on the other hand, is referred to as Richard Roe. The good news is that they are neither anonymous nor unknown. God knows exactly who we are and what we need. The laws of our land provide that we are innocent until proven guilty. Our laws are for the protection of our rights, not inspection of our rituals.

When God gave Moses laws for life, the Ten Commandments, they were not called the ten suggestions. God expected His people to follow the rules to live lives of greater freedom, not less.

As parents provide parameters around their children's behavior, this discipline produces character later learned and appreciated. The child rebels at first, but ultimately rejoices.

As children of God, we are no different, or at least we shouldn't be. We should love His laws, not loathe them.

KeyPoints to ponder:
- How have you broken God's laws lately?
- Are you still suffering the consequences?
- Is it time to turn back to your Heavenly Father who disciplines you because He loves you?

"You cannot break the law of God; you can only break yourself upon it."– *D. James Kennedy*

LEMONS

I have a love and hate relationship with lemons. I love lemons squeezed in my iced tea, on fish, in my salads, and even on top of broccoli. I hate "mechanical" lemons which represent some cars I have owned in the past, or my vacuum cleaner that never seems to work right. Do you have an appliance like that?

The ascorbic acid of a lemon makes it sour. In some cases it brings balance to our taste buds; but in other cases, it represents experiences of life which have become sour and bitter.

Jesus came to this earth to take the lemons of life and turn them into something sweet. He wants to restore your sour and bitter life with something spiritual and better. The key to unlocking His love is faith. Do you believe in Him? Have you received Him personally? The Bible says God "has turned for me my mourning into dancing; you have put off my sackcloth, and clothed me with gladness ..." (Psalm 30:11 NKJV). For this to happen, we must trust in Him.

Quit griping about life's lemons and look to the Lord for His security, sweetness and stability.

KeyPoints to ponder:
- What's gone sour or become bitter for you recently?
- Is it your family or your finances?
- How about your job, or even your joy?

"It weren't too long before I seen something in me, had changed. A bitter seed was planted inside of me. And I just didn't feel so accepting anymore."– Kathryn Stockett, The Help

LEWD

The word lewd today connotes something or someone who is sexually unchaste and all but evil. However, it originates from an Old English label for a distinct difference of a layperson as compared to one of the clergy. It later came to describe those who were unlearned, hence common.

Isn't it strange how the meaning of words can deteriorate through the decades? Christ came to make us as one in Him and with one another although, of course, we are different in personality and profile (John 17:21). God sees us as His creation, made in His own image, to uplift and not to denigrate one another (Genesis 1:26).

What we sometimes describe as lewd, our Lord sees as lovely. He judges the heart and soul of individuals, not their resumes or ranking in society.

Jesus reached out to the outcasts and sinners because He knew their value and potential. We would do well to hear His heart as He said, "Whatever you did for one of the least of these brothers of mine, you did for me" (Matthew 25:40).

KeyPoints to ponder:
- Do you know someone you might label as lewd?
- Are you?
- What efforts will you take to treat others as you wish to be treated?

"Three things in human life are important: the first is to be kind; the second is to be kind; and the third is to be kind." – Henry James

Good news! Life expectancy is climbing, at least statistically. The bad news is that all of physical life has a termination point, no matter how long or short it may be. Life is a mixture of love and loss, health and hurry, success and failure. The way we live our lives determines their direction. What we do with the time we have guides our destiny.

Jesus said, "I have come that they might have life, and have it to the full" (John 10:10b). He later explained who He was in connection to that abundant life as He exclaimed, "I am the way and the truth and the life. No one comes to the Father except through me" (John 14:6).

Is your life full of stuff or substance? Is it a joy or a job? Through trusting Christ with all of your life, you can turn your trials into triumph and trade your emptiness for abundance. Life is for living to the max – not limping. Live for the Lord today so that you might be prepared for eternal life tomorrow.

KeyPoints to ponder:
- Are you limping in life?
- How much longer do you expect to live?
- And then?

"When I stand before God at the end of my life, I would hope that I would not have a single bit of talent left, and could say, 'I used everything you gave me.'"– Erma Bombeck

LIGHTNING

Most of us run for cover when lightning strikes and rightfully so, since the average bolt raises the air temperature along its way to 50,000 degrees Fahrenheit. Lightning is a meteorological miracle charged with electrical current, streaking across the sky. Benjamin Franklin is said to have flown a kite with a key in a storm when lightning struck to provide proof of electrical current. Whether you're a golfer, swimmer, or just a casual outdoor person, you're looking out for lightning when storms start.

The truth is that all of us should be looking up for a sign when lightning starts to streak. Jesus said, "For as lightning that comes from the east is visible even in the west, so will be the coming of the Son of Man" (Matthew 24:27). Christ's return will not only light up the sky, but most importantly, He will light up our lives and give us a forever future in a heavenly home.

The next time you see lightning, remember God's promise for the return of our Redeemer.

KeyPoints to ponder:
- Have you ever been struck by lightning or know someone who has?
- Did it change his life or yours?
- If your life were taken today, where would you spend tomorrow?

"To be ever looking for the Lord's appearing is one of the best helps to a close walk with God." – J. C. Ryle

LISTEN

There is a huge difference between hearing and listening. We hear noises all around us, but we selectively listen to some. Our ears are finely tuned instruments that hear frequencies of sound which dictate our responses.

Our problem comes when we fail to listen to the right noises before danger strikes. Jesus said, "He who has ears to hear, let him hear" (Mark 4:9). He was talking about our willingness to tune into the truths that He was teaching.

We all have ears and most all of us can hear, but do we really listen? Christ spoke directly to his disciples when he stated, "My sheep listen to my voice ..." (John 10:27). Solomon proclaimed, "Let the wise listen and add to their learning" (Proverbs 1:5). With so many noises surrounding us, they either blast us or bless us, depending on how we choose to listen.

Tune into God's voice and tune out the wasted words of some who seek to rob you of your time and serenity.

KeyPoints to ponder:
- What do you hear?
- Are you listening?
- How will you determine to decipher the difference?

"Hearing is one of the body's five senses. But listening is an art."
– Frank Tyger

LISTS

Lists – we love them, don't we? Sure we do. Our world is flooded with factoids and filled with long lists: 36 amazing things for free; 20 minutes a day for total bodybuilding; 3 ingredients which add 10 years to your life; 5 things I know for sure. We think that if we complete our lists of important things in life, then we will be happier, complete, and satisfied. You know, however, it's not always so! Checking off one's daily list is addictive. You can set goals for the greatest accomplishment but fail to remember that your lists get longer the more you accomplish.

Jesus kept it simple. When approached by religious leaders of His day for the spiritual "to do" list of commandments, He responded with a short list focused on love. "Love the Lord your God with all your heart and with all your soul and with all your mind." He only added one addendum – "Love your neighbor as yourself" (Matthew 22:37-39).

Before you get stuck in the daily drudgery of lists, remember the words of Christ and the power of their priority.

KeyPoints to ponder:
- Is your life becoming simpler or more complex?
- Would Jesus appear on your "to do" list today?
- If He does, what would you plan to do to please Him? Be specific.

"I am beginning to learn that it is the sweet, simple things in life which are the real ones after all." – Laura Ingalls Wilder

LOSERS

Our world applauds winners but belittles losers. Nobody likes to be last, and almost everyone is frustrated when they aren't first. Losing leaves us lacking in some areas of life, but hopefully learning from our losses.

The Detroit Lions are the oldest existing NFL franchise to have never appeared in the Super Bowl. George H. W. Bush has been the only U.S. president over the last 25 years to fail in his bid for reelection. Yet both of these are still winners in life.

What do we do with what Jesus said? "The first will be last, and the last first" (Mark 10:31). It's really a matter of perspective. Sometimes our greatest loss becomes our greatest gain. We must understand that true winners are wise winners who see life through God's eyes, not their own.

Christ proclaimed, "I am the First and the Last" (Revelation 1:17). When we allow the Lord to become first in our lives, we will then perceive that there is no loss that will ever brand us as losers. God's loss of Jesus on a criminal's cross became our greatest win over sin.

KeyPoints to ponder:
- Do you consider yourself a winner or a loser?
- Do you ever remember a time when you lost, but later you saw it was a good thing?
- What have you learned recently from losing?

"Winning starts with beginning." – Robert Schuller

LOUNGE

To "lounge" means to refrain from labor or exertion. It can mean a kind of couch on which to rest. There's nothing wrong with rest unless it leads to laziness. A lazy lounger makes for a weak worker, unwilling to fulfill a role of responsibility.

God created us for a higher calling than to merely coast in life. The Bible boldly states that, "Whatever you do, work at it with all your heart, as working for the Lord, not for men" (Colossians 3:23). That's a tall task, but it is achievable when you ask for Christ's help. For six days God worked to put our world together and on the seventh day, He rested (Genesis 2:2). He didn't quit; He just got quiet. Our problem seems to be that too many people look for shortcuts in life to lounge around and become lazy.

The God-given ability to work is never to be taken for granted. He has equipped you, given you unique skills, and intends you to have pleasure and not just earn a paycheck. When we let go too soon and allow laziness to lead us, we violate what the apostle Paul wrote, "Being confident of this, that he who began a good work in you will carry it on to completion until the day of Christ Jesus" (Philippians 1:6).

KeyPoints to ponder:
- Are you a willing worker or a lazy lounger?
- What has been left undone because of your procrastination?
- Is there an even greater work to which God has called you? If so, are you willing to go?

"We often miss opportunity because it's dressed in overalls and looks like work."– Thomas A. Edison

LUMBER

Lumber is both a verb and a noun. If I move in a slow or awkward way, I lumber. If I take my truck to the local building supply store to get boards to build a fence, I buy lumber. There's even a term in Great Britain wherein the word represents household furnishings which have out-served their usefulness and inconveniently take up needed space. They are called lumber.

As a teenager, I worked in a lumber yard in Atlanta. When I would load the heavy boards, I knew they would soon be used to build something substantial. No longer would they be stacked in neat rows waiting to be purchased.

As every board or piece of lumber has purpose and potential, so it is with every person – in fact, even more so. Jesus expects us to use wisely what He gives us to build lives with luster, not those that limp or lumber.

Remember the parable of the talents? One received five, another three, and one had one. The one who buried his talent for fear of losing it was reprimanded by the master for wasting it when it could have been doubled in value through wise investment (Matthew 25:27-29).

KeyPoints to ponder:
- How are you using your spiritual gifts to build God's kingdom?
- Could anyone accuse you of wasting what God has given you?
- How will you help someone else today to make a wise investment with his God-given talents?

"Be frugal of your time. It is one of the best jewels we have."
– Sir Matthew Hale

LUNCH

It's been well stated that "there is no such thing as a free lunch." We understand this to mean that somehow, somewhere you pay for what you get.

The truth remains that we all need lunch or food. Our appetites take no vacation and remind us when it's time to eat. This is a God-given craving that cannot be ignored; but for all of us, lunch won't last. We still get hungry later, and the cycle begins again.

The question remains, "How much does lunch cost?" It depends on the cuisine and the company you're with. For the disciples of Jesus, lunch cost their lives. Several left their fishing and promise of food for a ministry with a man who worked miracles.

Christ even cooked for them one time and invited them to dine on the shore of the Sea of Tiberias (John 21:9-14). As they gazed at their God, they had a choice to make. So do you. Accept God's offer of His forever food and be nourished throughout eternity.

KeyPoints to ponder:
- What's cooking in your life right now?
- Does it have lasting value or is it spiritual junk food?
- How can you get on God's diet and bring others to the table?

"The perfect menu of spiritual food: God's Word, prayer, and listening to Him."– Unknown

M

MAKE

To "make" something is to bring something into being by combining, shaping or transforming materials. When I say make, I might mean to fabricate, fashion, form, or frame. Of course I could be "on the make," if I try to be something or somebody different from who I really am. This would demand that I transform myself and my identity, which might require some makeup!

Whatever your take is on make, it took someone special to make it all happen in the beginning. The Bible says God made the world and all its inhabitants (Genesis 1:31).

It also states that each of us is made in His own image (Genesis 9:6). God gave us the ability to make the most of life by living up to our potential with every possibility to make Him proud of us, as we were "fearfully and wonderfully made" (Psalm 139:14).

What do you make of all this? Do you only call on God in times of panic or with lips of praise? Is He your Savior in life or someone who just gave you life?

What you do with Jesus makes all the difference on earth and for eternity!

KeyPoints to ponder:
- What will it take to make you a stronger believer in Christ?
- Do you need a makeover?
- Will you be willing to state what will make God pleased in your life?

"When you cease to make a contribution, you begin to die."
– Eleanor Roosevelt

MARK

If I say, "Mark" some people may begin to think of a man's name. Others may imagine writings or scribble created by pen or pencil. The writer of one of the Gospel accounts of the life of Christ was named Mark. And, to "make one's mark" is yet another expression of the word.

At one moment in time, that phrase meant simply to distinguish one's work from another. More specifically, it was the practice of smiths and artisans to mark their wares with a special symbol or logo. Once the mark became well known, the artist was known in his community to have "made his mark." Yet, while many hope for success in life, not everyone makes their mark known.

Do you know that you're well known? God sees you when you're resting, when you're working, when you're playing – at all times. What He sees, He loves, even when He might not like it, because He put His mark on you. He loves you even if you don't love Him. If you'll give Christ your life, He'll mark you for eternity to experience a future beyond belief.

KeyPoints to ponder:
- What mark have you made recently that is making a difference?
- Have you put your mark on someone special?
- How is God using you to leave His mark on your world?

"So the Christian, too, belongs not in the seclusion of a cloistered life but in the thick of foes." – Dietrich Bonhoffer

MEEK

To many, meek means weak. Not so with God. He said, "The meek will inherit the land ..." (Psalm 37:11). Jesus preached, "Blessed are the meek, for they shall inherit the earth" (Matthew 5:5).

That's interesting, isn't it? We can get more from God by giving out less of ourselves. God's blessing goes to those who don't grab and claw their way through relationships. It's not that we're to be weak-spirited or Jell-O-like in our convictions; rather, meekness is a sign of security. We trust God to answer for us instead of railing with rebukes and rebuttals.

A synonym for meekness is gentleness, and Christ is described as having both attributes (2 Corinthians 10:1). He was so strong in character that He was meek in manner. Today is a great day to take the test of meekness. If you ask God for help, He is certain to respond. Blessed are the meek!

KeyPoints to ponder:
- Are you meek?
- Would people describe you as secure and sensitive?
- Is there calmness in your character?

"Meekness is power under control." – Warren Weirsbe

MEETINGS

In my earlier days of ministry, while raising our three sons, my boys saw my daily routine and tried to copy it. One day my wife told me that her day with them had been quite different. Apparently, the boys decided to be like Daddy and play a game called "meeting" all day. What they did we don't know, but I got the picture and became more sensitive to my times away at my meetings, realizing I might better serve my sons at home. To add to the tension, I picked up a book published with a very convicting title: "Death by Meetings". I was learning. Slowly.

Jesus met frequently with His disciples, but it was for a powerful purpose – to show them the ways of God. Maybe that's the difference in what He did and what we do. Christ chose to bring life and meaning to His meetings, as each encounter had a divine agenda.

The Native American Indian powwows of yesteryear were noisy celebrations that took place after successful wars or hunts. Our modern-day powwows at work or home are usually lifeless and dead. So remember what the Savior said, "I have come that they may have life, and have it to the full" (John 10:10b).

KeyPoints to ponder:
- Are you ready to meet with the Master today?
- What's on the agenda?
- Will there be a purpose as you gather with people?

"If you had to identify, in one word, the reason why the human race has not achieved, and never will achieve its full potential, that word would be 'meetings.'"– Dave Barry

MERCY

I remember playing a game with my high school friends called "Mercy." You consent to grab hands with your buddy, face to face, fingers interlaced with each other, and then squeeze. I don't mean politely squeeze, I mean squeeze the hand of your opponent until you get screams of pain that cry for "mercy!" It's a contest of strength and a plea for relief. When you've had more than you can stand and your pain is overpowering, you plead for mercy.

The Lord is full of compassion and mercy, according to the brother of Jesus (James 3:17). The Bible tells us that it is His mercy through salvation that extends to those who fear Him from generation to generation (Isaiah 50:39).

Do you fear God? I'm not asking you if you're afraid of God. To fear God is to respect His strength, to cry out to Him in your sorrow, and to accept His mercy for your times of pain.

God is not interested in hurting you, but He is interested in sharing His mercy in times of your hurt.

KeyPoints to ponder:
- Is it time for you to ask for mercy from our great God?
- Are you merciful to others?
- How?

"It is mercy, not justice or courage or even heroism, that alone can defeat evil." – Peter Kreeft

MILK

Whether you like milk or not is a matter of taste. Some babies cannot tolerate their mother's milk and have to substitute soy products or even goat's milk. Milk seems to be a staple on the shelves of stores and a supplement in almost every dairy diet in the world.

Geneticists are attempting to develop cows that will produce milk easily tolerated by the billions of lactose-intolerant persons on earth. Meanwhile, thanks to current genetic engineering, today's cows provide 10 gallons of milk per day, several times the natural amount.

Milk brings nourishment. When God gave the nation of Israel a promise of a better land away from Egyptian slavery, He called it the "land of milk and honey" (Exodus 3:8). Milk reminds every form of mammal life that we cannot live without liquid, and we must have a source of strength.

The milk and meat of God's Word are supernatural sources for survival. With the next glass of milk you drink, remember God is the Giver, and we get the gain from that.

KeyPoints to ponder:
- Who is your Source today?
- Where do you get your strength?
- Are you a supplier or a sapper for others?

"Pray for someone. Create a prayer book. Connect with friends. Share with friends."– Unknown

MIND

What comes to mind when I say, "mind"? If you think like a parent you may scold a child to mind or obey, or maybe you simply use your mind to think and remember.

It's not how big your brain is that makes your mind work wonders. Albert Einstein's brain was smaller than average. Strangely enough it was removed prior to his cremation and secretly stored by Dr. Thomas Harvey, who performed the autopsy on this body part of the genius in 1955.

One organization's commercial states that, "A mind is a terrible thing to waste." I agree and so should you. What kind of mind really matters? The Bible says, "The mind of a sinful man is death, but the mind controlled by the Spirit (of God) is life and peace" (Romans 8:6).

It's interesting to know that we can actually have the "mind of Christ" (1 Corinthians 2:16). To think like He does gives us actions and attitudes that lead to good and Godly choices and away from sin and sorrow. Think about that today!

KeyPoints to ponder:
- So, what do you think about most often?
- Is it pleasing to the Lord?
- Do you need a new state of mind?

"You cannot tailor-make the situations in life but you can tailor-make the attitudes to fit those situations." – Zig Ziglar

MOON

While the moon is the largest object in the sky when seen from earth, it isn't the biggest natural satellite in the solar system. That honor goes to Ganymede, one of Jupiter's moons. Astronomers believe our moon may be home to as many as 25 billion gallons of water, in the form of ice hiding in the shadows of craters on the surface.

During creation "God made two great lights – the greater to govern the day and the lesser light to govern the night" (Genesis 1:16). God's promise of protection comes from the Psalmist who wrote, "The Lord watches over you ... the sun will not harm you by day, nor the moon by night" (Psalm 121:6).

Next time you glance at the moon, remember that you are looking at God's handiwork. This vast universe is a product of His power and given for our habitation and enjoyment. As the moon's light is a reflection of our sun, so we should reflect God's Son. Our solar system points to a Savior whose greatest desire is to recreate us in His image.

KeyPoints to ponder:
- What or who are you reflecting right now?
- Around what or whom do you rotate?
- How are you going to make your light shine even brighter for the Lord?

"Life can only be understood backwards; but it must be lived forwards."– Soren Kierkegaard

MOUNTAINS

For some, mountains bring motion sickness; for others, mountains bring memories. However, mountains are always a challenge for everyone who seeks to ascend and travel downhill on the other side.

The ups and downs of life are inescapable and inevitable. One day we feel on top of the mountain; the next, we are underneath it. So, which is it for you today?

Moses got the Ten Commandments for life on a mountain (Exodus 24:18), and Jesus rejected temptation by the devil on another (Matthew 4:8). On mountains, miracles are made real. Even Isaiah preached prophetically concerning the role of John the Baptist, saying that because of his righteousness, "Every valley shall be filled in, every mountain and hill made low" (Luke 3:5).

Good news! God makes the mountains of life and gives us the power to remove them (Matthew 17:20). But often, we would rather complain about our mountains than scale them. The Bible reminds us that with God, nothing is impossible; but without Him, no mountain can be made low. What you do with your mountains will either make you or break you, so climb on!

KeyPoints to ponder:
- Are you on the way up or down?
- Who is helping you to climb?
- Where are your best resources that will enable you to climb without falling?

"Only those who will risk going too far can possibly find out how far one can go."– T. S. Eliot

N

NAG

Nobody likes a nag. This annoying, irritating word comes from the Scandinavian word "*nagga*," which means "to gnaw." During the Middle Ages, rats and squirrels infested parts of Europe, making nerve-racking sounds through the night as they nestled in thatched roofs.

Nags gnaw today at nerves and emotions. Instead of offering a positive solution, nags remind us of everything they don't like and why. Nags come in all forms and fashion. They can be your neighbor, your nephew or your niece; but to be sure, they are not nice. A holy household can quickly be turned into a horrible home. The Bible reminds us, "A quarrelsome wife is like a constant dripping" (Proverbs 19:13). The same is true of a husband whose heart is self-centered and stingy.

Who's nagging you today, or worse, who are you nagging? Instead of criticizing, why don't you try complimenting those whose lives need help? "A gift opens the way for the giver and ushers him into the presence of the great" (Proverbs 18:16).

KeyPoints to ponder:
- Are you a nag?
- Do you know a nag?
- In what ways can you help them to stop?

"Any fool can criticize, condemn, and complain - and most fools do." – Dale Carnegie

NAME

There's a wonderful family named Stein –
There's Gert, and there's Epp, and there's Ein;
Gert's poems are lame;
Epp's statues bring shame;
And no one can understand Ein.

– Unknown

The name game is nothing new. What we name our children sticks for a lifetime. American journalist Park Benjamin once wrote, "Strong towers decay, but a great name shall never pass away."

Do you live up to your name or have you been running from it forever? Today's tradition is to find a name which either reflects or brings fame. Think of the trends: using old names for new or returning to our roots or sound-alikes with same beginning letters or rhymes.

More important than what others call you is to understand God's call upon you. The wise writer of Proverbs stated, "A good name is more desirable than riches; to be esteemed is better than riches or gold" (Proverbs 22:1).

KeyPoints to ponder:
- So, how rich are you in following the "name that is above every name" – the Lord Jesus Christ? (Philippians 2:9)
- How well do you wear the name of Christian before others?
- Are you living up to your name?

"Carve your name on hearts, not on marble." – Charles Spurgeon

NATURE

There are nature walks, nature talks, nature books, and nature looks. Nature is the most natural term ever. However, our view of nature varies radically. Some worship it, some wonder about it, some wander in it, and others whine about it. What's your view of nature?

The first-century church must have been filled with supernatural expressions concerning the miraculous Messiah who had come from God to visit our globe. During one encounter of the Apostles Peter and John with their complaining critics, they were warned to be quiet but the warning made them bolder, rather than bashful.

When the apostles' friends heard the report of their release from prison, "They lifted up their voices together in prayer to God," thanking Him as the "Sovereign Lord ... you made the heaven and the earth and the sea and everything in them" (Acts 4:24).

Did you just hear their definition of nature? Those who were closest to Christ gave God the glory and the credit for all of creation. In a day and time when it seems that nature is neutral, it behooves us to remember that the Divine developed all we experience and enjoy.

KeyPoints to ponder:
- Is sharing Christ natural for you?
- Do you credit God for the beauty which surrounds your life?
- Why not make a list today of blessings from which you benefit?

"I love to think of nature as an unlimited broadcasting station, through which God speaks to us every hour, if we will only tune in."
– George Washington Carver

NEWNESS

I love the way new books smell. Isn't that strange? My wife laughs each time she sees me read the cover, check out the table of contents, thumb through the pages, and then smell the inside. There's something about newness that attracts my total senses.

How do you handle new? Some people prefer old and ordinary. They run from anything new and different. One thing is certain – one day everything will be new for you. There will come a time when this life ends and a new one begins. The Bible tells us, "If anyone is in Christ, he is a new creation; the old has gone, the new has come!" (2 Corinthians 5:17). Your new life can begin today if you'll totally trust God's way of sending His Son as your Savior.

In the New Testament language, there are two words for "new". One means renewed; the other means altogether new-in-kind. We need both in life.

KeyPoints to ponder:
- Can you name three new activities you have begun this month?
- Do you feel stuck in a rut, with very little that is new for you?
- Why not ask God to give you a new attitude, followed by new actions?

"Are you stuck in a rut? What is a rut? It is a coffin with the ends kicked out."– Jim Holmes

NICE

To say that a person or experience is nice is favorable, but a bit bland. The funny fact about the word "nice" is that it came originally from the Latin "*necius,*" meaning ignorant. In the fourteenth and fifteenth centuries, the phrase "a nice person," actually referred to someone who was foolish, rather than agreeable. Isn't it strange how chronology and culture can change meanings and understanding?

When Jesus said, "I am the First and the Last" (Revelation 1:17), it sounds like double-talk. Then, when He stated that the "first will be last and the last first ..." (Mark 10:31), it seems to have a muddled meaning.

However, words do change, and people need to also. When your heart is in tune with Christ, you can clearly understand that His statements are divine declarations, meaning that He is our everything and He wants us to promote the good of others more than our own good. This is nice to know because it is neither ignorant nor foolish, but purely powerful.

KeyPoints to ponder:
- How nice are you to others?
- To yourself?
- To God?

"A kind word is like a Spring day." – Russian Proverb

NOSE

Our noses are primarily air vents. Our sense of smell comes from an organ about the size of a fingernail, far inside the nose. A dog's olfactory apparatus dominates much of his brain, affecting his instincts and reflexes – all connected to his sense of smell. Did you know that even fish follow their noses? Salmon headed upstream will turn back from water saturated by odors produced by men or bears.

But who really knows best about our noses? God does! He made them and directs their uses. He created big ones, little ones, fat ones, funny ones, cute, and even curious ones.

We use the idiom, to "have a nose for trouble," about people who have an unusual capacity for detecting difficulties. Even God has one of these. The Bible reminds us, "We are to God the aroma of Christ among those who are being saved and those who are perishing. To the one we are the smell of death; to the other, the fragrance of life" (2 Corinthians 2:15-16). Let Jesus guide your life and quit being so nosey about others.

KeyPoints to ponder:
- What kind of spiritual smell do you leave before others?
- Does your fragrance foster gladness?
- Is your odor pleasing to Jesus?

"Just as a flower which seems beautiful and has color but no perfume, so are the fruitless words of the man who speaks them but does them not." – John Dewey

Not is such a negative word. "I'm not going with you." "I'm not a great singer." "I'm not ..." (you fill in the blank). To say you are "not" infers that you either cannot or choose not to take action to the fullest fashion. You simply will not. But what if you add a "k" to "not" and change the meaning? You still say it the same, but it carries a completely different character and context.

I can tie myself up in knots (as with a rope) if I choose not to follow God's direction for my life. This misappropriated action creates a negative reaction when God's consequences follow.

When we know what to do from God's Word – the Bible – and yet reject it by not obeying, we get tied up in spiritual knots. This is not good.

KeyPoints to ponder:
- What are you not doing or not choosing to be today that you know Jesus wants from your life?
- Will you not follow His great command?
- What's not to like about God's gift of life and love?

"When the early disciples were confused over the commandments, Christ reminded them that the greatest was to love God and not to neglect loving their neighbors as they loved themselves."
(Luke 10:27)

NOTHING

When asked, "What's bothering you?" and the response is "Nothing," you can bank on that meaning something. "Nothing" is a relative term. If I say, "I have nothing to offer this discussion," what I really mean is that I have nothing worthwhile to share, not that I could not offer to say something.

What then did it mean when Jesus said, "Apart from me you can do nothing" (John 15:5)? Was he bringing discipline to his disciples or instruction? Both. Christ was reminding them of their true source of strength. He was admonishing them to stay connected to the living vine and to become fruit-bearing branches which can touch a world of worry with God's peace.

Do you feel like you have nothing in the midst of plenty? We are all ill at ease with emptiness and desperately want to be filled with faith. The trick is to trust in God, but really, it's no trick at all. It's a matter of stating your need, sticking close to God's truths, and staying connected with Christ. Remember, Jesus also said, "For nothing is impossible with God" (Luke 1:37).

KeyPoints to ponder:
- Are you up to nothing or something of substance?
- What is one thing in your life which would be impossible without God's help?
- Are you tired of doing nothing that demands trust and reason?

"[Nothing] means we're just going along, listening to all the things you can't hear, and not bothering." – Winnie the Pooh

219

NUTRIENTS

Did you know that cats cannot survive on dog food because of the different blend of nutrients? Our feline friends require five times as much protein as dogs do. Be careful what you feed your dog – in large quantities chocolate, onions, grapes and raisins can be poisonous to our canine critters.

It's been said, "You are what you eat." This phrase becomes a fact when we neglect our nutrition. However, what we eat and digest is so much more than through our mouths. The Bible says, "As a man thinketh in his heart, so is he" (Proverbs 23:7 KJV). We feed our mouths and our minds to nourish our stomachs and our souls.

How's your spiritual diet doing? What you put in your head will feed your heart. If you live by "stinkin' thinkin'" you're sure to starve your soul. If you are nourishing your heart as well as your head, you understand that "Man shall not live by bread alone, but by every word of God" (Luke 4:4 NKJV). So, the next time you take a bite of food, think strongly before you eat wrongly.

KeyPoints to ponder:
- How are you doing on your spiritual diet?
- What have you eaten today that will be of benefit to yourself and your Lord?
- Would you be willing to start every day feasting on God's Word?

"Put your nose into the Bible every day. It is your spiritual food. And then share it. Make a vow not to be a lukewarm Christian."
– Kirk Cameron

O
OBEY

If you tell someone to obey, it usually projects a negative picture. Obedience is not often a pursued desire because it demands effort. But obedience is one of the keys to survival and success.

When I was raising my three sons and one of them would ride his bike into a street full of speeding cars, I would yell, "Stop!" Their obedience saved their lives more than several times.

The same is true of our heavenly Father. He provides the rules and boundaries of life and warns us when we wander. When we ignore His wise words, we suffer the consequences. "To obey is better than sacrifice," the Bible tells us (1 Samuel 15:22). Jesus said, "If anyone loves me, he will obey my teaching" (John 14:23).

I learned a long time ago that obedience brings the blessing of God, and disobedience always brings conflict. Don't bring trouble on yourself when God has a world of privileges waiting for those who obey. As the hymn writer John H. Sammis wrote, "Trust and obey for there's no other way!"

KeyPoints to ponder:
- How do you feel when someone disobeys you?
- How do you think God responds to your disobedience?
- With whom will you share appreciation today for their model of obedience?

"Obedience without faith is possible, but not faith without obedience." – Unknown

OFF

The opposite of "on" is "off" – no power, no light, and no motion. To say that someone is a little "off" means not everything is just right with their thinking and their acting as compared to the norm.

Yet, not every idea of off is bad. We need off times. Our bodies, minds, and spirits scream for time to power down, to rest and rebuild. After all, the Bible says that God created the universe in six days and then he took the day off – to celebrate, to chill out. He expects the same from us.

For years, France has adopted a 32-hour work week, but one of the nation's newer presidents says that's too much time off and leads to poor productivity.

The best answer to bring "off and on" into all of life is balance. Jesus had the most balanced life of anybody. Since He was the sinless Savior, and yet God in flesh, we would do well to follow His ways.

KeyPoints to ponder:
- Is it time for you to turn something off in your life?
- Are you a balanced believer?
- Who will you encourage to get from a lazy lifestyle and on to positive productivity?

"Balance, peace, and joy are the fruit of a successful life. It starts with recognizing your talents and finding ways to serve others by using them." – Thomas Kinkade

ORGANISM

A fungus known as the honey mushroom (Armillaria ostoyae) in the Malheur National Forest of eastern Oregon, is the single largest organism on earth. It is roughly 2,400 years old and stretches 3.5 miles in diameter. With most of it hidden under the earth, that's an area larger than 600 football fields.

As amazing as that seems, there is yet a greater organism in structure and stability. It's the church of the Lord Jesus Christ. When the Apostle Peter proclaimed Jesus as the Son of the living God, Jesus affirmed him and declared, "on this rock, I will build my church." Then He exclaimed, "and the gates of Hades will not overcome it" (Matthew 16:18).

The church is not an organization of people grouped together to make a social statement. The church is a living organism linked to a living God who brings life to all who will believe. The church is not a club to join; rather, it is a fellowship who follow after God, their Father.

No earthly organization can compare to the Godly group that gathers faithfully to give God the glory which He desires and deserves.

KeyPoints to ponder:
- Are you an active part of God's great group called the church?
- What kind of statement is your church making within your community?
- How can you include others into your organism to learn and grow in grace?

"No man is an island, entire of itself; every man is a piece of the continent, a part of the main." – John Donne

OUT

"Out" is the opposite of "in." To be out sometimes means to be left out and alone. However, there are times when out is exactly where we need to be. For example, if a great job offer comes your way, you twist and turn to create every reason why you deserve the position, even if it will take time away from your family and fun. When you finally resolve it in your spirit you say, "I'm out."

Like a card player who lays down his hand on the table – you simply back out. You don't lose; you just don't choose to play the hand.

Are you in a situation at home, school, or work right now where you need to get out? Do you worry over what you'll lose instead of what you might gain if you do? Well, that's good. You are perfectly postured to go to a greater source for strength. Your answer comes from asking. Prayer brings power to get out of unholy habits, ungodly circumstances, unruly relationships, and unnecessary choices.

God says, "Call to me and I will answer you and tell you great and unsearchable things that you do not know" (Jeremiah 33:3). Sometimes the greatest growth we gain is by getting out.

KeyPoints to ponder:
- Are you feeling left out lately?
- Have you opted out of something in life recently?
- Are there those who need your help from feeling left out?

"As soon as you can say what you think and not what some other person has thought for you, you are on the way to being a remarkable man." – James M. Barrie

OVERWHELM

Interestingly enough, the word overwhelm means basically the same as whelm, though over adds more emphasis. It comes from the Middle English word *"whelmen"* meaning to overturn. It's like a capsized boat – upside down. From this thirteenth-century word we created overwhelm as meaning something completely covered over.

Did you feel overwhelmed today? Has something or someone covered you over with worry, hurt, anger, or stress? So many of us are in danger of drowning emotionally, but there is an answer. The Apostle Peter said, "Cast your anxiety on him (Jesus Christ) because he cares for you" (1 Peter 5:7). Our problem is not so much that we don't keep casting our worries on God, it is that we keep reeling them in again and again.

How you handle the hard times of life shows your level of learning and faith. Don't just go with the flow in life, swim against sin to the safe shores of a Savior who loves you. He is always ready for another rescue.

KeyPoints to ponder:
- Is life upside down for you right now?
- What is it that is overwhelming you today?
- Who needs your rescue from troubled times to become right-side-up?

"Our vision is so limited we can hardly imagine a love that does not show itself in protection from suffering ... The love of God did not protect His own Son ... He will not necessarily protect us – not from anything it takes to make us like His Son."– Elisabeth Elliot

P

PAIN

Nobody willingly invites pain – it just happens. Charles Kingsley once said, "Pain is no evil, unless it conquers us." A pain is an ache; a pang or a prick; a smart, sting or stitch; a tingle or a twinge. Say it anyway you want, it still brings discomfort, whether it is physical, emotional, mental, or spiritual. Pain hurts.

Are you in pain today? Is it your head or your heart that hurts? Do you have a broken relationship which pains you or maybe a bruised bank account? Every pain has its source in a problem; every pain also has a solution which can lead to an ultimate cure.

Jesus healed people's pain. "... and people brought to him all who were ill with various diseases, those suffering severe pain ..." (Matthew 4:24). However, Christ also experienced pain on our behalf. Not every healing is instant; many of them are eternal.
Because of Christ's death we have the opportunity to be forgiven of our painful sins and to experience an ultimate cure. Someday, the Bible states, every true believer in God's plan will be absolved of his or her pain.

Put your pain into God's hands and allow Him to use it as a reminder of His love which went to the cross for you. Because of His great pain, we have everything to gain!

KeyPoints to ponder:
- What pains you today?
- Have you sought His healing?
- How will you help heal others whose pain is greater than your own?

"All of our difficulties are only platforms for the manifestation of His grace, power and love." – Hudson Taylor

PANIC

On a recent airline flight, the intercom voice pierced the cabin as we reached 37,000 feet above land, 1,000 miles away from home, and travelling 600 miles per hour – "If there are any medical personnel on board, please report to the closest flight attendant." You could see the panic pour over the passengers on this Boeing 737 bound for California. Apparently the problem was resolved, or at least contained, after nearly an hour of commotion.

We all face times of testing. None of us are immune to panic. It may come from an announcement or an action, but it results in one of two responses. We either respond with fear or we react by faith.

For the Christian, the "panic buttons" of life should be replaced by "peace releases." In the midst of our worst fears, God, our Father, reminds us to hear the words of Christ, "Quiet! Be still!" This command of Jesus rested the troubled seas and calmed the disturbed disciples (Mark 4:39).

Before you have your next panic attack, try trusting God with your worries – He wants to help.

KeyPoints to ponder:
- What or who is bringing panic in your life?
- Have you asked God to give you His peace?
- Who needs you to be an instrument of peace to help them with their panic?

"We are not at peace with others because we are not at peace with ourselves, and we are not at peace with ourselves because we are not at peace with God." – Thomas Merton

PAPARAZZI

Suddenly the word paparazzi has become popular. Today it refers to any freelance photographer who aggressively pursues a celebrity for the purpose of obtaining that perfect candid shot. Though the origin of the term is quite different in translation, it is similar in its setting. From Italian, it means "buzzing insects." The parallel is obvious to our contemporary culture.

Do you know that God does more than glance at your glamour? He actually gazes on all you do. He aggressively pursues a lasting relationship with you, sometimes like a nagging gnat which demands your full attention.

Yet, God's motive is not to bug you, but rather to build you. He wants you to advance in all you do as His prized creation to give you His promise of greater possibilities. "For I know the plans I have for you," declares the Lord, "plans to prosper you and not to harm you, plans to give you hope and a future" (Jeremiah 29:11).

Much of our problem is that we run from Him, rather than toward Him. His interest is not to take from you, but rather to give to you. His gift is a life of peace, here and now, and a life of perfection in the hereafter. Jesus is only a prayer away from you.

KeyPoints to ponder:
- What or who has bugged you?
- Have you prayed over it?
- In what ways will you plan to run toward Jesus Christ and His peace today?

"We are never more like Christ than in prayers of intercession."
– Austin Phelps

PATIENCE

Everybody hates to wait, or at least they act like it. Recently in a restaurant I was ushered to a seat and sat and sat and sat. When the waitress did show up she said, "I'll be back in a minute, honey." So I sat and sat and sat.

Patience is not my strength but I persisted, almost to prove the point that I could endure. My waitress was not going to win this one. I think what made the waiting worse was that there were only four cars in the parking lot and seven people inside, five of whom already had their food.

Did I forget to tell you there were three staff waitresses? Oh well, sometimes what starts slow, ends great. It happened to me. The food was delicious and when I forced a smile at my waitress, she returned the kindness. I even qualified for a senior discount (barely), and I rarely take advantage of this. I think you call that "pride". I did leave her a big tip – she needed it!

God told us to wait on Him, so we can fly like eagles and walk and run without falling down (Isaiah 40:31). I believe His ways are much higher than mine. God tells us, "As the heavens are higher than the earth, so are my ways higher than your ways and my thoughts than your thoughts" (Isaiah 55:9).

KeyPoints to ponder:
- Are you a patient person?
- Can you name a recent event which either proves your patience or not?
- Will you work to swallow your pride and show patience to someone today?

"Patience is the queen of virtues."– John Chrysostom

PENSION

Don't you admire and even envy those whose life's work grants them pensions? Most of us work hard, try to save some money, and hope for a break from a slumping housing market and ever-escalating gasoline prices.

The word "pension" comes from the Latin "*pensus*" which means "weighted." Roman citizens of old were paid by weighing silver or gold – it was their payment. The English transliteration from the 1400s has come to mean any kind of payment or wage, particularly made to people after they retire.

Some people get pensions; many people don't. What may seem fair or unfair in the world's wages is made equitable by God's payment plan. It's simple: He gave His all so we might be rich in character and provision. "For God so loved the world (that's you) that He gave His one and only Son (that's Jesus), that whoever believes in him ... might have eternal life" (that makes us rich forever!) (John 3:16).

The next time you catch yourself complaining about cash, remember God's gift of the Christ – whose riches are abundant and eternal.

KeyPoints to ponder:
- Do you get paid what you're worth at work?
- How much more in wages would it take to make you happy?
- What value do you put on the price paid for your life through the crucifixion of Christ?

"The golden age only comes to men when they have forgotten gold." – G. K. Chesterton

PERFECT

Is there anything in life that is really "perfect"? If I were to call you today and ask, "How's your day going?" I'm sure most of the responses would not include the word "perfect." Why is that? Because perfection always seems slightly out of our grip.

The Psalmist declared, "The law of the Lord is perfect, reviving the soul" (Psalm 19:7). I do know that I could use some soul-restoration. The answer comes in following God's laws. That's the powerful promise we have. Sure, it's hard, but it is possible.

You'll never be perfect – no one will – but there was a sinless Savior who showed us ways to live life with purpose instead of seeking illusive perfection.

In fact, our times of greatest turmoil are when we can be strengthened most. The Bible says that God's "power is made perfect in our weakness" (2 Corinthians 12:9). I like that! Instead of pouting that today hasn't been perfect, think about God's perfecting power that is waiting to work through you.

KeyPoints to ponder:
- In what way is God perfecting you?
- Are you glad or sad in this process?
- Can you think of someone whose life is being affected by yours through a perfecting process?

"The acknowledgement of our weakness is the first step in repairing our loss."– Thomas a' Kempis

PERSEVERANCE

"Press on!" "Don't quit!" "Winners never quit!" "Quitters never win!" We've all heard these admonitions and encouragements at one time or another. And you've probably been guilted into doing more, as well as convicted by being slack. Where's the balance? How do we know when to push the pause button in life and when to live in fast forward?

God has some good ideas that he has chosen to share with us in scripture. Maybe it matters about the moment in which you find yourself in life. If you're under pressure right now, perhaps God's wisdom speaks to you: "Blessed is the man who perseveres under trial ... he will receive the crown of life that the Lord has promised to those who love him" (James 1:12). Maybe you're feeling unstable right now. God says, "My steps have held to your paths; my feet have not slipped" (Psalm 17:5).

What moment in life do you find yourself right now? Think of the powerful promises that God has given to you. Doubtless you have had feelings that make you want to give up, when the best advice is for you to go on, gear up, get moving, and be graced by God.

KeyPoints to ponder:
- Where are you stumbling spiritually right now?
- Are you someone who perseveres or procrastinates?
- Who needs a helping hand from you to keep on keeping on?

"The best way out is always through." – Robert Frost

PESTER

Roman farmers discovered that tying a drag or large log behind a horse's hoof helped keep the horse in place while grazing. It worked well and was called a "pestern hobble", later expressed in French as an *empester*. We use the word "pester" today to denote something or someone who bothers and restricts us.

What or who is pestering you? We become angry when interrupted from our routines, especially when someone pesters us. It's irritating, but it can become engaging. Here's what I mean. Just as farmers used a device to restrict their horses' range of motion, sometimes God will use a pestering person or event in our lives to keep us from wandering beyond His safe boundaries. He knows what we need better than we do.

I see all of life as a test. We are often tempted to cheat by taking short-cuts in life, which will result in ruin. God allows pesters to become testers to teach us patience and perseverance, which can ultimately lead us to His peace. "And we know that in all things God works for the good of those who love Him, who have been called according to His purpose" (Romans 8:28).

KeyPoints to ponder:
- Who or what is pestering you?
- How well are you handling the irritation?
- What might you be bothering?

"Character cannot be developed in ease and quiet. Only through experience of trial and suffering can the soul be strengthened..."
- Helen Keller

PHRASES

It seems funny how certain phrases stick in your mind. "Long in the tooth" comes from the condition observed as a horse's gums recede as a part of the aging process. The area containing the cheap seats in vaudeville theaters came to be known as the "peanut gallery" since patrons would sometimes pelt the act with empty shells if they weren't pleased.

"Pleased as punch" refers back to the Punch and Judy puppet acts, most of which ended with Punch victorious and smiling.

I like these phrases better – "God is good," "Prayer is the answer," and "Jesus is Lord." The origin of these phrases comes from the Bible and from life's experiences. Christians use these statements to reinforce their belief that God is in complete control.

Perhaps the most powerful and poignant phrase came following the resurrection of Jesus Christ. "He is risen!" (Mark 16:6).

KeyPoints to ponder:
- Do you believe that Jesus is still alive?
- Is He alive in you?
- Where will you share His life today in a world that is dying to hear it?

"The person of Christ is to me the greatest and surest of all facts."
– Philip Schaff

PIERCE

Are you pierced? Because of earrings, nose rings, lip rings, tongue rings, navel rings, and more, many would have to say, "Yes, I am pierced." Some people have so many body piercings, one man remarked to me recently, it looks like their bodies are magnets that walked by a tackle box. Whatever!

The truth is that our piercings are a statement of fashion, but the piercing of Jesus Christ was a statement of forgiveness. Prophecy from the Psalmist provides proof that the Messiah would be pierced in His hands and His feet (Psalm 22:16). On the day of His death, Jesus was wounded as the "soldiers pierced his side" (John 19:34).

All of this activity, which included the cruel crucifixion on a cross, was to prove God's love for you and to show us that our sins can be forgiven.

The Easter season is a sign of the surety of a Savior. He really came, He really cares, and He will really come again. His piercings were painful, and His resurrection is a reminder that "Jesus paid it ALL, all – all to him I owe!"

KeyPoints to ponder:
- What's pierced on your body?
- Have you ever had your heart pierced for Christ's sake?
- How many reminders can you think of which could guide someone to God today?

"At Calvary the naked truth is staring down at us, challenging us to drop the pose and own the truth."– Roy Hession

PLANT

It is said that the General Sherman Tree, a giant sequoia in Sequoia National Park, California, is the world's largest plant. It is about 272 feet tall and more than 100 feet in circumference. This plant is predicted to have grown for about 3,500 years.

A plant can be an object or an action. I can plant my foot to take a quick turn or I can even plant a plant with the expectation that it will grow. Plant is an interesting word.

God created "seed-bearing plants and trees on the land" according to Genesis 1:11, and God also planted His Son, Jesus, on this earth to rescue and redeem us from sin. Someday, this same Savior will return again to take all who believe to be planted in a place called heaven. The Bible says it will happen "in a flash, in the twinkling of an eye" (1 Corinthians 15:52).

No matter how long and how large we live here, God is calling us to live forever. He calls us to plant ourselves with Him through the object of His Son and by the action of our faith.

KeyPoints to ponder:
- Have you planted a seed of faith in your heart?
- Can you make a plant grow better than God?
- Who is He guiding to you that needs to plant a gospel seed?

"There are two things about the gospel – believe it and behave it."
– Susanna Wesley

POWER

Power is more than an electrical current accessed through outlets in your home. Power is the potential to overcome your every weakness, knowing that you will always need to come back again for more.

The power of God was personified through Jesus Christ. He has the power to pardon, to save, to redeem, and to redesign our lives. His wonder-working power was demanded by the people of His day and demonstrated by His resurrection from death.

The wise writer of 1 Chronicles reflected on God, saying, "Wealth and honor come from you; you are the ruler of all things. In your hands are strength and power to exalt and give strength to all" (1 Chronicles 29:12).

If you are not experiencing God's power today, then you probably are seeking it from the wrong source. Your greatest power is not in your position at work or pride in your own accomplishments. Your greatest power comes as a gift from God, who is waiting patiently for you to ask Him.

KeyPoints to ponder:
- Are you seriously plugged into the power of God?
- Do you feel powerless today?
- What areas of your life need more of God's power?

"There are in the world two powers – the sword and the spirit. And the spirit has always vanquished the sword." – Napoleon

PRAISE

When I pour on the praise for someone or something, it's because I believe in what they represent and what they've done. Praise should never be for personal favor, but only because it is deserved.

Who or what have you praised lately? Some sad lives are lived for years without caring enough to say something kind. It's a tragedy when you lose an opportunity to encourage someone who is special for who they are or through what they've done. It robs the recipient of a real reward!

Since this is true of our human relations, it is even more so for our great God. The Bible reminds us, ". . . great is the LORD and most worthy of praise, he is to be feared above all gods" (1 Chronicles 16:25).

Because God has chosen to bless you and protect you today – right now would be a great time to pause and praise Him.

KeyPoints to ponder:
- Do you need some praise today?
- Have you given God the praise He deserves?
- With whom will you praise the Lord so they will see Him working through you?

"Man's chief work is the praise of God." – Augustine of Hippo

PRAYER

Should we pray? Most people would respond, "Of course." Does prayer work? Many would say, "I hope so." Well then, do you pray? Some would retreat by replying, "Why bother?"

Prayer in its simplest definition is communication with God. It's an exercise of a relationship established between a Holy Father and His needy children.

Jesus called the temple (the church) "a house of prayer" (Luke 19:46). The Apostle Paul admonished us to "devote yourselves to prayer" (Colossians 4:2). Peter reminded husbands to understand and care for their wives "so that your prayers may not be hindered" (1 Peter 3:7). Sadly, prayer remains a universal opportunity with limited participation.

Prayer provides power. With God's help you can overcome discouragement, disasters, devastations, and get direction. With God's help we can be stronger, smarter, and more sensitive.

Let go of your pride and turn to God in prayer!

KeyPoints to ponder:
- What's holding back your prayer life today?
- Is it self-sufficiency or complacency?
- What are the needs in your life over which you can pause to pray right now?

"The chief purpose of prayer is that God may be glorified in the answer." – R.A. Torrey

PREPARATION

Preparation is never as fun as presentation. Getting ready rarely surpasses the thrill of being ready. It takes work and time.

Many people want a quick fix – a short cut – the easy road. Yet, this approach to life usually has limited results and less-than-best consequences.

What have you been putting off in preparation? Is it a work assignment or a school project? Could it be an unreconciled relationship or a fouled act of forgiveness? I know most of my areas of procrastination because I practice them too often.

God knows what it means to prepare. From the beginning of time, He has prepared a place on earth and in heaven for us (John 14:1-4). To meet His presence there takes preparation on our part as well. We must believe that Jesus was born to die – to live – to come again – all of which is God's prepared plan. Our part in the plan is to trust and obey.

Since God has a future place prepared for those who believe and receive His Son as their Savior, surely it is time to renew your preparation by getting ready and by getting right with Him.

KeyPoints to ponder:

- Are you prepared for Christ to come again and take you away?
- What have you delayed doing or saying that should be done today?
- Do you really understand that God has prepared you for His pleasure?

"Failing to prepare is preparing to fail." – Anonymous

PRESENTS

The word "presents" presents a problem. You might take it as a sense of physical awareness (presence) or as an offer of gifts (presents). The truth is that it means both, depending on the spelling.

When the Magi or Wise Men made their way to the Messiah, they were aware of His presence through the shine of a star. They were also bringing presents, which they carried from afar (Matthew 2:1-8).

The acute awareness that Christ is near and our desire to bring Him gifts is still needed. The Wise Men's trek was a reminder that God's promises are never broken. He said He would give us the gift of His Son to become our Savior ... and so He did.

Do you sense His presence on Christmas in the flood of presents bought and sold? Can you feel His love for your life as much as shepherds and seers sought His love in their lives? What gift do you bring before the Christ child born in poverty, destined to become good potentate?

When the Magi discovered the Messiah, they gladly gave. Today we demand a gift, rather than to give one. Whenever you give a present, allow it to bring a strong sense of God's presence over the pleasure of physical presents that will soon be hurriedly opened and forever forgotten.

KeyPoints to ponder:
- Do you have a gift for God this year?
- What is it?
- Who needs to receive the gift of everlasting life through you today?

"We should find no pleasure or delight in anything except in our Creator, Redeemer, and Savior."– *St. Francis of Assisi*

PRIDE

Pride is an interesting term. There's good pride and bad pride. There's pride in the accomplishment of a job well done; and there's false pride, which claims that I'm better than you.

The Bible warns that, "Pride goes before destruction, a haughty spirit before a fall" (Proverbs 16:18). In other words, when we think more highly of ourselves, it's a long way down when we fall from our self-made pedestals of greatness.

Children love to hear parents brag and say, "I'm so proud of you!" As a child of God, I want Him to be proud of me – don't you? The problem comes when we think we deserve recognition, when we demand attention, or when we are happy over the demise of others. That does not make our Heavenly Father a proud parent.

The Apostle Paul wrote, "Each one should test his own actions. Then he can take pride in himself, without comparing himself to somebody else, for each one should carry his own load" (Galatians 6:4). I love that imagery. We each have a load in life to carry and a responsibility to fulfill. "The brother in humble circumstances ought to take pride in his high position" (James 1:9).

Through God's love, His wisdom cries out, "I hate pride and arrogance ..." (Proverbs 8:13). Our proudest moments should be for others and not in ourselves.

KeyPoints to ponder:
- Are you a prideful person?
- Can you name others whose pride has caused them to fall spiritually?
- Will you confess your pride to God and ask Him to make you humble?

"Be not proud of race, face, place or grace." – Samuel Rutherford

PRISON

Around two million Americans are currently detained in jails and prisons across our country. There is no other nation with as many incarcerated people. An estimated 60% of federal inmates were placed there after being convicted of one or more drug offenses.

The point of these statistics is simple – you can lock up a criminal, but only God can release a soul for redemption. The prophet Isaiah spoke for our Redeemer when he said, "I, the LORD, will ... free captives from prison and release from the dungeon those who sit in darkness" (Isaiah 42:6-7).

You may consider yourself free because you are not locked behind bars, but you can be in greater bondage than those who are in prison. True freedom is on the inside of a person, not in his or her outside circumstances.

If you'll trust Christ, He will unlock your life so that you can experience lasting liberty.

KeyPoints to ponder:
- Are you really free today?
- Do you feel like a prisoner to your schedule or your setting?
- Which part of your life will you ask God to give you liberty?

"Liberty cannot be established without morality, nor morality without faith."– Alexis de Tocqueville

PRODUCE

The English language sounds strange to outsiders and insiders alike. For instance, is it pronounced rēad or rĕad, tomāto or tomäto, prŏduce or prōduce? Let's deal with the latter comparative. We buy prōduce at the grocery store, but we prŏduce when we work or labor.

The Psalmist said that "the earth has yielded its harvest; God, our God, will bless us" (Psalm 67:6). Simply put, God is the giver of every blessing, no matter how much we work at getting more.

Jesus once told a story about a certain rich man whose land was "very productive." He had so much that he decided to tear down his older barns to build bigger ones. His motives were impure because he wasn't willing to share any of his wealth (Luke 12:16-21).

Let's face it – to be really productive in life is not to measure what you have in your barn, but instead to see how much you have given away of the substances with which God has blessed you.

KeyPoints to ponder:
- If you could produce one product successfully, what would it be?
- Are you a productive person?
- What can you produce today that will make a difference to this world and the next?

"Don't be yourself. Be superior to the fellow you were yesterday."
– Anonymous

PROFIT

In a meeting concerning financial planning, I listened carefully to the consultant's response to my opening question – "How's your day going?" She said, "Profitable!" I smiled.

Now that's a great comeback remark from someone whose work involves wealth, but it steered my thoughts toward the true profit in life.

The Book of Proverbs reminds us that, "All hard work brings a profit" (Proverbs 14:23). However, we all know that not all labor brings profit.

When Jesus illustrated this in the Parable of the Talents (Matthew 25:14-30), He was teaching all disciples that we should wisely invest whatever God gives to us. To bury your talent or treasure in fear of losing it is unacceptable.

God expects us to make the most of who we are and what He has given to us – no matter what proportion.

Take an inventory of your blessings today. Be honest enough with yourself and with God to let go of what you have to bless others who have not.

KeyPoints to ponder:
- What are you doing with what you have?
- Are you hiding it or hoarding it?
- How will you have fun helping others with it?

"There is nothing wrong with people possessing riches. The wrong comes when riches possess people." – Billy Graham

PURCHASE

Strange, but true – the first Wal-Mart, Kmart, and Target stores all opened in the very same year: 1962. Their popularity proves that everyone is interested in a purchase that brings value. Some people will push and shove to make a purposeful purchase.

Most people are interested in a good deal and will work to make it happen. Contrary to popular belief, the day after Thanksgiving is not the biggest shopping day of the year. Typically, it's the last Saturday before Christmas. Isn't it strange that we'll wait in line to save a dollar, but quickly spend five of those same dollars freely when it is a matter of convenience?

God's greatest purchase is actually an exchange. He sent His Son to die for us in exchange for our willingness to receive and believe in Him. Christ purchased our salvation through His sacrifice on a cross and proved God's power through His resurrection from a tomb.

All you have to do is believe to receive. That's a divine deal!

KeyPoints to ponder:
- Have you made a foolish purchase recently?
- Would you do it again knowing what you know now?
- How are you going to help others to make the "great exchange" of their lives for His?

"As you sit and gaze, it will be born in you that only a crucified Savior could meet your need." – William Sangster

PURIFICATION

I have a water purification system in my house. It works two ways. The water is filtered as it comes into the house and then filtered again at my refrigerator. I'm not paranoid; I'm just careful.

The sediments and contaminants which enter our house are much like those that enter into our hearts. If only it were as simple to filter the sediment in our souls. The prophet Ezekiel spoke for God when he said, "I will sprinkle clean water on you, and you will be clean. I will cleanse you from all your impurities ..." (Ezekiel 36:25). Wow!

Getting God's purification is better than a bath and stronger than a shower. We get clean from the inside out. What kind of system do you have in place to act as a spiritual filter in your life? It could be a friend, a family member, a pastor, or any number of people. Everybody needs somebody to help them stay clean.

KeyPoints to ponder:
- Is your heart clean?
- Are your thoughts pure?
- What impurities will you ask God to clean up today?

"Make and keep me pure within." – Charles Wesley

PURSUIT

A lot of people pursue a lot that is elusive. They want more than they have, or at least they want better. Our pursuit of pleasure is endless, particularly if we can escape the pain of the present. We chase dreams, we run after riches, and we seek safety when satisfaction from any of these is too often very shallow. What are you pursuing these days? Or maybe it would be better said, who's pursuing you?

The Bible has the answer and reminds us that the Lord is good to those whose hope is in Him. The good news is that we can go after God and find His favor. He promises, "You will seek me and find me when you seek me with all of your heart" (Jeremiah 29:13). He will fill your hollow heart and He'll satisfy your searching soul.

However, you must pursue Him. He's been after you from the time you were framed in your mother's womb and created you for His glory.

KeyPoints to ponder:
- What is on your list of your present pursuits?
- Is Jesus near the top?
- How will you reorder your list of priorities to bring God pleasure?

"If we seek God for our own good and profit, we are not seeking God."– Johannes Eckhart

PUZZLE

Puzzles have a purpose, which is to tease our thoughts and test our abilities until we either solve them or surrender to them. Everybody wants to work one, but no one wants to be beaten by one.

In the 1980s, I remember working hard to solve my first Rubik's Cube. This puzzle was comprised of 27 sub-cubes that rotated on horizontal and vertical axes. It was invented by a teacher of architecture and designed at the School for Commercial Artists in Budapest. His name was Erno Rubik.

No matter how difficult a puzzle may prove to be, there must always be a purpose behind it. The same is true of life. Many don't understand God and why He does what He does. They see Him as a puzzle, when instead God's greatest desire is to bring us purpose. We can't solve God's complexity, so we should surrender to His sovereignty.

The Bible tells us to "be transformed by the renewing of your mind. Then you will be able to test and approve what God's will is – His good, pleasing and perfect will" (Romans 12:2).

KeyPoints to ponder:
- What's puzzling you?
- Have you worked it out?
- How will you seek to gain God's help in solving it?

"Every great achievement was once considered impossible."
– Anonymous

Q

QUICK

If I say, "You're quick," it might mean that you're fast or you are bright with your brain. However, if I say, "You cut me to the quick," it means what you did was to tap into the most personal and emotionally sensitive part of myself.

This latter definition comes from the raw exposed flesh area under the fingernails. Its derivation comes to us from the Anglo-Saxon word "*cwicu*," meaning "alive or living." If you've had a hangnail, then you know the pain that persists when you peel back the quick of your skin.

Jesus said He was to be quick about His return to earth. The Bible says that He'll come "in a flash, in the twinkling of an eye ..." (1 Corinthians 15:52).

When Christ comes, He won't wait until we are ready; He will come quickly to take every believer to a heavenly home. Ready or not, here He comes!

KeyPoints to ponder:
- Are you quick to obey God?
- Has someone cut you to the quick recently in your emotional or spiritual life?
- What will you do or say to make it right with them and before God?

"Obedience is the key to every door." – George MacDonald

QUIET

Being quiet is about as much fun as being still. Some consider it a pleasure and for others it's pure pain. We're not made to run 24/7 in body, mind or spirit. Even God chose to rest and be quiet after creating our planet and two persons.

The Bible boldly reminds us to, "Be still, and know that I am God" (Psalm 46:10). It's God's way of telling us to unwind, get quiet, listen instead of talk, and remember to reflect.

Most of us are caught in a "doer's net." We believe that busyness will increase our business and that the more we do, the better we'll be. The journey of Jesus to earth proved just the opposite. He came from the calm of God's glory to spend time in the chaos of our world (His creation).

In the midst of men's mad rush, however, He taught his disciples to get away and pray – to move from the rush to get rest – to learn that it is better to be a God-lover than to do everything trying to prove you are one. The prophet Isaiah said it best, "... in quietness and trust is your strength ..." (Isaiah 30:15).

Stop now and listen to our Lord; He has a lot He is ready to tell you.

KeyPoints to ponder:

- Have you gotten quiet today?
- Who talks more in an average conversation – you or your friend?
- What do you think you can learn better from listening more?

"Silence nourishes patience, charity, discretion." – Elisabeth Elliot

QUIETNESS

Quietness is not always the absence of sound. It may be better defined as stillness within our souls, an inner peace, or perhaps even a pause. Our loud world does not applaud quiet and certainly does not understand being still. But we need it – desperately!

God guides us to stillness. The Scripture says, "Be still, and know that I am God" (Psalm 46:10). Job understood that the greatest lessons for life come in the quiet. He prayed, "Teach me and I will be quiet; show me where I have been wrong" (Job 6:24).

I like Isaiah's instruction, "The fruit of righteousness will be peace; the effect of righteousness will be quietness and a confidence forever" (Isaiah 32:17). We scream for help, but God gives us his best help in the stillness of the moment. Moses reminded God's people, "The Lord will fight for you; you need only to be still" (Exodus 14:14).

Try keeping quiet and learn to listen for someone bigger than yourself.

KeyPoints to ponder:
- How long has it been since you have spent an hour in silence before God?
- Could you do it?
- Will you do it and when?

"Humility is the perfect quietness of heart." – Andrew Murray

R
RADIO

Over the last twenty years, the number of FM stations has doubled, while AM stations in the U.S. have remained stable. Authorized by the FCC, stereo FM broadcasts began in 1961. Radio reaches more persons over the age of 12 on a weekly basis than any other media form. That's more than 95 percent of adults who listen to radios at least once a week.

I wish the same were true with God. Too many are tuned out or turned off to His voice. There's a large segment of our society who consider God's words as irrelevant and antiquated, but they are wrong.

God has broadcast His message through mankind in verbal and written languages since the creation. Two millennia ago, God chose to send a Messiah as the strongest message of His love.

The voice of Jesus Christ has been broadcast throughout the world in almost every language and on every continent. "For the word of God is living and active ... it judges the thoughts and attitudes of the heart" (Hebrews 4:12).

KeyPoints to ponder:
- Are you daily tuned in to our Savior?
- Have you been broadcasting His message?
- What do you think it will take for our world to get on God's frequency?

"We trust that their hearts will be melted by that love, and that they'll listen to the gospel."– Ken Ham

RAIN

It was during the heaviest of rains in seventeenth-century England that the remains of dogs and cats were often seen floating in the streets. The reason for this was poor drainage systems and even poorer health control laws. As these unprotected animals drowned during times of flooding, it was then said that it had "rained cats and dogs."

Rain is a good thing. It brings nourishment to our earth. We drink it, we wash with it, it generates power, and it has huge potential for good. Yet, it can prove destructive without boundaries.

Once God chose to let it rain forty days and forty nights. Noah and his family were the only ones spared because they were the only ones who believed in the Source (God) of the rain and His warnings (Genesis 6:8).

Though the rainbow is a promise of God's goodness that a worldwide flood will never occur again, it should also remind us that God "... sends rain on the righteous and the unrighteous" (Matthew 5:45).

KeyPoints to ponder:
- How are you handling the rains of life right now?
- Are you all wet?
- What's good about this; what's bad?

"God never promises to remove us from our struggles. He does promise, however, to change the way we look at them."
– Max Lucado

RAINFALL

The Bible says that the rain falls on the righteous and the unrighteous alike (Matthew 5:45). Rainfall is indiscriminate and unpredictable; it brings both nourishment and nuisance. We either love it or loathe it depending on our need.

In the beginning of time, rain was unknown until the Genesis account of the first flood. This is a reminder to us that rain can bring ruin when we are unprepared. A farmer's worst fear comes when it rarely rains, knowing that the crops can wither and die.

Is rain falling on you today? Is it a blessing or a curse from above? If you'll remember the Source of the wet substance and not focus on the symptoms, your day will be brighter. God knows what we need and when. He sends tough times our way as well as times of ease and enjoyment.

Look up! If storm clouds surround you, thank God for the strength to endure them and even enjoy them. We cannot always determine the form of God's gifts, but we can develop an appreciation for the Giver.

KeyPoints to ponder:
- What is stormy for you right now?
- How well are you handling the rainfall of rough times?
- What are you planning to do about it?

"Many men owe the grandeur of their lives to their tremendous difficulties."– *Charles Spurgeon*

REED

The word reed can be pronounced as reed or read (red), depending on your desire and definition. If it's a book, you read it. If it's a dried, hollowed-out plant, it's a reed. The interesting thing about a plant reed is that it was one of the many symbols used to describe Jesus. The Bible predicted that He would be like "a reed swayed by the wind (Matthew 11:7). The purpose of this passage was to present the coming Christ as One whose life would be beaten and broken – as a reed.

It happened just as the prophets predicted. Jesus came in the body of a man, was bent by those who did not believe and was crucified by those who thought they could break Him. What they failed to understand is that this Reed became a Redeemer. His death led to life – His own and ours as well.

The problem remains this day as it was yesterday. Some will reject Him, and others will receive Him. To those who receive, God gives the promise of eternal life hereafter and the power of abundant life here and now (Romans 10:9; John 10:10b).
What you read about God's Reed will only make a difference if you receive.

KeyPoints to ponder:
- Have you ever been broken in life?
- Do you believe God's power is greater than your problem?
- Will you trust Him completely today?

"You can't break what's already broken."—LeAnn Rimes

REST

Rest is both regular and elusive for all of us. It's regular, as we need a nightly time to recover from our daily routine. It's elusive because most of us wrestle with truly being able to unwind.

Many of us run from rest for fear of being unproductive, when the truth is that we produce more and better following real rest.

An acronym that has helped me to rest is:
R-E-S-T
- **R**elax
- **E**at right/**E**xercise
- **S**leep
- **T**rust

I've discovered you cannot completely rest until you learn to relax in body, mind, and spirit.

As we eat and exercise, we fulfill the admonition to care for our bodies as the "temple of God" (1 Corinthians 6:19).

Sleep is not just important; it's essential. Enough is needed to gain strength for another day. To trust God with all you have and all you are is a challenge, but it is obtainable.

KeyPoints to ponder:
- Whose rest have you disturbed recently?
- How well have you rested lately?
- What will it take for you to completely rest in the Lord?

"He who cannot rest, cannot work; he who cannot let go, cannot hold on..."– Harry Emerson Fosdick

RESULTS

We all want results because those around us expect them. We work for results, performance, and paychecks. We play for results – recreation and relaxation. We even sleep for results – rest and restoration. Results are a big part of all of our lives for all of our lives.

One problem we face is the lack of results from others. Many times we demand more of strangers than we do of ourselves. We want fast food, and we want it fast. We want instant coffee instantly, and we want tomorrow's results today.

The Bible tells us, "Whatever you do, work at it with all your heart, as working for the Lord … it is the Lord Christ you are serving" (Colossians 3:23-24). If we would follow this admonition, we would have less ruin and richer results. Our lives would be filled with less demands and more delight. We would discover lasting results instead of fading failures.

KeyPoints to ponder:
- Are you driven by results?
- Do you drive others (family, friends, co-workers) for results?
- What are the results that you think God really wants from you?

"Godliness is devotion to God which results in a life which is pleasing to Him."– Jerry Bridges

RETIRE

Many people work for forty-plus years with the driving hope that someday they can retire. We have this distorted notion that retirement means rest and relaxation. The word actually comes from the French meaning "to withdraw," which later took on the English translation of getting away from the world.

However, if you go deeper with the meaning, you can discover the root of the word is *"tirer"* which means "to pull," shortened from *"martirier"* from which we get the word martyr or witness. A martyr's limbs were once pulled from them in response to their stance for God. This tortuous death was a result of the person's unrelenting faith which was in direct contrast from the world's ways.

Most of us believe that peace is the absence of conflict when in reality a life of retiring toward God may bring friction. However, the joy which comes from this retirement is worth the journey.

Jesus said, "My peace I give unto you. I do not give to you as the world gives" (John 14:27).

KeyPoints to ponder:
- Could you ever be accused or indicted for your God-fearing faith?
- Have you ever endured the shame of verbal or physical attack because of your love for Jesus Christ?
- Do you think a Christian should ever really retire from service?

"Faithful servants never retire. You can retire from your career, but you will never retire from serving God." – Rick Warren

RETURN

To return is to go back from where you came. Not all returns are readily received or welcomed; however, like Dorothy in "The Wizard of Oz", many of us would easily proclaim, "There's no place like home."

Jesus said that He would someday return to retrieve those whose trust is in Him. The trumpet sound of God will signal our Savior's arrival. The Apostle Paul stated that the dead in Christ will rise first and then, "we who are alive and left will be caught up together with them in the clouds to meet the Lord in the air. And so we will be with the Lord forever" (I Thessalonians 4:17).

In other words, Christ's return will initiate our earthly removal and our ultimate reception into the heavens prepared for God's children.

For some this scene will signal fear; for others, it will be a fulfillment of their faith. If you have doubts, it's time for you to return to the One who redeems all who repent and receive Him.

KeyPoints to ponder:
- Will you be ready for His return or will you run from such a sight?
- Is it time for you to return to Jesus before He returns to us?
- What will you do to prepare for His coming?

"And what is the hope of a true Christian? It is just this – that Jesus Christ is coming again." – J.C. Ryle

REVISION

I love eating Ben and Jerry's ice cream but was surprised to learn that Ben Cohen and Jerry Greenfield first wanted to go into the bagel business. It seems that the $40,000 start-up costs for equipment discouraged their attempt. Instead, they revised their plan as the two opted to take a $5 correspondence course in ice cream making.

Life is filled with revised plans, or it should be. When you hit a hard spot you don't quit; you find another way to get through. It is God's design for you to take a detour and sometimes even a U-turn in life. Our stubbornness can develop into a sin, if we are not willing to change for Christ's sake.

Jesus came to revise our plans or to restore our pursuits. He left His heavenly home to fulfill His Father's will through His sacrifice for our sins. Should we do less in our willingness to change?

Jesus preached, "Repent, for the kingdom of heaven has come near" (Matthew 4:17). This is more than a statement of curiosity – it is a command. When we revise our plans, God revives our lives and promises to restore us to permanent peace.

KeyPoints to ponder:
- What needs revision in your life right now?
- Are you willing to change to make it happen?
- Who is waiting on you to help them revise their relationship with God?

"The question isn't were you challenged. The question is were you changed?"– Leonard Ravenhill

RING

One can wear a ring or ring a bell. It can be an ornament or an action. A bride-to-be flashes her engagement ring and squeals, while a boxer throws punches until the bell peals, thus ending the round. Rings always bring response.

Kings once used their rings as symbols of authority and rule. A document was made official when the ruler pressed his ring into a hot wax seal, signifying his approval.

God is King of the universe and pressed His approval toward us by sending His one and only Son to be our Savior. Our response to God's action determines our present and our future.

If we refuse God's gift and ignore his ring of redemption, we have rejected an awesome offer and created an awful offense. Jesus said, "My yoke is easy and my burden is light" (Matthew 11:30).

KeyPoints to ponder:
- Have you made Christ the king of your life?
- Are you engaged with God through your faith in King Jesus?
- What outer symbols of your faith can others clearly identify?

"Christ in you, on the grounds of redemption, this is the Gospel!"
– Major Ian Thomas

ROAR

The roar of a crowd captures our attention. The roar of the ocean captures our imagination. But the roar of a lion captures us in fear. Roars are sounds which start in our ears, move to our minds, and then motivate our hearts. A roar is rarely ignored, no matter its source.

The Bible says that, "Your enemy the devil prowls around like a roaring lion looking for someone to devour. Resist him, standing firm in the faith ..." (I Peter 5:8-9a). I like what an inscription over the mantle of Hind's Head Hotel in England says, "Fear knocked at the door; faith answered. No one was there."

How is it with you when you hear the fearful knock of Satan as he roars at the door of your life? Do you succumb to fear, or do you answer his threats with faith?

Remember the words of the apostle John who reminds us that, "... the one who is in you is greater than the one who is in the world" (I John 4:4). If Christ lives and rules in your heart, He is in you and will help you to defeat the devil who only wants to "steal, kill and destroy" you in this world (John 10:10). Shout back at the roar and say, "No more!" and let faith melt your fears into peace.

KeyPoints to ponder:
- Whose roar are you hearing today?
- Does it bring faith or fear?
- What specific actions will you take to resist the devil?

"A believer is to be known not only by his peace and joy, but by his warfare in distress." – Robert Murray M'Cheyne

ROCK

"Rock" is a solid word. When you hear about rocks, you think about what is hard and heavy. We say, "rock-solid," "rock-hard," and "rock-foundation." Rocks aren't soft or supple; they're strong and solid.

Rocks are used to build walls, gates, gardens and borders. They aren't the last element to add to a house, but the first.

The Psalmist said, "The LORD is my rock, my fortress and my deliverer ..." (Psalm 18:2). God is our solid-rock foundation for life.

Jesus taught about a man who built his house on a rock and a man who built his house on sinking sand (Matthew 7:24-27). His point was simple. Solid is strong; sinking is weak.

It's time to come back to the Rock of God Who will redeem you and refresh you. It's time to build your life on the Rock of life – your solid source of strength. "Rock of Ages, cleft for me, Let me hide myself in thee..."– Christian hymn (Augustus M. Toplady)

KeyPoints to ponder:
- Are you standing on a Rock or throwing one?
- How solid is your foundation of faith right now?
- Who needs your rescue from their sinking sand?

"On Christ, the solid Rock I stand; All other ground is sinking sand."
– Edward Mote

RULE

During high school and college summers, I worked several construction jobs in the Atlanta area. The foreman would say to me, "Bring me the rule." What he meant was for me to get the tape measure or ruler. A ruler is used for measuring, and the same is true of someone who rules or has a larger measure of authority over others.

God gave us authority to rule over animal life in the Book of Beginnings (Genesis 1:26). Later, in early Bible times, the people of Israel asked God for a king to rule over them (1 Samuel 12:12).

Yet, the greatest rule is not animal or people rule, but God's rule and measure of our lives. He wants to "Let the peace of Christ rule in your hearts ..." (Colossians 3:15).

A rich request from the Apostle Paul to every Christian was that we should "never boast except in the cross of our Lord Jesus Christ" (Galatians 6:14) and His rule. In fact, He promised "peace and mercy to all who follow this rule ..." (Galatians 6:16). God's measure over us will always stand supreme.

KeyPoints to ponder:
- Who rules your life?
- What areas of your life does God need the authority to rule?
- Will you ask Him and then let Him?

"Christ is not valued at all, unless he is valued above all."
– Augustine of Hippo

RULES

Rules are what we want others to obey. A rule can also be something done to show authority and keep order. Contrary to many people's opinions, rules are not made to be broken, but are usually made to better our behavior.

A barnyard rooster certainly fits the description of one who "rules the roost," but actually this saying comes from an entirely different source. Its original form was first recorded as "rule the roast." Coming from old England, it referred to the master of the house who sat at the head of the table and served his guests. He set the rules and faithfully served his family and friends, using his seat of authority.

God has a right to rule over all. He took the form of a servant in becoming a man to show us that His rule was one of humility, love, and forgiveness. God's best rule is received when we show Him and others how much we care. Let's follow His rule from the Bible that tells us, "Let us not become weary in doing good, for at the proper time we will reap a harvest if we do not give up" (Galatians 6:9).

KeyPoints to ponder:
- Who rules your household?
- Is it a person, a pocketbook, or a promise?
- What rules are you setting for others to follow our Lord faithfully?

"The very word authority has within it the word Author."
– R.C. Sproul

RUMMAGE

To rummage or to "stir around" came originally from the noun "roomage" and was, by definition, a storage place for cargo in a ship's hull. The verb came about as a result of searching that particular roomage place. If you picture the roomage of the ship, you get a clearer idea of what rummage was intended to be.

What are you searching for in the storage areas of your life? Maybe you have saved so much stuff that when you look at it all, this causes confusion for you instead of clarity.

Christ is also looking and stirring around in our lives. He searches our hearts for something special. David, the psalmist, pled, "Create in me a pure heart, O God, and renew a steadfast spirit within me" (Psalm 51:10).

KeyPoints to ponder:
- Is your heart pure or putrid?
- Is God pleased with what you have stored in your soul?
- Will you make some time to take a spiritual inventory and get rid of what is bringing ruin inside you?

"A divided heart loses both worlds." A.B. Simpson

S

SABOTAGE

The word sabotage comes from the French – sabot – meaning "wooden shoe." When weaving looms were first introduced to the French during World War II, the workmen protested the loss of their jobs to machines by jamming wooden shoes into the looms. From the destruction that came about from a wooden shoe in yesteryear, we get sabotage today.

At times we all have felt sabotaged. We get undermined at work, in our family, in school, community, and recreation. It's not unusual that people get opposition from reactive forces who wish them harm. God knows this feeling, as well as the fact. When He sent Jesus His Son to earth, He felt the pain of betrayal, denial, and refusal. He watched while the Christ was subjected to ridicule and ultimate rejection.

Though God's plan led Christ to a cross to pay the penalty for our sin, there were many who wanted to sabotage the Savior, and there are still many who wish to wreck His redemptive plan.
Be God's source for support to others and not a saboteur.

KeyPoints to ponder:
- Have you been sabotaged recently?
- How did it feel?
- Are you a saboteur?

*"Christianity is the story of how the rightful King has landed . . .
And is calling us all to take part in His great campaign of
sabotage." – C.S. Lewis*

SAIL

I love to sail and on windy days it's an incredible enticement to be on a boat rather than to be bothering with my day.

One day when Jesus was resting in his disciples' boat, a storm plagued the sea and pressed the sails to danger. His band of believers panicked and accused him of not caring that they might perish in the squall. In His peace-filled personality, Christ calmed the waves and rested the sails to safety. (Mark 4:38-40)

Two expressions become examples for us. First, He proved His power to control the elements. Next, He showed His compassion for his panic-stricken friends. What's the most important? Both. We need His peace and we need His power in the midst of our stormy seas of life. The Bible reminds us that God does not sleep nor slumber (Psalm 132:4).

He knows what we need and when we need it. His love is lasting in the midst of our doubts that lead us into dangerous waters.

KeyPoints to ponder:
- How stormy is life for you right now?
- Are you at peace in the midst of the storm?
- Do you think Jesus can do anything about it? Have you asked?

"I'm not afraid of storms, for I'm learning how to sail my ship."
– Louisa May Alcott

SALT

Anyone not worth his salt is worth very little indeed, and by some definitions, not worth the money that he earns. In ancient Roman days, rations of salt were given to soldiers and civil servants. These portions fell under the general category of "sal" (the word in Latin). When money became the substitute, the word "salarium" or salary was born.

Jesus said, "You are the salt of the earth. But if the salt loses its saltiness . . . it is no longer good for anything . . ." (Matthew 5:13).

Salt is used for seasoning and preserving food. The reason Jesus called His disciples salt was because He expected them to bring a spiritual seasoning to the world. He also knew that by spreading His fame, we would give opportunity for many to experience His permanent preservation.

The English phrase "true to his salt" refers to one who is faithful to his employer. We do want to be found faithful to the Lord and salty for our Savior.

KeyPoints to ponder:
- Have you lost your saltiness?
- Do you taste better this year than last or more bitter?
- How can you be truer to your Lord as you labor?

"Any supervisor worth his salt would rather deal with people who attempt too much than those who try too little." – Lee Iacocca

SCAPEGOAT

Today a scapegoat is synonymous with one who takes the blame for another. The original scapegoat is biblical in origin and associated with the Jewish Day of Atonement (Yom Kippur). It refers to one goat presented as the Lord's live offering and allowed to go free, symbolically taking the people's sins with him.

Too many of us play the "blame game" as we deflect our deficiencies on others. We writhe and wiggle to get out of our wrongdoings when all the while we know we won't win.

The Bible says, "You may be sure that your sin will find you out" (Numbers 32:23). In other words, we can run today, but someday we will be caught. God not only knows who we are, but what we do and why we do it. In His knowledge, He still loves us with a love beyond compare.

When you're tempted to tell a tale which distracts from the truth – save some time and ask Jesus to help you through your trouble. To shift your sin will only bring more pain than pleasure.

KeyPoints to ponder:
- Who or what are you blaming in your life?
- Who's blaming you?
- How will you begin to take responsibility instead of demanding your rights?

"The search for a scapegoat is the easiest of all hunting expeditions." – Dwight D. Eisenhower

SCENT

Do you think much about how you smell to others – your scent? There's a billion-dollar business built around this concern with tens of thousands of choices.

Scent comes from the Latin word "sentire" meaning to feel or perceive. Originally it referred to the sense of hunting dogs detecting their prey by smell.

Every one of us emits an odor – some better than others! The Bible says God is even interested in how we smell. When we are a person seeking to build up His kingdom, we are like a sweet-smelling savor unto the Lord. Even our gifts to God have a sacred scent and are pleasing to Jesus (Philippians 4:18).

Next time you dab on perfume or splash on cologne, think about the lingering smell which you offer to a greater audience than your circle of daily contacts. Think of how your scent smells to the Savior. Ask Him to let your life be pleasing and acceptable to His favor even more than to your family and friends. Now, that smells good!

KeyPoints to ponder:
- Do you smell something?
- Is it sweet or sour?
- Is it you?

"Prayer - secret, fervent, believing prayer - lies at the root of all personal godliness"– WIlliam Carey

SEAS

Admit it – the ocean holds an appeal for most of us. Maybe it's the mystique or perhaps the vastness of water. Three-quarters of our earth is covered with water and most of it is the sum of our seas.

"High seas," by definition, are those seas which are purely public – they're the property of no country. As I understand the rules, apparently no country can lay claim to the water which is beyond 3 miles from its borders.

On a recent trip to the Georgia coast, I saw this as a certainty. Day and night there was a very large, cruise-type ship which navigated between the small islands. I discovered it was a floating, gambling casino which legally bridged the local laws because of the separation by sea.

The last book of the Bible, a Revelation from God, reveals that someday there will be "no longer any sea." This "new heaven and new earth" will not permit separation, nor segregation (Revelation 21:1). Our new heavenly homes will be places of peace and prosperity unparalleled on earth as we know it now. The key to unlocking this new abode is to believe in Christ and you, too, can come.

KeyPoints to ponder:
- Are you sailing on stormy seas?
- Do you feel separate from God and others?
- What will it take from you to get connected again?

"Peace comes not from the absence of problems, but from the presence of God." – Alexander Maclaren

SECRET

Remember the game played in school when a "secret" was shared from one student to another and was whispered in the ears of the class members row-by-row? It was always funny to hear how it had changed from the original words to the concluding revelation.

A secret is something you wish to keep private – away from public knowledge. Back in the Dark Ages, it was long held by superstition that a doctor could not cut into the body of a dead person, for fear of disturbing its ghost. As a result, cadavers became hot items on the black market for doctors longing to study human anatomy. When grave robbers began to supply the goods, many a good doctor became suspected of having a "skeleton in his closet," which gave us today's meaning of private or hidden secrets.

The Bible says, "Would not God find this out? For He knows the secrets of the heart" (Psalm 44:21). There are no secrets to God. He knows you, yet He loves you. He sees you, yet He forgives you. He longs for us to come clean so we can cling to Him forever.

KeyPoints to ponder:
- What's your biggest secret?
- Does anyone know it but you?
- Is God pleased with it or is He bruised by it?

"Nothing is ever hidden from God. Not an activity, not a book you read, not a word you say, not a thought you think, not a place you go." – Jack Hyles

SEEDS

Seeds are a source of life. Plant a seed, water it, wait for it to grow, and witness a miracle. A single seed can produce a powerful harvest.

Jesus said, ". . . unless a kernel of wheat falls to the ground and dies, it remains only a single seed. But if it dries, it produces many seeds" (John 12:24). This was more than a lesson for life. It was God's way of reminding us that from death comes life and a life worth living.

When Christ died on the cross, His seeds of eternal life were sown for all time and for all people. Without His death and burial, there would have been no sure sign of His love for you and me.

Surely there is something which needs to die in your life to produce more of God's power. Would you be willing to sacrifice your physical sense of security or your substance or even your stuff? Our spiritual security and sustenance come from the seeds of God planted deep within our lives through faith in Jesus Christ.

KeyPoints to ponder:
- What's growing in you right now?
- Has your soil been nourished by the watering of God's Word?
- How will you plan to plant seeds of faith in others today?

"Don't judge each day by the harvest you reap but by the seeds that you plant."– Robert Louis Stevenson

SERVING

Serving seems so demeaning if you think of it as a chore, rather than a privilege. Growing up in the South, I watched the racial tensions mount as friction festered between those who served and those being served. All the while I wondered why the model was so muddled. After all, God gave us great good in sending His Son to serve us.

There's a huge difference in being a servant and being subservient. A servant cares for the one he serves; one who is subservient is under the harsh hand and demand of the one to whom he is enslaved.

Think about which one you are. We are given guidance from God as He tells us, "Serve wholeheartedly, as if you were serving the Lord, not men" (Ephesians 6:7). If you are a disgruntled employee or a spouse with suspicions, this is a tough assignment. Your natural desire is to get out of disagreements and certainly not to serve the one who makes life so sour.

Take the challenge to turn your thinking into thanking by giving God an opportunity to change you – maybe before He changes your circumstances or relationships.

KeyPoints to ponder:
- Do you seek to serve others or be served?
- Whom are you serving?
- Who else will you begin to serve for Christ's sake?

"I don't know what your destiny will be, but one thing I know: the only ones among you who will be really happy are those who have sought and found how to serve." – Albert Schweitzer

SHIELD

Several years ago, when I went to Africa, I saw shields of all sizes, shapes, and descriptions. The warrior's shield is a device of defense, intended to ward off any attack. A shield becomes a hiding place to prevent penetration. A shield is a weapon used in war.

Do you find it strange that the Bible would refer to God as "my strength and my shield"? (Psalm 28:7) We are told to "take up the shield of faith" (Ephesians 6:16) and be reminded that God's "faithfulness is a shield" (Psalm 91:4). All of these passages provide a sense of protection and peace for our lives. We don't have to fight our battles alone.

Modern police and law enforcement officers are meticulously trained to seek cover when fired on by bullets. Their shields might be a door, a car, or a wall. When God sees you "under fire" from the devil's darts, He does not want you to get hurt. His provision and protection is the shield of our Savior. In Christ, you are safe; with God's shield, you can be secure – forever.

KeyPoints to ponder:
- Are you being fired on by somebody?
- Do you need protection?
- What will it take for you to take cover in Christ?

"Our 'safe place' is not where we live, it is in whom we live."
                                              – Tom White

SHINE

"Rise and shine" was my mother's call to me morning by morning. Getting up was a chore and still is for most of us. Yet, the sun does it day after day, and its shine is a signal of a bright new beginning.

Do you know that we also exude light? Jesus said, "Let your light shine before men in such a way that they may see your good works, and glorify your Father who is in heaven" (Matthew 5:16). There's a sense of shining in all of us. For some it's bright; for others it is dull and discouraging.

God also shines. There's a Bible blessing that says, "The Lord make His face shine on you, and be gracious to you" (Numbers 6:25). I think the reason that shining is superior is because darkness is depressing. We need light and need to be light in a dark world.

Shining lights draw attention. Examples are numerous: fire engines, police, billboards, traffic signals, strobes – Las Vegas!

The Apostle Peter said we would "do well to pay attention as to a lamp shining in a dark place . . ." (2 Peter 1:19). Let your light shine as a signal for our Savior!

KeyPoints to ponder:
- So how's your glow for God today?
- Are you casting a shadow on someone else's shine?
- How do you plan to grow in your glow for God's glory?

"It isn't necessary to blow out the other person's light to let your own shine." – Anonymous

SHIP

A ship can be a vessel or a verb. It happened as a part of our history. Until the locomotive came along, there were no land vehicles able to haul heavy goods at a low cost. Transportation was dominated by ships for so long that our vocabulary was permanently affected. We still "ship" goods – whether by ship, train, truck, or plane.

How do you handle your heavy goods of life – those tough times when it seems you're going nowhere? Who helps you transport your troubles? Don't you have days when you wish you could ship your suffering to another state? Sure, you do. We all do.

This is why Jesus came to earth in order to heal our hurts. His life and death are a sure cure for sin when we trust in Him. Like a ship, our Savior became a vessel and a verb.
He is God's vessel of victory through His forgiveness and His favor. He is our ship of security as He transports our sins away. "Therefore my friends, I want you to know that through Jesus the forgiveness of sins is proclaimed to you" (Acts 13:38).

Don't wait until your "ship comes in." Trust God now and He'll move you away from your misery.

KeyPoints to ponder:
- What needs to be shipped out of your life?
- Do you sometimes feel like you are on a slow boat going nowhere?
- When will you release control of your rudder and let God be your Captain?

"God brings men into deep waters not to drown them, but to cleanse them." – James H. Aughey

SHRIMP

Shrimp come from the sea, but not all shrimp are small. Prawns are shrimp as big as a human hand. I guess that's where they get their name – jumbo shrimp.

It's funny how words can have one meaning and yet be mixed and mean another. For instance, we park on a driveway and we drive on a parkway. What's up with that? To most of us, the word shrimp means small. We say, "He's such a shrimp," or "That girl is shrimpy."

How would someone describe your faith today? Is it shrimpy, skimpy or simply wimpy? If so, you need to know that we have a great God who made no mistake when He made you. You were created to be big in every way. God designed you to think big, act big, love big, forgive big and live big for Him.

Our Savior was no shrimp. He didn't back down when critiqued. He didn't back away when criticized. He didn't break down when crucified. Our great God has a great plan for your life if you will just choose to live it for Him.

KeyPoints to ponder:
- Do you feel like a spiritual shrimp?
- Are you ready to grow in the grace and knowledge of our Lord Jesus Christ?
- What will you ask God to help you with to make this a reality?

"All growth that is not toward God, is growing to decay."
– George Macdonald

SHOP

How we shop has been altered through the years by inventions such as the cash register (1884), the shopping cart (1936), and the bar code (1952). Yet, no matter what's new, we still continue to "shop 'til we drop."

Our lives are driven to find something different from what we have or to obtain what we've exhausted in supply. Sometimes we even shop for God. Many times we go to the wrong places in our quest to fulfill our query for who He is and what He has to offer.

God is not bound to a church building or even one denomination. However, He is linked to one Lord, one Christ, and one salvation source. Jesus came to earth to show us the way so that we would not have to shop for a Savior. In fact, He cleared the confusion when He emphatically stated, "I am the way, and the truth and the life . . ." (John 14:6).

We all look for good deals when we shop and we want value for our efforts. God's deal is simple, but spiritually solid. "Confess with your mouth that Jesus is Lord and believe in your heart that God has raised Him from the dead and you will be saved." (Romans 10:9)

KeyPoints to ponder:
- Are you shopping for salvation right now?
- Have you found the real deal of Jesus Christ as your personal Savior?
- How will you share Him with others who need to stop shopping?

"Every choice you make has an end result." – Zig Ziglar

SHORE

Shore is a fun word. I can take my family to the shore to swim or I can shore a broken table with screws and nails. If you're from the South, you can even get away with complementing the cook by saying, "That 'shore' was good!"

Let's choose to use the second definition which lends itself to mending what is broken. We all were born broken (Romans 3:23) by being separated from God through sin. It's not what you did as much as who you are. We're broken people with broken lives which God alone can shore-up.

He gave Himself as the solution for our sin by sacrificing His Son, Jesus Christ. His purpose is not to make us good, but to fix us from our failures.

Some people spend a lifetime trying to prove they are good when God already knows this – we just need to get a faith fix. This repair can come quickly but lasts a lifetime.

The Bible says, "If you confess with your mouth that Jesus is Lord and believe in your heart that God raised Him from the dead, you will be saved" (Romans 10:9).

KeyPoints to ponder:
- Aren't you ready for the Savior to shore you up?
- Won't you help others to rebuild their broken lives?
- How has God rebuilt you recently?

"When God forgives, He at once restores." – Theodore Epp

SILENCE

Someone once said that silence is golden. Most of us act as if silence is stifling. We run from it and feel uncomfortable without some semblance of sound.

But the Bible reminds us from the wise writer of Ecclesiastes that there is "a time to be silent, and a time to speak" (Ecclesiastes 3:7). Our problem is that we don't always understand which is best for what time.

The phrase "to pipe down" means to be quiet. It was originally a command from a ship's captain to his crew. It meant to clear the decks and head below to safety. Once the crew had complied with the command, the ship was left silent and still, at least in appearance to other vessels.

We would do well to pipe down more often. "Be still and know that I am God," says the

Scripture (Psalm 46:10). We move our mouths so much and surround ourselves with sounds at the expense of deafening the divine voice of God. Shhhh . . . let's listen.

KeyPoints to ponder:
- In an average conversation, do you speak more often than listen?
- How well would you handle an hour of silence?
- Have you been quiet and still enough to hear the voice of God recently? When?

"Silence is a fence around wisdom." – German Proverb

SILENT

"There is an appointed time for everything," says the Bible (Ecclesiastes 3:1), including "a time to be silent, and a time to speak" (Ecclesiastes 3:7). The problem rests in knowing when to do what. Do I speak or do I listen? Do I answer or remain silent?

Sensitivity to silence is a learned lesson of life. When Jesus stood before Caiaphas, the high priest, who asked for His response to the accusations that He was the Christ, the Bible states, "But Jesus kept silent" (Matthew 26:63). Sometimes the loudest answers are the quietest.

When you live your life in such a way as to prove yourself, words are hollow in comparison to actions. It is what you do when accused falsely and how you handle unjust criticism that prove your inmost character. Most people will either deny the charges, defend themselves, or seek to destroy the accuser's credibility. But there are times to be silent; let God be your counselor, and let the Lord become your defense.

Today you will be challenged by someone over something that will not seem fair. Before you raise your voice or your hand against another, seek to silence your tongue, speak a silent prayer, and spend a moment thanking God for the right time to answer.

KeyPoints to ponder:
- How have you handled a slanderous comment against you recently?
- Did you try to bite back or it give it to God?
- Who could use a word of encouragement from you today?

"Slander is worse than cannibalism." – John Chrysostom

SINCERE

You can be sincere in your concerns and expressions and still be sincerely wrong. Here's what I mean. A child pleads for his parents to let him play outside his yard. Though he's been told time-after-time that the boundaries are not to be breached, he remains persistent with such strong expressions, which could even persuade the Supreme Court to reverse its stance.

The parent stays strong in her discipline, knowing that danger is waiting to harm her little one. A speeding car, an unleashed dog, or even an abusive stranger could take the love of her little one from her.

The Bible says, "Love must be sincere" (Romans 12:9). Is yours? Maybe you love to be loved or maybe your love is only a syrupy, superficial lip-service to gain favor from another. Be sincere but be sincere about what is right and good and godly.
When we do this, we are following the biblical admonition to "draw near to God with a sincere heart . . ." (Hebrews 10:22).

In your sincerity today, be certain your motives are pure, then your outcome will be powerful.

KeyPoints to ponder:
- Who do you know with a sincerity problem?
- Is it you?
- Will you sincerely ask Jesus to help you and others to sincerely speak the truth in love?

"Temptation is a trial of our sincerity." – Thomas Watson

SKIN

Do you know that there are more living organisms on the surface of the skin of a single human being than there are human beings on the earth's entire surface? In fact, an average adult's skin has a surface area of 16-22 square feet, each square inch of which houses 20 million microorganisms. The body is an unbelievable creation from God's hand, in God's image, for God's glory.

He didn't make a mistake when He made you. Although your body is not perfect, each one of us has an opportunity to enjoy and improve it every day. Our skin may be smooth or it may feel scratched, but it works as a protective coat over our organs.

To those who trust in Christ there is a promise that someday we'll get a new body – a heavenly one with no disease and no death (Revelation 21:4). My body is screaming for help! My skin is crawling for a cure!

The good news is that there is hope for those whose faith is focused on Jesus Christ, the One who gave up His earthly body for each of us to have an everlasting one. His sacrifice of His skin gave us salvation from our sin.

KeyPoints to ponder:
- Are you comfortable in your skin?
- Do you believe God made you the way you are for His purpose and your pleasure?
- Will you pause to thank Him, for you are fearfully and wonderfully made?

"More men fail through lack of purpose than lack of talent."
– Billy Sunday

SKY

The sky is a vast celestial ceiling. It's gilded by God to display his divinity. Look up. If you're outside you'll see a constantly changing display of clouds and climates. Even the best meteorologists cannot completely determine their direction.

King David reflected God well as he proclaimed, "Your love, Lord, reaches to the heavens, your faithfulness to the skies" (Psalm 36:5). All around us is evidence of God's handiwork. His fingerprints are all over creation. The upper regions of our earth are a heavenly umbrella perfectly proportioned for our protection. We don't get too much sun to sizzle us and we don't get too much rain to rot us. The sky is a giver of life and a sustainer of strength.

The next time you go outside, take time to gaze on God's glory through your eyes on the sky. It provides powerful proof that God created all and is recreating Himself through us and for us as we model his ministry around us.

KeyPoints to ponder:
- When you look up, what do you see?
- Is it another dreary day or an opportunity to allow God to work through you?
- Whom are you pointing to the sky to give them full vision of their potential under God's protection?

"The great thing in the world is not so much where we stand, as in what direction we are moving." – Oliver Wendell Holmes

SLEEP

Getting a good night's sleep seems to be a problem for too many these days. Either our lives are too full or is it that our minds are on overload? Our fast-paced world presses us to be more and do more than ever, and it keeps us from sleep.

The only One with a good excuse is God. The Bible tells us, "He watches over you" and "will not let your foot slip" because He "will neither slumber nor sleep" (Psalm 121:3-4). Now, that's good for God and great for us!

We need sleep. Our bodies are built to work, play, and then rest. God is not opposed to rest at all. He created it and expects it for us while on this earth, but someday, "we will not all sleep, but we will be changed – in a flash, in the twinkling of an eye, at the last trumpet" (1 Corinthians 15:51). When the Apostle Paul wrote this inspired and startling statement, he was using the word "sleep" for death.

Though we need sleep now, someday God promises to change us, rearrange us, and exchange our mortal bodies for eternal bodies. But for now, rest in the Lord. Rely on His watchfulness, and sleep well tonight in the knowledge of God's love.

KeyPoints to ponder:
- Do you have trouble sleeping?
- Instead of counting sheep, have you asked the Shepherd to help you rest?
- Why not end your day with thanking God for His blessings rather than thinking through all your business?

"A ruffled mind makes a restless pillow." – Charlotte Brontë

SMELL

Smell is one of our five senses that God gave us to fully experience His gift of creation. Our noses are perfectly positioned in the center of our faces and near the top of our bodies to get the full effect of smell.

Did you know that you emit an aroma? Sure you do. The Bible says to the faithful that you "are to God the aroma of Christ" (2 Corinthians 2:15). Does that sound strange to you? This same passage provides a deeper purpose as it states that the smell we emit is for those who are perishing because of their unbelief.

Have you ever been so hungry that you could smell food cooking, even when it wasn't? Better yet, if food was already on the stove, your salivary glands respond in readiness to eat. That's the way it is for those who are hungry for God. They smell the faithful, and it's an attractive aroma. Just as you yearn for food, there's a divine implant in you to yearn for God. When you smell Him on others, you yearn to take a taste and enjoy all God has for you.

KeyPoints to ponder:
- How well do you smell to others?
- Are you sweet and savory or repugnant and repulsive?
- How can people smell God on you?

"I know well what I am fleeing from but not what I am in search of." – Michel de Montaigne

SMILE

Ever notice how a smile can cheer even the most corrupt? It can convey acceptance and openness. A smile brings joy for life's journey and helps others over their bumps and bruises. Physicians say it takes nearly three times the muscle strain to frown than to smile. No wonder there are so many worn out worriers! Maybe the answer to our agonies could be found in a simple smile.

Not long ago I saw someone whose life was well worn – maybe even homeless, and definitely helpless. I wanted a way to offer hope, so I stopped and shared a smile. The results were amazing; this small gesture opened an opportunity to share some good news about God's love. Because of a simple smile, Jesus gave me a new friend whose hurt was helped to heal. The Bible states, "A happy heart is good medicine" (Proverbs 17:22).

What's your attitude right now? Are you found with a frown or shining with a smile? The bumper sticker may be trite, but it's true – Smile, God loves you!

KeyPoints to ponder:
- Whose smile brings you great pleasure?
- Are you someone who smiles sometimes or more times?
- Who needs your smiles today to experience the joy of Jesus?

"Let us always meet each other with smile, for the smile is the beginning of love."– Mother Teresa

SNOB

Ever wonder where snobs come from? The origin is from the Scottish "snab" meaning boy or servant.   In the 1600's, Cambridge University began to admit commoners as students. They registered as Sine Nobilitate meaning "without nobility" and abbreviated to S.Nob. It came to be written snob to signify a commoner who wished to mingle with the nobles.

The power of prejudice is as real today as ever. We categorize and classify people as if they were pawns. If a person doesn't seem to follow our social setting, we call them a snob. If we don't fit someone else's style, they call us one.

Aren't you glad that God is not a snob? He accepts us as we are and invites us to become more like Him. Jesus elevated the role of slaves, foreigners, women and workers and offered the gospel to every group regardless of race, ethnicity, gender, culture or color.

His powerful promise is this, "There is neither Jew nor Gentile, neither slave nor free, nor is there male and female for you are all one in Christ Jesus" (Galatians 3:28).

KeyPoints to ponder:
- Are you at one with God in Christ Jesus?
- Are you a snob sometimes?
- Who's a snob to you? Will you pause to pray for them right now?

"I think there's just one kind of folks. Folks."
– Harper Lee, To Kill a Mockingbird

SOMETHING

We've all heard that you can't get something for nothing. While that's usually true, there is a gift that cost another, but we get the gain. It's the gift of life.

We got our first life from our parents as a result of the God-gift of creation. We get new life as a present from the Creator when he sent his Christ to suffer crucifixion on a cross. This new life is one of abundance and eternity. Because Jesus gave up His life, we don't have to do more than to believe and receive. The Bible is filled with terrific truths telling us, "we reap what we sow." This is true, but there is a time in life when you can have something without working for it. Salvation is a gift from God.

Sound too simple? Perhaps, but the real deal comes when you understand God's complex love that will last beyond your ability to be good or even do good. That is something strong to think about and something stronger for which you can thank God.

KeyPoints to ponder:
- Is there something you need to confess to God?
- Is there something for which you want to thank God?
- Is there someone who needs something more from you today? Who?

"God is love. He didn't need us. But he wanted us. And that is the most amazing thing."– Rick Warren

SPEECH

What we say many times defines who we are. Our speech is the audible expression of what is in our heads and in our hearts. Our tongues tell where we are in every dimension of our lives, unless we lie. And then, lying also shouts about our shallowness.

Scripture says, "He who guards his mouth and his tongue keeps himself from calamity" (Proverbs 21:23). Yet, silence is not always golden. There is much to gain when we give God an opportunity to use our lips. We're reminded, "A gentle answer turns away wrath" (Proverbs 15:1).

Many times we need to say something to bring about correction. To be quiet here would be cruel. How we say it can either make or break our purpose. The Apostle Paul spoke well as he advised, "Speaking the truth in love, we will in all things grow up into him who is the Head, that is, Christ" (Ephesians 4:15).

The key to salient speech is love. The language of love is understood without any need for interpretation and it lasts much longer than any tongue-lashing.

KeyPoints to ponder:
- What have you said recently that you wished you had not?
- Is your language seasoned with love?
- Isn't it time to ask God to tame your tongue? Will you?

"Integrity is telling myself the Truth. And Honesty is telling the Truth to other people."– Spencer Johnson

SPIRIT

When I hear the word "spirit," my mind moves in several directions. In high school, we had a "spirit stick" – when raised high, it became a signal to cheer. In the world of intoxicants, spirits are something which many claim they must have to have anything to cheer about. At Christmastime, we claim the spirit of good will and sharing.

The biblical expression of the word "spirit" is a direct reference to God. It was His Spirit who hovered over a formless earth in anticipation of creation (Genesis 1:2). The prophet Joel predicted that God would pour out His Spirit on all mankind toward the end of time (Joel 2:28).

We are told by Jesus that we are blessed if we are "poor in spirit" (Matthew 5:3) but instead to be filled with God's Spirit (Ephesians 5:18). We are even warned not to believe every spirit (1 John 4:1) but to hear only what the true Spirit speaks (Revelation 2:7).

God grant us the Spirit of Christ without the spirit of compromise this Christmas.

KeyPoints to ponder:
- What spirit do you follow?
- Is it secular or sacred?
- How can you make it holy?

"God knows what each one of us is dealing with. He knows our pressures. He knows our conflicts. And He has made a provision for each and every one of them."– Kay Arthur

STAFF

When I say "staff" some think I'm referring to a group of employees. Others' minds race to a type of infection, and then there are those who visualize a shepherd's tool. The 23rd Psalm lovingly reminds us that God's rod and His staff bring comfort to us (Psalm 23:4), so we need not fear.

As God's sheep, we need direction and correction. We get off course easily and choose our own paths. We stray from God's best to pursue our own pleasures.

A staff has long been a symbol of spiritual strength as well. God gave Moses the gift of a staff to show His strength and power. When Moses used it for good, God blessed him; when he used it angrily, God's strength was removed.

Our Lord yearns for you to use your influence for His good and to bring Him glory. If we refuse and wander away like stray sheep, we lose the power and potential placed in our hands. God, as your Shepherd, is leading you into greener pastures. He calls you to follow.

KeyPoints to ponder:
- Are you a wayward sheep?
- Are you following the Shepherd in fear or by faith?
- What other sheep can you help to find their way to greener pastures?

"It is His business to lead, command, impel, send, call or whatever you want to call it. It is your business to obey."– Jim Elliot

STARE

Sometimes a stare indicates a dare and sometimes it brings on a scare. It all depends on who's doing it and for what reason. A funny fact: if you stare at your forefingers pointing toward each other about a half-inch apart, it looks as if a third finger appears in the middle. My point is simple: a stare can bring about deception or at least distraction from reality.

I think the devil stares at us with distorted eyes, but I know that God gazes at you with love and affection, because you were created in His image and for His glory. The stare of Satan is one of hate and hurt; the gaze of God is for your good and gain.

When you look at others who are different in color, custom, or culture – don't stare. Instead, use prayer as the power to overcome your prejudice. Look at them as God does; see them for their potential, not their problems. The Bible is more than a good book – it's great, especially as it reminds us "so in everything do to others what you would have them do to you" (Matthew 7:12).

KeyPoints to ponder:
- Is your gaze on God and your glance on your problems?
- Do other people stare at you because you're different?
- What will it take for you to dismantle any unholy prejudice you harbor?

"Our Savior kneels down and gazes upon the darkest acts of our lives. But rather than recoil in horror, he reaches out in kindness and says, 'I can clean that if you want'".– Max Lucado

STARK

Stark is an in-your-face word. We use it to explain a striking contrast like a stark sky or a stark glare or even a stark expression. It always conjures an image of shock and cold – at least to me it does. The opposite of stark might be soft. This presents a picture of warmth and acceptance – like a soft face, soft fur, or a soft smile. Our world is filled with stark people with stark language, living stark lives. They need a soft touch, a caring conversation, and an act of kindness. That's what God did; that's what God does.

God gave us Himself by sending a Savior into our stark world to save us from our sin. However, many have chosen to reject this gift, thinking you cannot get something for nothing, which is true. Christ paid the price of His life so that you and I would believe and receive His solution from starkness. It will cost you your life as well – not physically, but spiritually.

If you trust in God's goodness and believe in His Son, you will feel His softness expressed through salvation and you will experience the freedom which comes from forgiveness.

KeyPoints to ponder:
- Is it time for you to come out of the stark to the Savior?
- In what ways will you do this?
- In what ways can you help others to do the same?

"We don't serve God to gain His acceptance; we are accepted so we serve God."– Neil Anderson

STARS

"Where is the one who has been born King of the Jews? We saw his star in the east and have come to worship him" (Matthew 2:2). This question of the Magi wise men still rings with truth and tenderness. They were searching under the star for a Savior who could offer salvation and serenity. What are you searching for during these days of Christmas?

Stars are luminaries which have always attracted attention. We seek the brightest stars in the heavens to gaze on them or wish for luck. The truth is that stars are a craft of creation intended to express order from the Creator.

"In the beginning, God created the heavens and the earth" (Genesis 1:1). And on the first day God said, "Let there be light . . . and the light was good" (Genesis 1:3-4).

God is good, and in His goodness He shines His stars to draw our attention to Himself.

KeyPoints to ponder:
- What lights attract you most this Christmas season?
- Is it the glitz and glitter of the holiday?
- How can you make the glory of God shine more brightly?

"It is well to remember that reading books about the Bible is a very different thing to searching the Word for oneself." – Harry Ironside

STILL

Most of us hate being still. We prefer the busyness of life to anything idle. Our lifestyles are chaotic with a sprinkling of the creative. We desperately need to slow down.

I like what Job requested of God. "Teach me, and I will be quiet; show me where I have been wrong" (Job 6:24). In order to get what God has to tell us, we need to follow His command that states, "Be still, and know that I am God" (Psalm 46:10).

As difficult as this seems, it can be a delight. When we sit still, we listen. When we listen, we learn. When we learn, we grow. When we grow, we can go on to get what we wanted in the first place – which is peace.

Take a moment to meditate and move away from the commotion of life to discover a fresh new devotion for God.

KeyPoints to ponder:
- How still are you today?
- What can you eliminate from your day's schedule to get still?
- Is there anyone who needs you to be an instrument of peace in their life?

"Yieldedness is vital in listening to what He has to say."
– Charles Stanley

STILLNESS

The word still has multiple meanings. It can be used as a conjunction indicating that there is still more to say or do. As a young boy, I remember coming across a moonshine still in the woods of North Georgia. And then, there's the understanding that to be still is the opposite of being busy. It's here where I want to stop. We desperately need serenity – we need to be still at times.

"Be still and know that I am God; I will be exalted among the nations . . ." says God to us today (Psalm 46:10). If we won't slow down, sometimes our Chief Shepherd has to force us. "The Lord is my shepherd, I shall not be in want, He makes me lie down in green pastures, he leads me beside still waters" (Psalm 23:1-2).

Do you know why God does this? Sheep will not drink moving water. It's God's way of nourishing us and protecting us as His sheep. His love is so strong that He offers us a way to serenity through stillness.

KeyPoints to ponder:
- Will you follow Him there?
- Is there someone who needs you to bring them there?
- How has God been guiding you beside still waters lately? Did you take a drink?

"Just remaining quietly in the presence of God, listening to Him, being attentive to Him, requires a lot of courage and know-how."
– Thomas Merton

STOCKINGS

"The stockings were hung by the chimney with care in hopes that Saint Nicholas soon would be there." This Clement Moore classic Christmas poem sets the standard for expectations that stockings at Christmas are sacred. Actually, the tradition dates back thousands of years as families hung stockings fireside nightly in readiness for the next day's wear after washing them.

In the fourth century, a priest named Nicolas ministered to the poor in his hometown of Patara, which is on the southern coast of Turkey. Tradition tells us that he tossed a gold coin into the stocking of a young betrothed girl to save her the plight of being sold for marriage in poverty. The coin became her dowry and remarkably appeared in each of her two sisters' stockings as well. All of this benevolence kept the family together and was proof that God's servants are givers.

Today's stockings are filled with candy, money or gifts. Occasionally, an orange is included, representing the gold of Nicolas's gift or maybe an apple for good health. However your stocking is filled this year, it's more important that you check your life more than your loot. What fills your self is better than that which fills your stocking. Jesus really is the reason for the season!

KeyPoints to ponder:
- Are you looking to give more than to get this year?
- Will you share the greatest Gift of God in Christ Jesus?
- With whom will you share today?

"Don't assume you have to be extraordinary to be used by God. You don't have to have exceptional gifts, talents, abilities, or connections. God specializes in using ordinary people..for His greatness and glory." – Nancy Leigh Demoss

STROKE

When you hear the word "stroke" several thoughts come to mind. In swimming, there's the breast stroke, back stroke, side stroke, butterfly and crawl stroke. A heart stroke can take a life or even disable it; this happened to my dad. If a stroke is linked to a touch, it can either be one that is tender or tough.

God strokes us with His love. But He loves us enough to stroke us with discipline as well. As a parent loves a child, so God loves us by stroking us for sin or to keep us from harm. Our Savior cares about you enough to stroke you, and this is good.

Scripture states that this is a good thing, ". . . because the Lord disciplines those He loves as a father . . ." (Proverbs 3:12).

Don't doubt or duck from the divine touch of God, even if it is tough at times. This is the Lord's way of showing you His love, even if His strokes may be strong or when they are subtle.

KeyPoints to ponder:
- What needs stroking in your life?
- Do you sense specific ways that God is disciplining you for love sake?
- Will you pause to pray for His direction and your obedience to it?

"God is interested in developing your character. At times He lets you proceed, but He will never let you go too far without discipline to bring you back." – Henry Blackaby

STRAIGHT

Straight can be defined as a line with no variance between where you are and where you wish to go. In comedy routines, the "straight" partner seems more serious and less likely to vary his or her disposition. In terms of relations, one is "straight" if he is heterosexual and monogamous in practice. The point is simple. Straight can determine your fate.

The Psalmist pled for God to guide and "lead me in a straight path" (Psalm 27:11). The wise words of Solomon say that as you "trust in the Lord with all your heart and lean not on your own understanding . . . he will make your path straight" (Proverbs 3:5-6). To protect your purity, you are admonished to "let your eyes look straight ahead" to prevent you from spiritual slippage (Proverbs 4:25).

A straight answer prevents problem, and a straight response procures respect. Next time you are tempted to turn a direction through diversion – stay straight. It's quicker, cleaner, and takes less creativity. Remember the words of Peter who warned against false teachings – "They left the straight way" (2 Peter 2:15).

KeyPoints to ponder:
- Is that straight with you today?
- Have you wandered off the straight and narrow path of Jesus?
- Who needs your help to go spiritually straight?

"Love provides the motive for obeying the commands of the law, but the law provides specific direction for exercising love."
– Jerry Bridges

STREET

The great highways systems of America were built by our fathers and grandfathers as the first form of rapid transit across our nation. However, streets are nothing new. A street provides a straight way from one location to another. Streets will be a part of life as long as there are people.

The difference between our streets and the streets of heaven is enormous. The Bible tells us, "the great street of the city was pure gold" (Revelation 21:21). Imagine that. No asphalt, no concrete, no steel reinforcement – it's pure gold! Whether you believe this or not is irrelevant. The fact is, God has a better path, a purer path, and a more glorious path or street than we have ever experienced. Here's the catch – you have to believe it, to receive it.

Trusting in God's Son opens a spiritual street for you now and later. The journey with Jesus is worth the wait; it's more than a wish and a prayer – it's a promise.

KeyPoints to ponder:
- How's your journey toward Jesus?
- Is it crooked or straight?
- Who is coming with you? Whom have you invited?

"If you're going in the wrong direction, turning around is the only right direction." – Woodrow Kroll

STRENGTH

It's strange, but true: experts recommend you allow NiCad (nickel-cadmium) batteries to completely run down at least once a month. Otherwise they'll begin to suffer from what's called "memory effect," reducing their life span and strength. If you think about it, that's the way we are as well. Each day we let our bodies run down in strength, and we sleep so we can once again gain new strength the next day.

It's also true when we go through the toughest of times in life. We feel weak and worthless until we wait to gain strength again. The Apostle Paul confessed, "For when I am weak, then I am strong..." (2 Corinthians 12:10). How's that? He knew that only God can recharge our lives. When we think of ourselves as strong and invulnerable, it is then that we are at the greatest risk. We need God's strength – we need God's Savior!

Whatever you might be experiencing today, when you feel totally weak, consider this to be a good opportunity to turn your troubles to God whose strength never saps.

KeyPoints to ponder:
- How strong are you?
- How weak do have to be to get strong again?
- Will you name your weaknesses so God can turn you toward His strength?

"Worry does not empty tomorrow of its sorrow. It empties today of its strength."– Corrie Ten Boom

STRONG

When Lou Gehrig was the first to be featured on the front of a Wheaties box in 1924, it was because of his strength as a baseball player. Michael Jordan's basketball strength has put him on the Wheaties box 18 times – more than any other athlete. However, we all know that strength comes in many other forms such as academics, emotions and spirituality.

Recently, I visited a museum which featured "the strongest man in the world." His name was Paul Anderson who grew up in Toccoa, Georgia, and won this strength title as an Olympic champion many times. Yet it was his inner strength in caring for children that made him a greater champion. This athlete's compassion was better than a box of cereal and lasted longer than his gold medals.

God looks on our inner strength and supplies more when we're weak (I Samuel 16:7). The Apostle Paul reminds us of the true source of our strength when he writes, "I can do everything through him who gives me strength" (Philippians 4:13).
If you think you can do it on your own, you're wrong and weak. If you ask God to make you strong, you can't go wrong.

KeyPoints to ponder:
- What's your claim to fame?
- What's your source of strength?
- Who needs you to lead them to the true Source of strength today?

"In all my perplexities and distresses, the Bible has never failed to give me light and strength." – Robert E. Lee

SUBSTITUTION

I remember substitute teachers when I was in elementary school. We loved them. You could relax from writing, redirect them from reading, and abort lessons in arithmetic. "Subs," as we called them, gave the class a chance to clown around.

But not all substitutions are as harmless and ineffective. For instance, Robert Parker from Circleville, Utah and Harry Longbaugh from Phoenixville, Pennsylvania chose to substitute their common names to become common criminals. History exposes them as the diabolic duo of Butch Cassidy and the Sundance Kid.

A more effective and eternal substitution was made at the crucifixion cross of Jesus Christ nearly two thousand years ago. The Bible says that God "made him who knew no sin to be sin on our behalf" (2 Corinthians 5:21). God gave us a Savior to become a substitute for our sin in order to bring us eternal security. Wow! That's a great gift from a Great Giver.

Don't make the mistake of substituting any other god for the One and Only God of the universe.

KeyPoints to ponder:
- What have you substituted for the real deal recently?
- Did it last and was it worth it?
- How will you get real with Jesus today?

"If in preaching the gospel you substitute your knowledge of the way of salvation for confidence in the power of the gospel, you hinder people from getting to reality."– Oswald Chambers

SUNSET

There's something about a sunset that draws us like a magnet. Maybe it's the colors; it might be the surrounding clouds which appear to catch on fire; or it could be the calm which it brings to our soul. A sunset is a statement of conclusion, but also one of collision. Here is what I mean.

Obviously, the end of each day concludes with a sinking sun in the western sky, but it is also a reminder of our concluding lives. We love beginnings, but for some reason, we loathe conclusions. However, if we end well in life, there should be celebration and not sadness. Our "sunset years" can be our best. A sunset is also a collision. It seems that the sinking sun crashes into the horizon.

Perhaps a greater way to view the colliding sunset would be as God kissing the earth with a heavenly kiss – a mixture of His mercy with our mistakes. "At sunset, the people brought to Jesus all who had various kinds of sickness, and laying his hands on each one, he healed them" (Luke 4:40). The Savior still heals our sickness of sin at sunset as God's kiss brings life to our lostness.

Next time you see a sunset, think of how your life is concluding and how God's kiss is colliding to bring a weary world the cure which comes through Jesus Christ.

KeyPoints to ponder:
- How well is your life concluding?
- Is the sun about to set for you?
- What will you do to make it conclude with celebration?

"How strange is this fear of death! We are never afraid of sunsets."– George McDonald

SURF

Surf is an interesting word for many, with many interesting meanings. For some, it has everything to do with waves and water. For others, it's a matter of computers and communication.

Whatever your take, it's all about movement from one place to another. That's what Jesus wants for all of our lives -- movement. He's not interested in stagnation and status quo. Christ presses us to go to the next level and to move beyond mediocrity and discover the next adventure.

There is an answer to your angst. His Name is God Almighty - the One who can take you from boredom to freedom. The Savior of the universe has a superior surf for you to discover which will move you to a place of peace and spiritual prosperity.

"Submit to God and be at peace with him; in this way prosperity will come to you" (Job 22:21).
So jump in the water of life and get on God's wave!

KeyPoints to ponder:
- How's your surfing these days?
- Do you feel stuck in the sands of life?
- In what ways will you submit to God to gain his prosperity?

"It is nothing to die. It is frightful not to live."
– Victor Hugo, Les Misérables

SWITCH

A switch is a change of direction, especially for a train, an electrical current or a lifestyle. Another kind of switch is used as an instrument of correction. I experienced this switch often in my early childhood. The switch my mother used was strategically placed on the top side of our refrigerator and used when needed on the backside of her back-talking boy!

Discipline is never easy for the parent, and especially less for the child, but it is needed. The Bible tells us that God disciplines those whom He loves (Proverbs 3:12). Since that is true from our Heavenly parent, I have to assume it is true for my earthly parents as well. My mother sure must have loved me a lot!

Our Savior bore the marks of men's switches, not for discipline but from derision. When God allows correction, it is for our good. When enemies force correction on us, it is usually for their gumption.

There is time today to switch your love and loyalty to Jesus.

KeyPoints to ponder:
>   Are you being disciplined by God?
>   Are you taking His correction correctly or by coercion?
>   What habits do you need to switch in your life to make matters right before Jesus?

"God does not will He should follow what man has initiated. Other than following God's direction, we have no right to direct Him. We have no ability to offer save to obey God's guidance."
>   *– Watchman Nee*

SWELL

When someone feels really good about you, they might just say, "Hey, you're looking swell!" Swell is a combination of the two words so and well – swell.

Life's question revolves around whether or not you are so well. Is it swell for you? Do you find yourself down and out today or up and ready? Are things well or worse than they were this time last year?

God's got a plan for you to succeed and to claim satisfaction. He sent His one and only Son to bring you what is well in a worrisome world in which we live. Jesus has a powerful promise to bring you a positive solution for your life. It's all a matter of trusting Him. The Bible declares, "Trust in the Lord with all your heart and lean not on your own understanding; in all your ways submit to him, and he will make your paths straight" (Proverbs 3:5-6).

Will you trust Him today? Won't you turn to Him right now? He'll turn your suffering into something swell. He'll take your hurts and bring you healing.

KeyPoints to ponder:
- Are you living so well these days?
- What specific changes do you need to make to make it right?
- Will you cry out to Jesus for His help?

"How wonderful it is that nobody need wait a single moment before starting to improve the world." – Anne Frank

SWORD

My youngest son has a knife collection that fills several shoe boxes. Some of the knives are actually swords from around the world where I have been privileged to travel. Swords are offensive weapons used by the aggressor to thwart hostile attack.

In the Christian community, a sword is synonymous with the Bible – God's love letter to mankind. In some churches, a Bible verse contest is still called a "sword drill." Whatever your thoughts are about swords, one element is agreeable from all accounts – swords are sharp, or at least they should be. If a sword becomes dull, it loses its potential for power. The same is true of our spiritual prowess. No wonder we are admonished to daily and prayerfully "take . . . the sword of the Spirit, which is the word of God" (Ephesians 6:17).

Each day begun by reading God's Word brings power for living. Every time we get back to the Bible is a time to treasure. Our greatest hope is not in the wisdom of man's words, but the everlasting hope discovered in the sacred sword of scripture.

KeyPoints to ponder:
- How sharp is your spiritual sword?
- Have you read your Bible today?
- Will you admit your dull edges before God so He can sharpen you?

"Remember you are God's sword – His instrument."
– Robert Murray McCheyne

T

TAX

Around April 15 each year we think about taxes. None of us like them. All of us benefit from them. Taxes are terrible to pay, but terrific for progress. They build roads, bridges and parks, provide lights, extend our liberties, and even offer free lunch to the needy. Tax time is a tough time, but we must accept it as a necessary nuisance.

When Jesus was asked about paying taxes to Caesar, it was a trick to catch Him in a political ploy. He read the hearts of those asking the questions and went to the heart of the matter when He said, "Give to Caesar what is Caesar's, and to God what is God's" (Matthew 22:21). He did not deny the government its giving, nor did He ignore God who deserves even more of the glory.

We would do well not to complain or criticize at tax time. A better approach is one of appreciation and thanksgiving for a land of liberty founded by pioneers whose motto remains on every coin – "In God We Trust."

KeyPoints to ponder:
- Do you trust Him today?
- Do you appreciate the freedoms we share as a blessed nation under God?
- How will you show your love for the Lord by what you give back and give away?

"The Income Tax has made more liars out of the American people than golf has."– Will Rogers

TEARS

Tears are not always a sign of weakness; many times they are a sign of meekness. Jesus cried real tears over the death of His friend, Lazarus (John 11:35). He also wept over the city of Jerusalem, knowing that its inhabitants were busy on the outside but lost on the inside. His heart hurt for those who rejected His holiness (Luke 13:34). He still weeps over us.

Crocodile tears are quite different from the tears of Christ. Those insincere tears are actually quite literal in origin. When a crocodile eats its meal, his food is pressed to the very top of his mouth, causing pressure against the lachrymal glands. This pressure causes a tear-like substance to secrete and flow from his eyes. It has nothing to do with a croc's sensitivity or his heart, just his appetite.

God gave us emotions for a reason. We don't need to ignore them – we really need to embrace them. Big boys do cry!

KeyPoints to ponder:
- How long has it been since you wept over a friend in need?
- Have you ever cried about those without Christ as Savior?
- How do you think God may weep over you?

"I wept not, so to stone I grew within." – Dante

TENSION

It's no secret that we're living in tense times. Have you noticed that tension and troubles can either lead you to turmoil or toward triumph? It's true. Though we don't like tension, we need it. It creates dependence on God and on others.

When tension squeezes you, the natural response is to cry out for something or for someone. We were created to respond, but some of us don't respond well. We complain and curse when we need to be controlled and compassionate.

Tension is a test. When we get crushed, the hidden character of our life comes out. God never promised a perfect life, just the opportunity for a peace-filled life. If you live your life based on circumstances alone, you'll ride a never-ending emotional roller coaster.

Most everyone is ready for relief. Turn your tension toward the One who can take your chaos and bring you calm. Jesus shouted at the storm, "Quiet! Be still!" (Mark 4:39). Can you hear Him saying the same to you?

KeyPoints to ponder:
- What is the greatest tension you are experiencing?
- Has it led to turmoil?
- How will you give it to God to allow the Prince of Peace to speak strongly to your need?

"No God, no peace. Know God, know peace." – Author unknown

TEST

Very few people like to be tested--we have an affinity to failure. Yet, tests are a natural part of life as each of us respond in ways that mark our understanding and comprehension.

The greatest test results of life's deeper purposes are revealed when we are questioned with the toughest challenges which we all face. This regular routine of testing goes far beyond our days of schooling and reaches into the level of our personal and spiritual maturity.

Everyday tests come into play as we choose what to wear, where to go, how to handle dilemmas, and how to respond to communications. It's all a normal part of life. We cannot avoid these decisions.

Jesus put many people to a test. He challenged them to live rightly and to choose wisely. When testing His disciples, He once asked, "Who do people say that I am?" One of His chosen responded, "You are the Messiah, the Son of the living God" (Matthew 16:15-16).

The test for our lives is similar. Jesus is giving us this familiar test and waiting for our response. How will you answer? He continues to ask us because He's longing for us to answer correctly.

KeyPoints to ponder:
- Can you name the biggest test of life which you are facing at present?
- Are you failing or passing in your response?
- Are you willing for God to test you?

"You can't really know what you are made of until you are tested."
--O.R. Melling

THANKSGIVING

Robert Caspar Lintner once said, "Thanksgiving was never meant to be shut up in a single day." The Bible says, "Give thanks in all circumstances" (I Thessalonians 5:18). Plutarch proclaimed, "The worship most acceptable to God comes from a thankful and cheerful heart." What do you say?

Years ago our country's president declared that a day be set aside to be thankful as "one nation under God." Usually we gather with friends and family to "talk turkey" and then we eat it! This is a terrific time to be thankful, but not nearly enough.

God has given us all that we have. Every breath and benefit is a gift from our great Giver. Being thankful only adds to our lives instead of subtracting from us when we take the time. If we believed what the Psalmist said, "Give thanks to the Lord, for he is good" (Psalm 106:1), then we would behave differently. We'd observe Thanksgiving as a holy day and not just another holiday.

Now more than ever, we should be thankful for Who holds us instead of complaining what we get to hold.

KeyPoints to ponder:
- For what are you truly thankful?
- Is anyone thankful for you?
- In what ways will you give thanks to God for His benefits and blessings for you?

"Count your blessings; Name them one by one. Count your many blessings, see what God hath done." – J. Oatman, Jr.

THERE

It's neither here nor there, but if I had a choice, I'd probably rather be "there."

Frequently, on our family trips with our three stair-step sons, the call would come from the back seat, "Are we *there* yet, Daddy?" There is a great place to be, especially when you've labored in the process. It's a goal accomplished; a quest fulfilled; a map marked to completion that brings satisfaction to the soul.

Don't you wish you were *"there?"* Work would be weariless, families would be fun, schedules would be successful. Please don't misunderstand me. There's no guarantee to glee, but God's got a greater plan than man. And it's usually just around the corner, over *"there"* – waiting for you.

Utopia might be a description of *"there,"* but only God has the key to this locked-up life. The Bible tells us that if we'll trust Jesus with our lives, He'll take us *"there."* Heaven is the home for those whose hearts are made whole through faith in the Savior's salvation. Hey – sure hope to see you there!

KeyPoints to ponder:
- Are you there yet?
- How far is it to there?
- Who will you bother to take with you there?

"Destiny is not a matter of chance, it is a matter of choice..."
  – William Jennings Bryan

THIMBLE

Sometimes word origins are just downright practical, and the word "thimble" definitely falls into this category. The thimble was invented to protect the thumb of the seamstress so that needles would not prick or poke. Of course, this was when all sewing was done by hand alone.

Originally, the thimble was called a "thumb-bell" because of its shape and purpose in protecting the thumb from a sharp prick from the needle.

We need protection in all areas of life, don't we? As inventive as we are, there are still areas of vulnerability which allow hurt and harm. If only we had the power to protect ourselves from injury, then we would rarely need any help from anyone or anything. How sad that would be!

God gives us areas of angst so that we can build a better dependency on Him. Without hurts in our life, there would be no happiness and no need for healing.

KeyPoints to ponder:
- What hurts most in your life?
- Do you need divine protection?
- When and how will you get it?

"God never does anything to you that isn't for you."
– Elisabeth Elliot

THIRST

Water, water everywhere, but not a drop to drink. That's what it was like for me one time as a boy. During summer camp in North Carolina, on a blistering hot summer day, my sailboat became stranded off the coast. I was thirsty and dry though surrounded by an ocean of water unfit to drink.

Our earth is made up of about 75% water, and human bodies contain nearly 60% of H_2O. Yet, we still get thirsty.

Jesus said, "If anyone is thirsty, let him come to me and drink" (John 7:37). If we believe in Him, "streams of living water will flow from within" us (John 7:38).

God has a better design for your day. He wants to build a relationship with you and get you out of a ritual of religion, or maybe your routine of ruin.

KeyPoints to ponder:
- What do you thirst for today?
- Success? Significance? Purpose? Power? Pleasure?
- Will you come to Him and drink?

"Don't be afraid to give up the good to go for the great."
– Kenny Rogers

THOUGHTS

When I think of thoughts, it sounds strange. It's like doing double duty. Thoughts are the brain's activity of moving us into action. We think thoughts because we are creatures of response. Our thoughts are our response to stimuli, both external and internal.

Who or what controls your thoughts? The Bible says, "the mind controlled by the Spirit (of God) is life and peace" (Romans 8:6). Since many of our thoughts are not peaceful, we would easily assume that they are not under God's control, nor are we.

The good news is that, "The Lord knows the thoughts of man ..." (Psalm 94:11). Since this is true, then why do we try to hide them? I like what the prophet Isaiah had to say about God's guidance, "You will keep in perfect peace him whose mind is steadfast, because he trusts in you" (Isaiah 26:3). Did you catch the connection? Our thought life leads us either to peace or panic in life. It's a matter of who or what we trust.

KeyPoints to ponder:
- What are you thinking about right now?
- Is it pleasing to God?
- If not, do you know it's a path that might prove to be very painful?

"Our life is what our thoughts make it." – Marcus Aurelius

TIRED

America is tired, our economy is tired, and likely you are tired too. When you are tired you become lethargic or lazy. When you are tired, you lose focus and momentum. We need energy. We need enthusiasm! Actually, the word for enthusiasm comes from two words "*en theos*," meaning "in God."

Perhaps our problem with being tired and unenthusiastic is that we do what we do without God. In God we have the promise of energy. In God we have the potential of power. In God we have the practical means to perform a meaningful life.

Aren't you tired of doing the same thing the same way with the same results? Don't you want to wage war against weariness? Isn't it time to go to God for results? He is ready, you know. He says these words through Christ our Lord, "Come to me, all you who are weary and burdened, and I will give you rest" (Matthew 11:28). This is an opportunity you cannot afford to ignore, because as you trust in God, you have every advantage for advancement.

KeyPoints to ponder:
- How tired are you?
- Are you burdened beyond belief?
- What will it take for you to take your troubles to the One who will give you rest?

"If He bids us carry a burden, He carries it also."
– Charles Spurgeon

THRESHOLD

In yesteryear, life actually depended on the annual harvest. Among the Anglo-Saxons, no ceremony was more important than the *"threscan"* where families would eagerly trod on piles of dry wheat to separate the harvest grain from the stalks. This act of shuffling feet so much resembled the wiping of one's feet at the doorways of a home that the area began to actually take the name threshold.

How you enter a door tells a lot about who you are and where you're going. If you come in clean, then it shows you care. If you cross the threshold with little concern, you violate the homeowner's hospitality.

Jesus said, "I am the door" (John 10:9 KJV). He invites us into His home but expects us to clean up first. Our Lord also said, "My Father's house has many rooms ... I am going there to prepare a place for you" (John 14:2). Because our lives are unclean with sin, we need to confess, ask forgiveness, get clean, and then we are ready to enter into the door which takes us to God's house (I John 1:9). The Bible says, "You do not have, because you do not ask God" (James 4:2). So, ask and enter in.

KeyPoints to ponder:
- Are you ready to cross the threshold?
- Are you clean enough to enter?
- Have you asked Jesus to open His door to you?

"The best is yet to be." – *John Wesley*

TOMORROW

Years ago, the movie "Annie" made the word "tomorrow" a household song. But the truth is that tomorrow has always been around. For the procrastinator, it's a relief; for the debtor, it's a cause for anxiety. Tomorrow holds both promise and pressure, depending on your perspective.

The Bible warns us not to boast about tomorrow because "you do not know what a day may bring forth" (Proverbs 27:1). In other words, there are no guarantees – except, of course, eternity. That deal is made when we trust God by trusting in His Son as Savior.

Jesus said, "Do not worry about tomorrow, for tomorrow will worry about itself" (Matthew 6:34). He said this to keep us calm. He also said this in the context of a command to seek God's kingdom first, before we try to build up our own estate. The payoff is powerful if we obey – "all these things will be given to you as well" (Matthew 6:33).

Simply put: tomorrow belongs to God, but He wants to share some of it with us today.

KeyPoints to ponder:
- Will you let go of your present priorities and trust God with your tomorrows?
- How will you choose to stop procrastinating?
- Who can keep you accountable to stay on task?

"How soon not now, becomes never." – Martin Luther

TOUCH

A touch can be tender or terrifying. It's tender if it's from someone you love; it's terrifying if it involves a threat or potential violation. One kind of touch is therapeutic; another is catastrophic. There's no doubt as to which we would want. When we are threatened, we scream, "Don't touch me!" When we are in need, we welcome touch. It warms us and brings comfort in our times of chaos.

Once when Jesus was walking through a crowd, He felt the touch of a bleeding woman. Her faith was fulfilled when she touched just the hem of His garment. This touch brought her healing and wholeness (Luke 8:43-48).

Another time when Christ met two blind men who followed Him, He asked, "Do you believe I am able to do this?" "Yes, Lord," they replied. Then He touched their eyes and said, "According to your faith it will be done to you" (Matthew 9:28-29).

Many are bleeding emotionally from a broken relationship or a bruised heart. Some have been blinded by others who want them out of their way in pursuit of their own goals. If you pursue God in faith, He will touch you in such a way as to bring spiritual wholeness and physical protection.

KeyPoints to ponder:
- Have you been touched by God?
- What is the bleeding or blindness in your life?
- Who will you touch for Christ's sake?

"The world doesn't care what you know until they know that you care." – David Havard

TREASURE

My wife loves yard sales. She comes home with treasures that the seller considered trash. A treasure's truest value is determined by its owner. One person's treasure has at times become another's trouble!

Jesus warned us not to "store up for yourselves treasures on earth" but rather to "store up treasures in heaven, where moth and rust do not destroy, and where thieves do not break in and steal" (Matthew 6:19-20).

It's strange how far we'll go to protect our treasures. We'll risk our lives for them and some even take the lives of others. We'll work hard to accumulate them and then spend even more to add to our collection.

Christ had another wise warning when he said, "For where your treasure is, there your heart will be also" (Matthew 6:21). If we treasure those things that God has valued, our heart is in tune with His. If our treasures are for the temporary and trite, our hearts are hollow and become hungry for more.

Turn your heart and your treasure toward the Savior who has promised to provide your every need (Philippians 4:19).

KeyPoints to ponder:
- What are your greatest treasures?
- Would you fight to protect them?
- What would you do if you discovered they were stolen?

"The man who has God for his treasure has all things in one."
– A.W. Tozer

TREE

Universal acceptance of the Christmas tree as a holiday essential occurred less than two centuries ago, but the tradition of bringing an evergreen into one's home can be traced back to more than one thousand years ago.

Legend has it that the Protestant Reformer, Martin Luther, was once so struck by the beauty of the starlight streaming through fir tree branches that he felt moved to duplicate the effect in his home. He taught his friends and family that the green tree represented the eternal love of God and that the candlelight was a picture of Christ as the light of the world.

By the 1880s, Christmas trees were so popular that many worried the seasonal rush might make fir trees extinct! Still today, the tree's popularity is evidenced in homes, businesses, schools, and churches. The evergreen of the tree represents eternal life offered through Christ, and the lights on the tree are forever a reminder of Jesus, the light of the world (John 8:12), who brings illumination to our darkness and hopelessness.

KeyPoints to ponder:
- Have you planted a tree of hope in your heart?
- Isn't it special that a tree can bring truth in the midst of our troubles?
- How will you use your Christmas tree as a witness to others who need hope?

"There are two kinds of light – the glow that illuminates, and the glare that obscures."– James Thurber

TREES

Trees are amazing. They live, then die, then live again. Just when I think they are at their best when green and lush, they turn colors, and then turn loose. Even dead-in-the-winter trees are beautiful with finger-like limbs pointing to the sky. It's as if they are thanking the Creator for the promise of new life that's forthcoming, and maybe they are.

The Bible tells us that we are blessed if we are "like a tree planted by streams of water, which yields its fruit in season and whose leaf does not wither." In fact, the Psalmist goes deeper by declaring, "Whatever they do will prosper" (Psalm 1:3).

I want to be this kind of tree, don't you? No matter what season of life you are in, you can prosper when you are planted in God's soil.

You can count on His nourishment, His root system, His fruit, and even His pruning to help you grow.

KeyPoints to ponder:
- Is your life blooming today or is it buried in burdens?
- What needs to be pruned from your life to encourage your spiritual growth?
- Why don't you give it to God and grow up like a strong tree for His glory?

"Growth is the only evidence of life." – J. H. Newman

TRIBULATION

Everybody goes through tough times; none of us are exempt from trials and tribulation. It is not *if* we will face them, rather it is *when*. What do you do when you go through these painful periods of life?

The Ancient Romans once had a device for threshing grain called a tribulum – a board with sharp points on the underside. From this threshing tool came the verb "tribulare" meaning "oppress or afflict" from which we extract the word tribulation.

Our days of oppression and affliction are surely hurtful but can also prove to be helpful if we know where and who to turn to. God has enough grace to get you through and promises His power at your times of weakness (2 Corinthians 12:9). Our problem comes when we curse our difficulties instead of seeking to discover their cause.

Some tribulation we bring on ourselves; others may be caused by our culture. Regardless, there is an answer and a solution to our suffering. When your days get dark, it's time to turn to the light of God's love. He's ready to give you triumph over tribulation. The question is, are you ready to receive it?

KeyPoints to ponder:
- What tribulation troubles you today?
- Are you the cause or is it coming from somewhere else?
- How will you give it over to the Lord for Him to handle?

"They gave our Master a crown of thorns. Why do we hope for, a crown of roses?"– Martin Luther

TRIP

A "trip" can be a journey or a stumble depending on how you use the word. To take a trip is to go somewhere that is a distance from where you are. To have a trip will take you the distance from where you walk to where you land after falling. Either way you think about it, trips put you in another place from where you are right now.

The greatest trip of life was expressed through Jesus when He said, "I go and prepare a place for you ... that you may be where I am" (John 14:3). His journey to earth was culminated by His return to a heavenly home (Hebrews 4:14). He invites us to take the same trip with Him. Our greatest problem is that we trip over sin in our lives, thinking that we can never be fully qualified to be with God in His glory. God knows our insecurity and He assures us that forgiveness comes to those who ask.

"All the prophets testify about him that everyone who believes in him receives forgiveness of sins through his name" (Acts 10:43).

KeyPoints to ponder:
- What's your next trip?
- Will you plan it yourself or go with God to His prepared place?
- Who needs your invitation to come along on the journey toward Jesus?

"It is easier to prepare and prevent, than to repair and repent."
– Author unknown

TROPHIES

You probably know about the trophy that was named for Frederick Arthur. He was known as Lord Stanley of Preston, and his trophy was, and still is, the Stanley Cup – the top trophy for hockey. Do you know the Major League Baseball pitcher to win the most games but who never won the Cy Young Award? It was Cy Young!

Trophies come in all sizes and shapes and are for all seasons of life. Some carry financial reward, but most carry emotional response. We are thrilled to be recognized for achievement. We rather like it when people look up to us.

God has a reward system for those who follow Him faithfully. The Bible says, "The man who plants and the man who waters have one purpose, and each will be rewarded according to his own labor" (1 Corinthians 3:8). The difference between man's trophies and God's is the "tarnish factor." Our trophies will rust and fade, but God's will remain forever. What we do on earth is not nearly as important as for whom we do it. Check yourself to be sure you are not striving for the plaque of pride.

KeyPoints to ponder:
- Have you ever won a trophy?
- Did it make you proud?
- Have you put it aside for the greater trophy of winning people to Christ?

"God sends no one away empty except those who are full of themselves." – Dwight L. Moody

TRUE

When a person is about to pass from life to death, there is a true revealing of his or her character and purpose that will usually be expressed. The dying words of any man tell the truth of how he lived, much more than a funeral's eulogy or an overstated obituary.

When Joshua was ready to depart his life's journey, he said, "Now I am about to go the way of all the earth. You know with all your heart and soul that not one of all the good promises the Lord your God gave you has failed. Every promise has been fulfilled; not one has failed" (Joshua 23:14). This was a magnificent moment of truth in the midst of mourning. Joshua was revealing what every one of us wants to know – that is, that God is true to His word and will not fail us.

In a world filled with so much that is false, it is time to tell what's true and to live it out. Jesus said, "I am the way and the truth and the life. No one comes to the Father except through me" (John 14:6).

KeyPoints to ponder:
- What would you say if this was your last day?
- Are you living a lie?
- Who needs to hear the truth about Jesus Christ from you today?

"Peace if possible, truth at all costs." – Martin Luther

TURN

Have you ever wondered what causes house plants to turn toward the light? It's because of growth hormones called auxins. When light falls on one side of a plant, the auxins tend to concentrate on the shaded side, causing the cells on that side to grow larger. As a result, the plant gradually leans toward the light.

I wish we were as responsive as plants to the light of God. We live in a dark world that tends to get more of our attention than the light.

Too often our tendency is to turn away from what is right and what represents God's light. If we were genetically coded to seek light, we would have less stumbles in life and less stress in living.

Jesus put this in proper perspective as He said, "I am the light of the world. Whoever follows me will never walk in darkness, but will have the light of life" (John 8:12).

KeyPoints to ponder:
- What is dark in your life right now?
- Are you ready to turn toward Him today?
- What ways can you ask God and others to help brighten you up?

"Darkness cannot drive out darkness; only light can do that."
– Martin Luther King, Jr.

U

UMBRELLA

An umbrella is a cover, usually to shield from the rain. Some people use it as a protector from the sun and even snow. Sometimes people purchase umbrella insurance policies that cover a broader area of their belongings. Umbrellas are used for protection.

We need protection during these days of turmoil. We need it emotionally, financially, physically, and spiritually. Though some say life has no guarantees – it does.

God guarantees to protect those who trust in Him. A wise proverb tells us to "Trust in the Lord with all your heart ..." (Proverbs 3:5); the prophet Isaiah stated, "I will trust and not be afraid" (Isaiah 12:2) and Jesus declared, "Trust in God; trust also in me" (John 14:1).

The proven power of God's protection is found in the cry of Christ before His crucifixion. His promise to God was, "I protected them and kept them safe" (John 17:12). This doesn't mean that nothing bad will ever rain in our lives; it simply states that we have His protection, if we turn and trust in Him. The more you get under God's protective care, the more God will cover you over with His promises of peace.

KeyPoints to ponder:
- How's your umbrella with God these days?
- Does it have any holes in it?
- How will you bring others under the protective care of Christ?

"The center of God's will is our only safety." – Betsie ten Boom

UNITY

What would you say is the most powerful and important number in existence? Is it a billion, a million, a thousand, a hundred, seven, or three? I believe the simplest is the best. What could be simpler, and yet more difficult, than the number one? The power of oneness supersedes any other conglomerate in all of creation.

The reason for its power is because we have such a problem proving that it's possible. The uniqueness of unity is yet to be completely understood. Why is something that is so easy to define so difficult to discover?

One is wonderful. The Bible says, "There is one body and one Spirit – one Lord, one faith, one baptism; one God and Father of all, who is over all and through all and in all" (Ephesians 4:4-6). There's a clarion call to all to get together and remain together. "How good and pleasant it is when brothers live together in unity" (Psalm 133:1).

If we could only learn to listen to the Lord in this area, we could become sources of strength to our world, our families, our friends, and ourselves.

KeyPoints to ponder:
- Are you experiencing unity with your family and friends?
- Are you at one with Jesus?
- If there is disunity in your family, what will you do to make a divine difference?

"Unity in Christ is not something to be achieved; it is something to be recognized."– A. W. Tozer

UTOPIA

Utopia is a place of perfection – a promise of something bigger and better. It was Sir Thomas More in 1516 who gave us this word, though few people know how he came by the name. Sir Thomas named his imaginary island of perfection using the Greek words *"ou"* – meaning "not" and *"topos"* – meaning "a place." Put them together and you have a visionary heaven that is, in reality, "no place" on earth. Utopia had such an impact on the literary world that its title soon became a word unto itself, meaning "ideal."

Are you longing for utopia? Is there an itch for the ideal which never seems to get a scratch?   God knows that the world in which we live is filled with wrong, worry, and woes. That's why He has prepared a place of perfection for those who trust in Him by faith.

Jesus said, "I go and prepare a place for you, I will come back and take you to be with me that you also may be where I am" (John 14:3).

A heavenly home is waiting for those who are willing.

KeyPoints to ponder:
- What's your picture of utopia?
- Is it a place for which you can prepare?
- How will you begin to get ready for the journey?

"This world is our passage, not our portion." – Matthew Henry

V

VANDAL

Vandals destroy, damage, and deface property today just as the original Vandal tribe did around AD 450. The first Vandals may be best remembered for sacking Rome and later persecuting Christians.

Technically, the word vandal means "wanderer," as the tribe was known for its wandering conquests throughout France, Spain, and Africa.

There is another vandal who seeks victory in your life. Jesus called him a "thief who comes to steal and kill and destroy" (John 10:10). However, the good news is that God spoke through Christ to assure us that He came to this earth to give us life – abundant and eternal (John 10:10b).

One of the ways in which Satan, the vandal, steals from you is by robbing your time. He destroys your day by substituting trivial concerns in the place of more powerful priorities. The devil vandalizes your sense of peace with worry and thwarts God's plan through distractions and delays. Since Jesus came to give you a life worth living, claim victory today instead of becoming the vandal's victim.

KeyPoints to ponder:
- Have you been the object of vandalism recently?
- What did they destroy or deface? Your property? Your personality? Or both?
- Will you take time to pray against the devil's destruction for yourself and others?

"The servant of Christ must never be surprised if he has to drink of the same cup as his Lord." – J.C. Ryle

VICTORY

V-I-C-T-O-R-Y, victory, victory is our cry! That's a cheer yelled by cheerleaders years ago when I was blessed to be a player on a state championship football team. We all love victory, but we hate the process of getting it.

We don't live in a world of ease. Life is tough and times get tough, even when we may be tender people. Victory on the football field is fun, but victory in life is even better.

Scripture teaches us about David's mighty men who won victory over eight hundred Philistines, though greatly outnumbered. "The Lord brought about a great victory that day" (2 Samuel 23:10). What's your day like today? Victorious or defeated?

Someday we will all die physically, but some of us will live again with God. The Apostle Paul penned the promise when he said, "Death has been swallowed up in victory. Where, O death, is your victory?" (1 Corinthians 15:54-55a).

Christ has a victorious plan for all who trust in Him.

KeyPoints to ponder:
- Have you?
- Will you?
- Won't you? How?

"When we pray for the Spirit's help ... we will simply fall down at the Lord's feet in our weakness. There we will find the victory and power that comes from His love."– Andrew Murray

VINE

A vine is an interesting plant. It twists and turns while it weaves and winds its way by growing. I have a vine that has grown so much that it covers my back patio porch. Every vine has branches that shoot out of their life-giving source, making the vine appear larger.

Jesus called Himself a vine and spoke of God as the gardener (John 15:1). He then referred to every believer as a branch. He understood that a branch can have no life without being connected to the vine. He wisely warned us that apart from Him, we can do nothing (John 15:5).

So why are you trying so hard on your own? If you have no God-connection, you're like a branch waiting to wither. If you have no graft into the "True Vine" of Christ, you will never bear spiritual fruit. This life lesson is sadly learned when we think we can tend our own garden and be our own vine.

God has a growth plan for you if you're willing to let Him lead.

KeyPoints to ponder:
- Are you withering right now?
- What will it take for you to get grafted into God?
- Who will you help to grow in God's garden?

"That is faith, cleaving to Christ, twining round Him with all the tendrils of our heart, as the vine does round its support."
  – Alexander MacLaren

VISA

I carry a Visa credit card in my wallet, and I have had to obtain many visas to gain permission to pass through foreign passport gates when entering international cities.

Actually, the word visa is short for the Latin phrase *"carta visa"* meaning "papers seen." Border controls around the world monitor visitors coming and going. Without a visa or official authorization, one cannot go into another country.

The same is true concerning our ultimate entry into heaven. The Bible speaks of a New Jerusalem with twelve gates, jeweled walls, and golden streets. The brightest light there is the light of the glory of God whose shine is eternal where there is no night.

Sound too good to be true? Not so, as it's really up to you. God has done His part in preparing the place, now you must believe, as well as behave, to gain entry as "Nothing impure will ever enter it, nor will anyone who does what is shameful or deceitful, but only those whose names are written in the Lamb's book of life" (Revelation 21:27).

Jesus Christ is your visa to God. Don't leave home without it!

KeyPoints to ponder:
- How would you respond if God asked, "Why should I let you into heaven?"
- Do you deserve immediate entry?
- Who needs your help in getting through God's gate?

"No man can resolve himself into heaven." – D.L. Moody

VISION

My brother was a dispensing optician in Atlanta, who had handily equipped our entire family with glasses with one exception – me. I had perfect vision through high school, two colleges, and into graduate school. Then it happened. I began to squint to see distant objects, and colors were no longer clear.

The inevitable hereditary gene kicked in, and I gave into my first pair of correction lenses. What was fashionable in the beginning became burdensome through the years.

The Bible warns that "Where there is no revelation, people cast off restraint..." (Proverbs 29:18). The literal meaning of this is that people who cannot see what's ahead become scattered in their direction. They lose focus and purpose.

There are at least two types of vision. One is physical – our eyesight. The other is spiritual – our insight. It's sad that many people can see clearly with their physical eyes, but their hearts are cloudy. What we need is God's insight into our circumstances of life.

There's an old hymn of faith that pleads for God to "Be Thou My Vision." If I could purchase a pair of glasses to see all of life as God does, I would race to get them. But then, His purposes would be short-circuited because the lessons are learned through living.

KeyPoints to ponder:
- How's your spiritual vision?
- 20/20 or worse?
- Are you ready to ask for God's glasses to see it as He does? Will you?

"When I think of vision, I have in mind the ability to see above and beyond the majority."– Chuck Swindoll

VISTA

A vista is a view, and while many of us have a great view of life, some of us don't. On a trip to California, my family and I made a 10-mile trip to the top of the highest mountain above the San Francisco Bay. We were literally above the clouds and could see the Bay cities on one side and the Pacific Ocean on the other. This breathtaking sight was a visible reminder of the enormity of God's world from a perspective many have never seen.

What's your vista? Do you live above the clouds and chaos of everyday life or find yourself in the fog of frustration? The lesson I learned is simple: the higher you go, the more you can know.

Each mile we travelled above the California coastline we saw a new scene which took us to the top. It's not so much what I saw with my eyes, but what I perceived with my heart. Our vistas are so small when we live below the clouds. Our view becomes better when we rise above them.

God wants to take you up to see life as He does. Jesus said, "Anyone who has seen me has seen the Father (God)" (John 14:9b). That's the highest view of all.

KeyPoints to ponder:
- Who do you see today?
- Will you go above the clouds of any current confusion?
- How are you going to assist others to take the higher hike with you?

"Perspective is worth 80 IQ points." – Alan Kay

W

WARM

Christmas cards I send and receive each year readily use the word "warm" – "warm wishes," "warm holiday cheer," "warm remembrances," "warm friendship and love." All these expressions bring a feeling of comfort, especially if it's cold outside. We like to be warm in winter.

As we face the promise of a new year, we would be wise to examine what we want in the coming months. God warns us against warmness. A church in the Bible was reprimanded that it was "neither cold nor hot" (Revelation 3:15). This lukewarm group was told that they were about to be spit out of our Savior's mouth!

The point is that physical warmth is attractive, but spiritual warmth is an abomination. God's goal for your life is not for you to be comfortable and cozy. He desires that our cold hearts become hot for Him. He is pursuing us with a passion and expects our rapid response. Determine to give God your goals for a hot and holy new year.

KeyPoints to ponder:
- Has your heart grown cold?
- Have you settled for what is comfortable over what is challenging?
- How will you handle this holiday season with a hot heart for God?

"Put your nose in the Bible every day. It is your spiritual food. Make a vow not to be a lukewarm Christian." – Kirk Cameron

WASH

I wash my face every morning and every night. I wash my clothes when the hamper smells ripe. Occasionally, I wash my car when the weather is right. And I even wash my hands more often these days with the threat of flu and ever-spreading germs.

Maybe the key question is, "Who is washing you?" Is it your conscience or is it Christ? The purpose of a wash is to be clean and most of us need cleaning up, both on the inside and the outside. If you look good to others but are dirty to God, then you need a bath from above.

The Bible says, "If we confess our sins, He (God) is faithful and just and will forgive us our sins and purify us from all unrighteousness" (1 John 1:9). Now this is good news from a great God! Your life's dirt can be washed by the divine desire of Christ to make you clean. Are you having trouble believing it's too good to be true? Try asking and not arguing with God's power over your potential to be washed from your sin to become a new self for God's glory.

KeyPoints to ponder:
- How well will you clean up today?
- What or who is keeping you from taking a spiritual bath?
- Won't you take time to ask Jesus to show you where you need the most scrubbing?

"Create in me a clean heart, O God, and renew a steadfast spirit within me." – Psalm 51:10

WATCH

When I say the word "watch," multiple images probably flash through your mind. Some of you are thinking about time because a watch we wear is all about keeping us on schedule. Other thoughts move toward sight. What we look at, or watch, affects our direction.

Jesus commanded His disciples, "Watch and pray so that you will not fall into temptation" (Matthew 26:41). He blended both time and sight together when He rebuked them, saying, "Could you men not keep watch with me for one hour?"
(Matthew 26:40). This was a tough time for Jesus because He was about to face His betrayal, His belittlement, and His burial. It's in the tough times of our lives that we need to watch most carefully.

If we follow His path, we can experience a powerful promise: "For the Lord watches over the way of the righteous, but the way of the wicked will perish" (Psalm 1:6).

KeyPoints to ponder:
- How will you choose to use your time today?
- Who watches over you to keep you accountable to God?
- Are there others in your life over whom you watch? Who?

"That which a man watches and prays against, he looks upon as evil to him, and by all means to be avoided." – John Owen

WEAK

To be weak can be wonderful! You don't believe me? Then let me share some simple stories. There have been times in each of our lives when we were weak through illness, a financial set-back, or maybe a broken relationship. When weak, we discovered we needed something or someone besides our own selves to gain help. If times got really tough, we'd cry out to God – and that's good!

God's response to us is found in the Bible. "My grace is sufficient for you, for My power is made perfect in weakness" (2 Corinthians 12:9). So then, do we seek to be weak to put on God's power? No! Weakness comes our way without an invitation – it just happens.

The weakest, most vulnerable of us all are children. When His disciples tried to discourage children from coming to Jesus, He turned to them with a stern statement saying, "Let the little children come to me, and do not hinder them, for the kingdom of heaven belongs to such as these" (Matthew 19:14).

If you feel weak today, then look up to God as a child to a Father. His promise can become your power.

KeyPoints to ponder:
- Do you wonder why you are so weak?
- Can you name a recent time when your weakness proved to be your strength?
- What are some ways you can encourage friends and family to be strong in the Lord?

"The gem cannot be polished without friction." – Anonymous

"Rich and poor have this in common: The Lord is the Maker of them all" (Proverbs 22:2).

We worry over our wealth or lack of it. We wonder if we'll ever have enough and what will happen if we don't. Our trust in stuff has overtaken our reliance on God, the Maker and Provider of all things, for all people.

It's not wrong to be rich, but we are told to "Honor the Lord with your wealth ... then your barns will be filled to overflowing ..." (Proverbs 3:9-10). Wow! No wonder we worry so much for what we may not have. Simply put: We probably won't get more than we're willing to give away, and if we do, it can then become our god.

The truth is found in the Bible that reminds us, "... we brought nothing into the world and we can take nothing out of it" (1 Timothy 6:7). Our continual clamor for cash can lead us to lose much more than we could ever gain. Jesus taught, by lifestyle, that less is more, first is last, and life on earth will soon end into an eternity where the only wealth worth having is life with our Lord.

KeyPoints to ponder:
- Do you consider yourself a person of wealth?
- What's in your account for Christ's sake?
- Can God count on to you to be a generous giver from the gifts He has given you?

"God only, and not wealth, maintains the world: riches merely make people proud and lazy." – Martin Luther

WEATHER

Weather is a weird word. Many of you might wonder whether I'm talking about the climate outside or the creation of a dependency clause determining your next action or attitude. Well, it all depends on how you spell the word or say it. For now, let's deal with the weather that has to do with the environment and its effect on our health. If you're feeling "under the weather" this refers to a phrase that sailors coined meaning seasickness. They would send inexperienced sailors under the ship's deck or "under the weather" where the motions of the winds and waves were minimal in order to help relieve their sickness.

I am thoroughly impressed with the meteorological predictions made by man, but I am more impressed by the great God who has the power to control all environmental elements, whether we appreciate the weather or not. And why not? He's a sovereign Savior with a miraculous mannerism, "clothed with splendor and majesty"
(Psalm 104:1), whether or not you like the weather.

KeyPoints to ponder:
- Is it stormy or clear for you at this time of life?
- Do you think you can control the circumstances, or do you need help?
- What will you ask God to do for you and with you to bring a calmer climate?

"As sure as ever God puts His children in the furnace, He will be in the furnace with them." – Charles Spurgeon

WEEDS

Weeds are almost always unwanted. They invade our gardens, lawns, fields, and pathways. We work hard to pull them or poison them. They are not a welcomed part of our daily work.

In His parable of the weeds, Jesus explained that unwanted weeds are like sin in our lives. If we sow good seeds or deeds, we won't have to worry over weeds. However, when weeds do grow in our lives, they must later be pulled, burned, and discarded. Christ warned that His angels "will weed out of his kingdom everything that causes sin and all who do evil" (Matthew 13:41).

Maybe we can better understand weeds as obnoxious plants when we remember where the word came from. The early Saxons used the word "*wiod*" which found its root meaning to be "wild." No wonder we have so much trouble keeping them under control.

The varieties seem endless: cudweed, duckweed, milkweed, knotweed, hogweed, ironweed, mugweed, and so on. Yet, the worst weed springs forth from our hearts when we plant sinful seeds such as lying, lusting, and laziness.

God, help us to plant and produce a life worth living – without weeds!

KeyPoints to ponder:
- What weeds are growing in your garden of life?
- How do you plan to get rid of them?
- To whom will you turn for help?

"Satan strikes at the root of faith or at the root of diligence."
– John Livingstone

WHY?

"Why?" is a query from the curious and an explanation from the intellectual. We can ask "why" or tell "why" depending on our level of learning. We need to know what's happening around us. No one wants to be ignored or left ignorant. God answered our biggest question with the solution of sending a Savior.

We all ask, "Why are we here?" or "Why do I feel so fearful?" When Jesus shared His stories and ministered in our midst, He answered the anxieties of all mankind as well as curing our curiosities.

Thomas wondered "why" one time as a disciple. He questioned Christ asking, "Lord, we don't know where you are going, so how can we know the way?" (John 14:5). Jesus told him the why and the way as he responded, "I am the way and the truth and the life" (John 14:6).

Next time you wonder why you are here and why you have been given life, listen to our Savior's answer, stop fretting, and start following God's answers.

KeyPoints to ponder:
- Do you know why you were born?
- Why do you care?
- How important is it that you get answers to why God responds as He does? Why?

"Large asking and large expectation on our part honor God."
– A. L. Stone

WIND

It blows, it howls, it destroys and even delights. It's wind. We can't see it, but we sure can feel it. The only control we have over it is mechanical. We can block it, channel it, and even create it, but in its natural element we cannot contain it. Hurricanes and tornadoes prove that.

Like wind, so it is with God. God's Spirit is compared to the wind with His invisible nature with very visible results (John 3:8). We are warned in the Bible not to believe every spirit as we are admonished to be mature. Not as "infants, tossed back and forth by the waves, and blown here and there by every wind of teaching ..." (Ephesians 4:14).

We need a Source bigger than ourselves to calm the storms of life that regularly blow us around. We need God's wisdom and not our sense of bewilderment.

God gives His wisdom to all who ask. But there's a condition attached to His promise. "But when he asks, he must believe and not doubt, because the one who doubts is like a wave of the sea, blown and tossed by the wind" (James 1:6).

As you feel the wind today, remember the Source and thank the Savior.

KeyPoints to ponder:
- What wind is blowing your life today?
- Is it the wind of worry? Discouragement? A broken heart? Despair or doubt?
- How will you allow God's breeze to break through for you?

"God provides the wind, but man must set the sails."
                    – Augustine of Hippo

WORD

We live in a world of words. The average female speaks 25,000 words each day, and guys like me share about 12,000 words. Although there's an obvious difference in volume, there is no difference in impact.

Words transform our world. Whether they are spoken, written, broadcast, whispered, or transmitted, words are life-changing.

The Bible tells us in the Gospel of John (1:1) that "in the beginning was the Word, and the Word was with God, and the Word was God." This is a direct reference to Jesus Christ, God's Word of love to all mankind.

Some days I get nearly a hundred emails. I'm flooded with words. Many of these messages I have to delete. They are irrelevant, irreverent, and some are irrational.

That's why I have a junk mail filter. It is a reminder to each of us that we need God's filter from filth.

Today when you speak, send an email, or text, use your words wisely. Don't waste them but use them to bless others.

KeyPoints to ponder:
- Who has spoken a word of blessing to you today?
- Are there recent words you have spoken that you wish you had not?
- Will you let the Word of God be your best source of speaking?

"Handle them carefully, for words have more power than atom bombs."– Pearl Strachan Hurd

WORK

Work is wonderful for some and worrisome for others. When someone asks, "What do you do?" the usual response is to tell them about your work outside of the home, the place where you put most of your time and talent. Rarely do we share who we are, along with our dreams and goals. Many folks would get nervous if we did.

Have you thought much about the greatest expression of work? Need some help here? Titus told us the truth in the Bible when he wrote, "Our people must learn to devote themselves to doing what is good, in order to provide for urgent needs and not live unproductive lives." (Titus 3:14)

Do you get it? Our work is not a matter of profit and pleasure, but rather purpose and productivity. This goes against the grain of life, but it goes toward God's goal for each of us.

When you do good, your needs will be met through the Lord's love for who you are, not just where you work. Remember that work is God-given and man-managed.

KeyPoints to ponder:
- How well is your work working in your world?
- Is it producing more purpose than profit?
- What can you do differently to make your work pleasing to the Lord and to yourself?

"Work designed for eternity can only be done by the eternal spirit."– A.W. Tozer

WORSHIP

Worship is a wonderful word, though many people do not understand it. For some it means an activity where we gather to meet God. For others it refers to an object of respect or reverence. For a few it's all about relationships – both vertical and horizontal.

Actually, the word comes from an old English derivation meaning "worth" and "ship." We carry out true worship when we understand that our actions lead us to revere the worth of the Almighty God more than ourselves.

The Psalmist wrote, "Ascribe to the Lord the glory due his name; worship the Lord in the splendor of his holiness" (Psalm 29:2). Perhaps our problem persists in that the act of worship has become more important than the attitude that must accompany it. If our hearts are hollow, then it's impossible to hallow the one true holy God of the universe.

It's past time for us to make our worship worthy of the object Whom we worship. It's not about me and my preferences; it's all about Him who longs to have your life.

KeyPoints to ponder:
- Can you be comfortable with worship in any context?
- Are your preferences in style of worship more important than the substance expressed during worship?
- How will you begin to make public worship an overflow of your private times of worship?

"The highest form of worship is the worship of unselfish service."
– Billy Graham

WRITING

Writing is a rapidly fading art form of communication. Hand-written notes and letters are becoming a thing of the past.

With the ever-increasing flow of emails and online publications, it's surprising that magazines and newspapers still hold their popularity. The average American household subscribes to or purchases six different magazines a year.

One would think that advertisers depend greatly on magazine coverage, but the fact is that Reader's Digest did not even contain one ad for the first 33 years of publication.

God has personally written a love letter to each of us, and He has a holy advertisement for eternity in its pages. It is called the Bible. The message of scripture is actually simple: "For God so loved the world he gave his one and only Son, that whoever believes in him shall not perish but have eternal life" (John 3:16). I doubt that you have read anything better than that!

KeyPoints to ponder:
- How long has it been since you received a personal, hand-written letter?
- When was the last time you wrote one?
- Will you take the time to do it today? To whom will you write it? Why?

"In good writing, words become one with things."
    – G. K. Chesterton

X

eXercise

Activity requiring physical effort carried out to sustain or improve our health and fitness is a fitting definition for exercise. Of course, it can also refer to a task done to practice or test a skill, such as a military drill or training maneuver.

We all know that God has created our bodies for exercise and that demands discipline along with a willing attitude. The problem is that most of America is grossly overweight and in desperate need of more exercise. An alarming fact is that obesity has increased from 30.5% to 42.4% in just the last decade.

Jesus knew that we need to retain balance and gain proper perspective in life. It was the Apostle Paul who reminded the younger preacher Timothy, "For physical training is of some value, but godliness has value for all things, holding promise for both the present life and the life to come" (I Timothy 4:8).

Spiritual exercise is essential for a balanced lifestyle. Our weakness in prayer, reading and memorizing scripture, serving others, loving the unlovely, helping the helpless and sharing our faith is even more alarming than our bloated bodies. Jesus is ready to coach you back to health.

KeyPoints to ponder:
- Have you become a flabby follower of our Lord?
- Will you be willing to commit to daily eXercise through spiritual discipline?
- Who do you think is waiting on you to help encourage and coach them?

"If you don't make time for exercise, you'll probably have to make time for illness."—Robin Sharma

X-RAY

Who would you be if you could see through walls or even into a person's body below their skin? Some might say, "Superman!"—all should say, "Jesus."

In 1897, X-rays were first used on a military battlefield during the Balkan War to find bullets and broken bones in patients. A German scientist became the first to discover this process by accident. This became a significant advancement, especially in the field of medicine. After all, X-rays make the invisible visible.

My father was a radiologist and looked at X-rays almost every day. He could diagnose a patient's problem and offer a potential cure. Why? Because he cared. The truth is that God, has always been able to see inside each of us. He cares enough to know us and He even "searches our hearts...because the Spirit intercedes for God's people in accordance with the will of God" (Romans 8:27).

This ought to make you cheerful and not fearful. God loves you whatever He sees in your life.

What does God see inside of you? Is it clean or cluttered? Is it diseased from sin or has it been made divine from the Savior? The Great Physician has a cure for every soul. His name is Jesus.

KeyPoints to ponder:
- What would you like to see in other people?
- What do others see on the inside of you?
- What does God see in your heart of hearts?

"He wished he had some kind of X-ray vision for the human heart."
—Kim Edwards, The Memory Keeper's Daughter

XMAS

A common abbreviation for the word Christmas is Xmas. Xmas and variants such as *Xtemass*, originated as handwriting abbreviations for the typical pronunciation.

The "X" comes from the Greek letter Chi, which is the first letter of the Greek word *Christos*, which became Christ in English.

Many people find the word Xmas offensive. However, the origin of this controversial term dates back to the mid-1500s. You will not find Xmas in church song books or even on many greeting cards. Some people associate Xmas as representing the holiday as a commercial, secular occasion instead of a particular cultural and religious ritual pointing to the birth of Jesus Christ.

Commonly, when we put an X on top of a word or near it, we think it may mean to eliminate it. God's clear intent is never to eliminate Christmas, but rather to accentuate it. We are also to illuminate the Christ child who was born to become our Savior. It was a miracle then and remains a miracle today.

The Gospel of Matthew expresses it best: "This is how the birth of Jesus the Messiah came about: his mother Mary was pledged to be married to Joseph, but before they came together, she was found to be pregnant through the Holy Spirit" (Matthew 1:18).

KeyPoints to ponder:
- Have you accepted the miracle of the birth of Jesus Chirst?
- Would you say that you have abbreviated your spiritual walk with God?
- Are you willing to help others understand the full meaning of Christmas?

"Christmas is the day that holds all time together." –Alexander Smith

Y

YEARN

Have you ever yearned for something so much that your body and/or your mind actually ached? You wanted something so badly that your mental desire became a physical detriment. It's not wrong to yearn for what is right, however, it can go wrong if you're chasing after what is wrong for you.

There's a big difference between what you want and how you go after it. For example, if you really want a new car and decide to steal it—then your yearning has turned bad from something that you thought would make you glad.

The Old Testament prophet Isaiah yearned for what was right and went after it rightfully. He wrote: "My soul yearns for you in the night; in the morning my spirit longs for you. When your judgments come upon the earth, the people of the world learn righteousness" (Isaiah 26:9). He wanted and yearned for more of God and he got it.

For what or whom do you yearn? If it's for your good, then go for it. If it is frivolous, then you need to forget it.

KeyPoints to ponder:
- What are you yearning for right now?
- Would you be willing to do most anything to get it?
- Is there anything that should prevent you from asking God to help you?

"There is something good in men that really yearn for discipline."
—*Vince Lombardi*

YES

Yes is an affirming word. We often say "yes" to our family, friends, and employers to show agreement. However, there are times when it is overused and even distorted. For instance, there are those who we label as "yes people" who repeatedly seek to earn favor by always agreeing with others. The problem with this is that they rarely speak their own mind and they poorly represent their true opinion.

How often do we say yes to God? Yes... to humility when with all of our being we want to be recognized for our own work, talents, and gifts. Yes... to joy when we are grieving. Yes... to strength when we are so exhausted we can barely put one foot in front of the other. Yes... to peace when there is chaos in our family, in our churches, in our world. Yes... to love when we have been hurt and wounded. Yes...to hope when all else seems to be lost.

When Jesus asked his disciples, "Who do you say that I am?", the Apostle Peter answered correctly as he said, "You are the Messiah, the Son of the living God" (Matthew 16:15-16). The response of the Savior was a huge YES!

The life-question that we must answer is: Who is Jesus to me?

KeyPoints to ponder:
- Saying yes to God changes everything, is it changing you?
- What have you said yes to in the past which you regret?
- Do you believe that God wants to say yes to what you ask Him?

"Yes is a world and in this world of yes live (skillfully curled) all worlds."—e e Cummings

YESTERDAY

Many people cannot remember what happened yesterday and struggle to know all that's happening today. Our yesterdays reflect the past and affect our future. If we didn't have yesterday, we would never be able to look forward to tomorrow.

As important as yesterday was, one thing is certain--we can't change it. However, we can build on it, grow from it, and make today even better.

Change is inevitable even though we might rebel against it. We wish some things would never change. Consistency is attractive; especially when it is reliable.

Scripture reminds us, "Jesus Christ is the same yesterday and today and forever" (Hebrews 13:8). His changeless character and consistent love is the highest level of stability. Our ever-changing world screams for someone who can offer us changeless consistency. This is the very reason that God sent Christ to come yesterday to impact today and give us hope for tomorrow.

What you cannot change from your yesterdays, you can change today by placing your total faith in the Changeless One.

KeyPoints to ponder:
- Are you holding on to yesterday?
- Is there anything about yesterday that you wish had never happened?
- What will you do today that you did not do yesterday so that tomorrow would make God smile?

"If you fell down yesterday, stand up today."—H. G. Well

YIELD

To yield means to produce or provide or, in a financial context, it means to generate a specific monetary return. When we yield to others, we relinquish possession or we give up something. Farmers offer agricultural yields from their crops that bring food and favor to our households.

We see yield signs on the roadways everywhere we drive. They express warnings and instructions to help us give way to other traffic in order to prevent accidents as we drive our vehicles. Many people do not like them because they slow their flow — all of us need to follow them. After all, if you are in a hurry, it is better to yield than to stop completely or to crash.

The Bible instructs us to yield ourselves to God: "Do not offer any part of yourself to sin as an instrument of wickedness, but rather offer yourselves to God as those who have been brought from death to life; and offer every part of yourself to him as an instrument of righteousness" (Romans 6:13).

What are you yielding for God this day? Make it large and not little. You'll get wherever you're going more quickly and safely.

KeyPoints to ponder:
- What are you yielding for others?
- Is there a good reason why you haven't yielded to God?
- Would you be willing to offer a good yield of yourself to benefit your circle of influence?

"True wisdom is marked by willingness to listen and a sense of knowing when to yield." — Elizabeth George

YOKE

A yoke is a wooden beam commonly used on the necks of a pair of oxen or other animals to enable them to pull together on a load. There are several types of yokes used in different cultures, and for different types of oxen. A pair of oxen may be called a yoke of oxen, and yoke can also be used as a verb, as in yoking a pair of oxen. The word is derived from *yugom* or the verb *yeug* which means to join or unite.

Jesus used a common concept of His culture to express an uncommonly known and misunderstood opportunity. He invited His followers to take His yoke. Today, Christ is inviting us to do similarly through joining Him by pulling together to lighten the load of our lives. He wants to come alongside you to teach you how to find rest for your weariness.

"Come to me, all you who are weary and burdened, and I will give you rest. Take my yoke upon you and learn from me, for I am gentle and humble in heart, and you will find rest for your souls. For my yoke is easy and my burden is light" —Matthew 11:28-30.

We have a choice. Either we can keep on trudging through life in our own efforts or ask Jesus to join us on the journey. What's your choice?

KeyPoints to ponder:
- With whom or what are you yoked?
- Is your burden heavy or light?
- Do you need rest for your soul?

"The yoke you wear determines the burden you bear."
        —Edwin Louis Cole

YOLK

A yolk is the yellow center of an egg. While some people find the texture of yolks repulsive, others take issue with the pronunciation itself. As you say the word out loud, notice how your throat twitches in confusion and anger when it has to pull out the odd sound.

Originally the word was spelled "yeck" from the Old English and actually has a link back to the word meaning *yellow*. However, figuratively the word refers to the innermost part of something.

God is concerned about the innermost part of our lives. The Bible tells us to love the Lord your God with all of your heart, mind, soul, and strength—our inside core (Mark 12:30). Jesus asked a great question which demands our honest response, "What good is it for someone to gain the whole world, yet forfeit their soul?" (Mark 8:36).

What you express outwardly in life is determined from what is inside of your life —your core, your soul, your "yolk." We must not forfeit God's best for what we think might be better. Our Savior offers salvation for your soul and expects sanctification from those who truly seek to serve Him.

KeyPoints to ponder:
- What does God see in your innermost parts of life?
- Do you feel secure in how you are serving our Savior?
- Have you substituted earthly goods for Godly gain?

"I am frightened of eggs... have you ever seen anything more revolting than an egg yolk breaking and spilling its yellow liquid?... Revolting."—Alfred Hitchcock

YOUR

When we use the word your, it means to belong or be associated with the person or people that the speaker is addressing. If we use the word informally, this denotes someone or something that is familiar or typical of its kind.

The word "your" comes from the Old English word "eower" and the Germanic word "ye." It is used as an attributive adjective referring directly to you; something belonging to oneself or to any person.

However you may choose to use the word, it most definitely signifies possession. For example, if you say, *"This is mine, but it's not yours"*, you are referring to something that somebody else does not have —it's yours! But just because it's yours does not mean that it cannot become mine —sometime.

Jesus possessed God's Spirit, but He chose to share it so that it could become yours as well. It was His to give to us so that it could be ours. "But the Advocate, the Holy Spirit, whom the Father will send in my name, will teach you all things and will remind you of everything I have said to you" (John 14:26).

God is the giver of every good and perfect gift from above (James 1:17). He wants to give you the gift of salvation and abundant living to become yours. Trust Him.

KeyPoints to ponder:
- Have you honestly asked Jesus to be your Savior and Lord?
- Can you identify the spiritual gifts which God has chosen to give you?
- Are you willing to share what is yours with others so that it can become theirs?

"Raise your words, not your voice. It is rain that grows flowers, not thunder." --Rumi

YULE

An archaic term for Christmas is Yule. It can also refer to a large log traditionally burned in the fireplace on Christmas Eve. Some people even bake a log-shaped chocolate cake eaten at Christmastime called a Yule cake.

The Old English word for Yule was *"geal"* which refers to a period extending from December 24 to January 6. This span of time is also called Christmastide or Yuletide.

Christmas is a special time for celebrating the birth of our Savior. Our gift-giving traditions will never surpass the greatest Gift of all in Jesus Christ. "For God so loved the world that he gave his one and only son, that whoever believes in him shall not perish but have eternal life" (John 3:16).

The compelling love of God for us prompted His covenant for us, that has provided His care for us, by offering His eternity for us in Glory. This season is a solid spiritual reminder that God still has a place for all of His creation made ready through redemption and forgiveness which is triggered by our faith and trust. However, we must believe it to receive it.

KeyPoints to ponder:
- Do you believe in God's Son as your Savior?
- Have you substituted cultural traditions for God's offer of redemption?
- Will you purpose to focus more on God's gift of Jesus than the gifts we give to one another this Christmas season?

"Yule log for the Christmas fire--tale-spinner of fairy tales that can come true."— *Yul Brynner*

Z

ZANY

The definition of zany is "amusingly unconventional or idiosyncratic." It also refers to a person who is erratic or eccentric. You probably know someone who is zany or, perhaps you are the one.

One beautiful thing about life is that it is filled with different personalities. One thing is certain, however. Not everyone acts as beautifully as you wish they would. The variety of characteristics which make up humanity is amusingly diverse and sometimes amazingly disturbing.

Jesus once encountered a man who had not worn clothes or lived in a house for a long time; instead he sheltered himself in the side of a mountain inside of tombs. When this man saw Jesus, he cried out and fell at His feet asking, "What do you want with me, Jesus, Son of the most High God?" (Luke 8:26-28).

After Jesus cured the man, He told him to return home and tell others what God had done for him. I believe God can cure the zany and the "inzane." He is able to transform anyone who will come to Him and ask for help. He cured me!

Have you asked Him? He's waiting on your response.

KeyPoints to ponder:
- Who do you know that is zany?
- What did someone say that you have a zany personality?
- Do you believe that God can use anyone for any reason at any time?

"All the best people are bonkers."
        —*Mad Hatter, Alice in Wonderland*

ZEALOT

The term zealot comes from a common translation of the Hebrew *kanai* frequently used in the plural form which means ones who are zealous on behalf of God. The term derives from the Greek word *zelotes* which means emulator, zealous admirer, or follower.

Historically, this group consisted of members of an ancient Jewish sect aiming at a world Jewish theocracy and resisting the Romans until 70 A.D.

Modern-day zealots are eager to stand for a cause and give energetic support to their passions —whether it be work, marriage, sports, hobbies or other interests.

A problem arises when zeal is misplaced or misguided. It is tragic when something is done for seemingly the right reason but in the wrong way. Zealots can be busy building up social order or destructive by tearing it down.

Jesus invites us to "Come, follow me and I will send you out to fish for people" (Matthew 4:19). His disciples responded with obedience and became spiritual zealots. After all, our Savior is worthy of our emulation as He declared, "I am the way, the truth, and the life" (John 14:6).

What and who we follow determines our direction today and for eternity.

KeyPoints to ponder:
- Who are you following with zeal?
- Is anyone following you?
- Are you ready to invite God to mold you into a spiritual zealot?

"For forms of faith let graceless zealots fight; his can't be wrong whose life is in the right."—Alexander Pope

ZENITH

Some people describe the zenith of their career as their time of greatest responsibility and highest earnings. Regardless, most will agree that it means a high point in life.

Everyone wants to stay on top because the view is so beautiful, but that's not reality. God understands the ups and downs of life and wants to help us up when circumstances have taken us to the bottom.

As people questioned Jesus' success as a prophet and a healer, they were admiring the zenith of his life and ministry. However, they wondered how He might keep it up and if He was truly authentic.

We all want to be on the top of our game, yet we know that's not an everyday happening. What we really need to do is to *look up* to God, instead of expecting to *be up* all the time.

The true zenith of our life is above ourselves, because Jesus is the One who cares more than we can even understand or comprehend.

KeyPoints to ponder:
- Who are you looking up to?
- Who is looking up to you?
- What are you willing to give up in order to get up for Christ's sake?

"Each man is always in the middle of the surface of the earth and under the Zenith of his own hemisphere, and over the center of the earth."—Leonardo da Vinci

ZIGZAG

The definition of zigzag is a line or course having alternate right and left turns. As an adjective, it means having the form of a zigzag veering right and left. If you were to use it as an adverb, it would mean veering to the right and left alternatively. As a verb, it would mean to have or move along alternating courses.

For many of us, life is a zigzag existence. At first we are going one direction and then, suddenly, we go to the opposite extreme. The twists and turns of life can put us into a state of confusion and consternation. We long for consistency and loathe changes.

The Apostle James stated, "Such a person is double-minded and unstable and all they do" (James 1:8). God was telling the people of an earlier age the same that he is telling us today— zigzag living leads to zero accomplishments.

How's your life lately? Do you feel like you are swerving without direction? Jesus came to give us a purpose and a plan that He invites us to follow. When we ignore Him or refuse to follow Him, we are doomed to remain unstable and the balance of life will be out of our grasp.

KeyPoints to ponder:
- What is out of balance for your life right now?
- Do you feel like you are swerving out of control?
- Won't you come back to God's perfect plan which leads to blessing and balance through your belief and trust in Him?

"When obstacles arise, you change your direction to reach your goal; you do not change your direction to get there."—Zig Ziglar

About the Author

Raised in Atlanta, Georgia, John Bryan was the youngest of five children born into a physician's family. After finishing college, his goal was to complete law school, however God had a different plan.

When he joined the staff of a downtown Atlanta church in his early 20s, this became the foundation for his teaching, broadcast and writing career over the last four decades. In addition to his many years of leading churches, he served nearly 20 years with the Georgia Baptist Mission Board, giving him a broader platform for ministry in thousands of churches.

John's longest single pastorate of 17 years was in Augusta, Georgia where he has returned and now resides. He has also been privileged to advance over a dozen churches in two states as their interim pastor.

John's love for his wife, three sons, and five granddaughters has been integrated with his ability to communicate practical applications to challenge multiple generations in America and around the world. His passion is for people to hear God's truths and respond to God's invitation for living a life with purpose.

Seasonal and Topical Index